Claudia Bauder

Canadian at Heart

My transatlantic childhood
in a German family

Dedication

For Nicolas

Introduction

The original German version was published in 2009, after five years of dedicated work. The goal was to tell the story of my transatlantic childhood, at a time when such a life was quite rare. First, I built a timeline—figuring out when and where we had lived. Much was a blur, and I had to interview people who were part of those times to piece things together. I spent an entire year on research and interviews.

Next, I sorted the collected information into the corresponding sections of the story. Then came the more personal layer—my own memories of events, people, and places. Usually, I would turn to my sister Carin and ask, *"Do you remember this happening?"*, which often led to long phone calls, emails, and pieces of the manuscript being sent back and forth. She suggested I write it in German—even though we are native English speakers. My written German wasn't very good back then, and even after decades, German grammar remains a mystery to me. But I had the incredible help of Hildegard Schmid, who had just retired and was not only interested in the project but became my biggest supporter—and harshest critic.

When I told people I was writing a book, the usual response was: *"You can't do that, you didn't study literature."* And I always replied: *"I'm not writing literature. I'm telling a story—my story."* I wrote an exposé and contacted potential publishers—on paper, as was the norm at the time. Hoping to catch the attention of a publishing house, I then waited. But no one was interested. Next, I investigated self-publishing, which was a relatively new idea at the time, and this became my solution. Having no editor, I asked people I knew to help: Friends, acquaintances, and even a child psychologist, who was very much interested in my work, offered feedback.

Despite a lack of available information and many negative comments, I persevered, until it was finished and self-published in 2009.
And in 2024, I finally took the time to translate my book into English!
Enjoy diving into an extraordinary family story.

In loving memory of my mother, **Magdalene Emma Bauder**, née Holl, who died much too soon. She was my anchor, my haven of peace in my early life, and I still miss her today.

Contents

From Europe to South America

My parents originally came from the small town of Heubach in Württemberg, about 60 kilometers east of Stuttgart, in the South-Western part of Germany. My father, Hans-Jörg Bauder, was born there in 1929, the third of seven children. My mother, Magdalene Emma Holl, known as Magda, was also born there, in 1930 and was the second of three children. My parents knew each other from an early age onwards, their families lived a few hundred meters apart. Their fathers worked in the same company, which was initially called Spiesshofer & Braun in the textile industry, later named Triumph International. The Second World War started in 1939 and ended a few days before my father's 16th birthday in 1945. That was his great good fortune, because young men were at that time drafted into the war, at the age of 16.

In the same year, my father began training as a sewing machine mechanic at Spiesshofer & Braun, specializing in industrial sewing machines. He then trained as a clothing technician before attending a private business school. He was very attractive, 1.87 meters tall, slim and athletic, wore glasses, had dark eyes and almost black hair, and a mischievous smile.

My mother was trained as a secretary at Spiesshofer & Braun. At first, she worked in a room with other women for various people and later, exclusively for Paul Bauder, who was not only the director of the company, but also the father of her boyfriend, Hans. She was 1.65 meters, had a very feminine figure and auburn hair, which she usually wore short. Her large, bright blue eyes were unmistakable.

As of February 1953, my father worked for the sewing machine manufacturer Pfaff in Kaiserslautern, also in the south of Germany, as a "specialist consultant for the sewing industry based in Germany, Holland and Denmark". As of October 1953, at the young age of 24, he was sent to Holland for six months, where he was involved in rebuilding the Dutch industrial business for Pfaff. He was chosen for this task because of his age, as he was too young to have been a soldier during the war and could therefore be sent to a country which had been invaded by German soldiers, just a few years earlier. My father lived alone in a furnished room in

11

Hertogenbosch in the Haverdonklan and studied the Dutch language in the evenings. It was during this time that he finally decided to marry my mother, and the two were engaged on New Year's Eve 1954. From the spring of 1954, he was again working in Germany and was able to spend most weekends in Heubach and thus see his fiancée more often, although she still lived with her parents. As of March 1955, my father was sent to Denmark for a year to develop the Scandinavian market for Pfaff. He lived in Copenhagen-Ordrup, in Ordrupvej. My parents married in October 1955 and when she got married, my mother stopped working and moved to her husband in Denmark, becoming a housewife.

Heubach, October 1955, Wedding of Magda und Hans Bauder.

Just six months later, in the spring of 1956, my father was brought back to Germany and my mother was already expecting her first child. There was still a housing shortage in Germany at that time and it was not easy to rent a nice big apartment. Since my father would still often be away on business trips and my mother would be home alone - and pregnant - she decided that it would be better if they lived in her parents' house in Heubach. There was enough space in the three-story house, and she wouldn't be alone during the week. Hans could travel without worrying, knowing that his pregnant wife was in good hands. Their first child, Susanne, was born in Schwaebisch Gmünd in October 1956. After the birth of the baby, my mother stayed with her parents for another six months and the marriage continued to be a weekend relationship. Then it was time to go far away, to South America.

From April 1957 on, my father worked for Pfaff International Corporation, which was based on Fifth Avenue in New York. However, his place of work was not in the United States of America, but at various locations in South America. As a sales promoter, he first moved with his young family to Porto Alegre, Brazil. Daughter Susanne was six months old. My mother was only 26 years old when she made the move to the second foreign country, in her second year of marriage, with her husband and now also with a baby. This time, however, she was very far away from her parents and completely without their support. My father had just turned 28 and was responsible for opening new markets for Pfaff products there and expanding the entire sales organization. My parents both learned Portuguese, the language spoken in Brazil. They liked to go out to eat and dance and enjoyed the local way of life. After just one year in Brazil, however, the family moved on, to Uruguay. In her third year of marriage, my mother followed her husband to the third foreign country.

Montevideo, Uruguay 1958

From 1958 to 1962, the family lived in Montevideo, Uruguay, where my father did the same job for Pfaff as he had done in Brazil. The family lived near Plaza Fabini and could see the sea from their apartment, which everyone was very happy about. During this time, they became members of a riding club and learned to do horseback riding, which was a normal thing to do there. In her "Cedula de Identidad" (identity card) from December 1958, my mother's full name is Magdalene Emma Holl Schurr de Bauder, because in South America these names were also part of the whole family name.

Susanne was two years old when her mother traveled to Germany for four months for medical treatment and took her with her. While my mother was in hospital, Susanne stayed with her grandparents, Hedwig and Eugen Holl, known as Grandma and Grandpa, or Oma and Opa. At the time, Susanne spoke more Spanish, or rather the Portuguese she had learned in Brazil, than German. At her grandparents' house, she would point to her shoes and say: "Mio zapatos, Oma zapatos, Opa zapatos". But the three of them managed to communicate despite their language differences.

After his wife's recovery, my father joined his family and they set off together on a major vacation trip, with stops in Copenhagen, New York, Toronto, Mexico, Panama, Colombia and Peru. My mother wrote in a letter: "Susanne has gotten used to flying." No wonder with so many flights! She went on to write about Susanne that when she arrived back home in Uruguay, she repeated everything she said to her in German and everything the nanny said in Spanish, she repeated in Spanish.

In November 1959, my father had arrived at the airport a little earlier than necessary for a trip to Rio de Janeiro. He was offered to fly on an earlier plane than planned, partly because the scheduled plane would be delayed. He accepted the offer, which was fortunate for him, as the plane he was supposed to board crashed, and there were no survivors. When he arrived at his appointment in Rio, everyone in the office stared at him and couldn't believe he was alive. They said, "Mr. Bauder, your plane has just crashed." It seemed like a miracle to everyone, including him, that he hadn't taken the planned plane. Shortly after my father had been very lucky to have escaped death, my mother wrote a detailed letter to her friend Margret, saying that Hans was traveling a lot and she was alone a lot and "we had to make a lot of personal sacrifices for the job, but when you see the benefits and successes afterwards, one is happy about it". She went on to write: "In August, we bought a 1957 Volkswagen for 4,000 US dollars, but unfortunately it was at customs and was not delivered. In the meantime, the airlines were offering 40% special discounts, so Hans came up with the idea of buying a flight to Tokyo instead of the car, for the fall of 1960. No sooner said than done. The flight tickets were Montevideo - Zurich - Copenhagen - Anchorage (Alaska) - Tokyo - Hong Kong - Bangkok - Calcutta - Germany - Lisbon - Montevideo."

But first my parents traveled to Chile in December 1959 together with Susanne, who was now three years old. Our parents were so enthusiastic about Chile that they kept talking about this beautiful country. My father also said later that he wanted to move there as a pensioner.

The planned trip around the world, which was to last for six weeks, began at the end of September 1960. First, my parents flew to Zurich with Susanne and from there took their daughter to grandma and grandpa in Heubach to be looked after. As times were still bad for many people in Germany 15 years after the end of the war, it seemed unthinkable to our grandparents that my parents could afford to go on a trip around the world. Nobody did that back then, because they were still busy rebuilding the country in Germany yet were still a long way from prosperity. That's why my parents had to promise not to tell any of their friends or relatives about their trip around the world. They had to pretend they were going on a business trip.

During this time, Susanne attended kindergarten in Heubach, which she loved very much. Meanwhile, our mother turned 30 and the trip around the world was her birthday present. On her birthday, my parents flew from east to west and at midnight they toasted her birthday. As they flew across two time zones during this flight, they were able to toast to her birthday twice more, which amused them both immensely.

At the end of the trip, my parents picked up their daughter in Germany and flew back to Uruguay. Our father later said that this trip was the best idea they had had in their entire marriage. They were still young enough at the start of the trip to really enjoy the adventure. They were able to ride camels and go out for dinner and dancing every night. And they took great pleasure in buying local objects and souvenirs, which would become part of our household for decades to come. All the other couples they met on this trip were much older, most of them retired, and didn't have as much fun as they did.

Back home in Montevideo, Susanne went to a private German Spanish kindergarten, to be able to continue learning both languages. My parents then also got the VW Beetle, but it didn't have a particularly long life. It ended abruptly after an accident in which the car was hit from behind by a truck and then pushed into the back of a second truck. The blow from behind sent my mother flying forward onto the windshield, which partially broke, and she had shards of glass almost everywhere in the front of her body, especially in her face. Susanne was very lucky that she wasn't sitting in the back seat at the very moment of impact, but behind her mother's seat on the floor, because she was looking for a toy. As a result, she was only pushed against the front seat and remained uninjured. As there were no ambulances as we know them today, the whole family was taken home by another private car, without receiving any treatment. Injured, bleeding and in shock, as they were, they were treated there by a doctor who had been sent for. Using tweezers, as Susanne remembers, he removed the glass splinters from her mother's face and treated all the injuries.

In the spring of 1962, our mother was visited in Montevideo by her best friend Margret, whose friendship started with the two of them being in kindergarten together. Margret really wanted to take a souvenir picture of the two girls from Heubach, so far away from home. But my mother was pregnant and didn't want to be photographed like that. Back then, women had a different body image and being pregnant was not considered as being attractive. So, Margret had to fly home without a picture of them together, halfway across the globe, but with lots of impressions and memories. During this time, my father was on business trips again and wrote a postcard to his parents-in-law from Port-of-Spain, Trinidad, West Indies, from the Trinidad Hilton Hotel, which was said to be the newest luxury hotel in the Caribbean at the time.

Their second child, Carin, was born in a British hospital in Montevideo, Uruguay, in July 1962. She should have been a boy and named Peter, that was certain. Our parents had to accept their disappointment at the "wrong" gender and decided to call the girl Karin. In Spanish, however, the letter "K" did not exist on the typewriter and so they had to change Karin to Carin with a "C". When little Carin was four weeks old, my mother traveled with her and Susanne to her hometown in Germany. She was exhausted and wanted to recover with her parents. The journey for the flight route Montevideo, Rio de Janeiro, Recife, Cap Verde, Lisbon, Zurich, Stuttgart took almost two days.

Susanne came to Uruguay when she was just two years old and for four years, she experienced it as her home and her first homeland. At the age of almost six, she was to say goodbye to her first home, as she would never return there. When she arrived in Heubach, she returned to the kindergarten she had attended two years earlier. In January 1963, after six months in Heubach, my mother and the children moved directly from Germany to Caracas, Venezuela.

Caracas, Venezuela 1963

As of January 1963, my father worked in the industrial machinery division of Pfaff Máquinas de Coser Industriales S.A., in Caracas, as sole managing director. He was responsible for the import and sale of industrial machinery. This job meant that he had to travel less than in the first seven years of his marriage and my parents were finally able to spend more time together.

In a letter from my mother to her friend Margret in November 1963, she wrote: "Susanne has been in first grade since September. The school bus comes at half past six in the morning and brings her back shortly after 1 pm. She has 30 hours of lessons a week with a proper timetable including science and Venezuelan civics. The children are given up to five or six different pieces of schoolwork every day. Every month there are report cards with strict grades and twice a year they must take real exams with written and oral tests. If you don't study intensively with the children at home, it is impossible for them to complete the workload.... Here in Caracas, the situation is a little better, there hasn't been so much shooting for about 14 days. There has been a lot of militaries in the streets for a few weeks now and that seems to be helping. Let's see for how long? Otherwise, things are going well, Hans has a lot of work and is very busy. Susi will be on vacation for 2 months next week because of the political situation. Most schools have been closed for a long time. And yet, the people here could have paradise on earth."

In mid-December 1963, the family traveled to Germany for Christmas. This trip was triggered by my mother's wish for a Christmas tree. It was summer in Venezuela at the time and there was no fir tree like the one our mother had in mind anywhere in Venezuela. It would have had to be flown in from North America. But that was so expensive that my father said somewhat exaggeratedly: "We can fly to Germany for the money." So, once again, said and done, they flew. From Venezuela, they made a stopover somewhere in North Africa with an overnight stay, as the journey still took two days. When Susanne got off the plane there, she was almost struck dumb: the people all had black faces! She hadn't been prepared for this at all and didn't even know that such a thing existed. Not only did they all have black faces, but they were also all wearing long robes! The child didn't know where she was, and she couldn't stop being amazed.

In mid-January 1964, my mother traveled with the children via Zurich back to Venezuela, where it was still summer and not winter like in Germany. The family sometimes spent a few nice days by the sea, near Maracaibo, and stayed in a luxury hotel there. My father filmed his family at the swimming pool and in the hotel garden and then filmed the hotel. There were armed men on the roof of the hotel. As my mother had written, there was a lot of military presence, and it was strictly forbidden to film them. But my father couldn't resist and filmed anyway.

In March 1964, my father's mother, Emma Bauder, died and he wanted to fly to Germany for her funeral. However, he was refused permission to leave Venezuela by the Venezuelan authorities on the grounds that he had just been abroad for a few weeks and was therefore not allowed to leave the country again. The refusal to grant him an exit permit was a very heavy blow for him. My father had loved his mother very much and really wanted to attend her funeral, but in this situation he was powerless. Although the country was so beautiful, my father gradually had enough of Venezuela and its politically difficult situation.

I was born into this travel-loving, truly cosmopolitan, yet very Swabian family. My parents were already in their eighth year of marriage when I was born on July 10, 1964, in the Clinica Caurimare, in Colinas de Bello Monte, Venezuela, as their third daughter. My mother was cared for by a German doctor who discharged us to go home after a week in hospital.

Caracas; Magda and Claudia, November 1964

The family lived in an elegant high-rise building in the Apartado de Correo in La Candelaria, Caracas. My sisters Carin and Susanne were 2 and almost 8

18

years older than me. I was also supposed to be a boy and my parents wanted to name their son Alexander. But as it turned out to be a girl this time too, my parents had to come up with another girl's name. This time, however, my father was no longer able or willing to hide his disappointment about the child's wrong gender - yet again. He said to his wife: "I don't care what the child is called. You do it." No sooner said than done. My mother chose the name Claudia for me on her own, without the help of her husband. My parents received a card from their friend Sven in Denmark saying "Congratulations, another son!"

My sister Carin was very happy about the baby and always said: "Mio baby", my baby. However, she was also jealous of the new addition to the family right from the start, because I - the baby - stole the show from her and she faded into the background. Maybe that's why one day she started running around the whole apartment with a new roll of toilet paper until it was empty. This was a lot of fun for her and got her the attention she wanted, even if it probably wasn't in the form she would have liked. My sister Carin was not only full of energy and cheeky, but she was also curious. One day she picked up something she didn't know from the floor, put it in her mouth and started chewing it to see how it tasted. When our mother heard cracking noises coming from her daughter's mouth, she asked Carin what she was eating. As Carin didn't answer, my mother had to open her mouth and take the half-chewed cockroach out of her cheek.

Susanne expressed her wish to be allowed to visit her grandparents in Heubach during the summer vacation. She didn't like the people in Venezuela very much, she found them less friendly than the people in Uruguay or Germany and she didn't have any friends in her new home country either. A few weeks after the birth of her second sister, her wish was granted. She flew to Germany accompanied by an acquaintance of the family at the time. Unfortunately for Susi, Mrs. Laux flew first class, but she was flying in second. This meant that although she was accompanied at the airport, she was alone in her seat for the entire flight. When she arrived in New York, her chaperone got off the plane and Susanne had to travel on alone. She remembers how lonely and abandoned she felt at the time and thought to herself: "What am I actually doing here? I'll never get to Germany!". Fear gave way to tiredness, and she fell asleep on the plane on the way to Europe. When she woke up, she was told that she had arrived in Germany and Susanne was enormously relieved to have made it after all.

19

The school vacations in Germany did not coincide with those in Venezuela, which is why Susanne had to go straight to school when she arrived in Germany instead of having the vacation she had been looking forward to. While she was there, our father got a transfer to New York, whereupon he obtained the relevant official documents for the planned move. So, it was known to the authorities that the family would be leaving Venezuela for good in December. As a result of this, when Susanne wanted to return to Venezuela in September, she was refused permission to return to the country, as her family would be moving to the USA just three months later. From the authorities' point of view, we were already leaving, and they therefore saw no reason to allow anyone from our family to re-enter Venezuela! Again, the family was powerless in the face of the authorities' decisions. As a result of this situation, the decision was made that Susanne should stay in Heubach with her grandparents for the next few months and continue going to school there. There was no other option. She was told that she would not be allowed to return to her family at the end of the vacations. She would be separated from her parents and sisters until after Christmas.

The grandparents were 62 and 64 years old at the time, but due to their approach to an active life and resulting good physical condition, they were still sufficiently agile to be able to spend a lot of time with a child of this age. They were also very grateful for this child, their grandchild, who was to live with them, as their own children were now all living abroad. Their sons, Martin and Gustav had emigrated to Canada. There was only Aunt Berta left in the house, who was old but still somehow interesting for a child like Susi. Susanne was now the only child in the house with three adults - instead of one of three children - and enjoyed the attention she received.

The adults wanted to make it as easy and successful as possible for her to start at a German school and therefore studied intensively with her. To improve her German, however, she also needed extra tuition. So, Susi went to school in the morning, had tutoring at lunchtime and then did her homework with her grandmother. It soon became too much for the child. One day, when she was supposed to do her homework, she stood in front of her grandmother and shouted "No!" at her. As a result, grandma chased after her around the table attempting to grab her and force her to sit down. But Susi ran and ran and screamed the whole time: "No!" The poor child was obviously overwhelmed. But so was poor Oma. And the parents probably knew nothing of all this.

It was a completely new experience for Susanne to be at the same school as a relative, a cousin. That wasn't possible living far away. But in her parents' hometown it was. Although Susi had to leave her family of origin, she had the opportunity to get to know other family members and to be warmly welcomed by them. So, there were positive aspects to this separation. In addition to the new family relationships, Susi was of course able to learn her parents' language intensively.

In October 1964, my father was away on business again. This meant that my mother was alone with the two small children and still had to prepare for another overseas move. On a card from Sugarloaf Mountain in Rio de Janeiro, my father wrote to his parents-in-law: "On my quick trip, I have also arrived here. Tomorrow I'm going back to Caracas" and he added in the margin "Greetings to Susi". Susanne was to leave Germany for good during the Christmas vacation to be reunited with her family. Little did she know that she would never see the home she had left in Venezuela again.

Caracas, November 1964, Martin Holl, Magda,
Pastor, Hans. baptism of Claudia.

I was baptized in the "Iglesia Evangelica Luterana en Venezuela", the Evangelical Lutheran Church of the Resurrection in Caracas. My baptismal motto was: "Lord, your word remains forever, as far as the heavens are." Psalm 119, verse 89. My uncle Martin Holl, my mother's younger brother, became my godfather. He came from Montreal, Canada, for the christening.

The move to New York was to take place after Christmas. In preparation for the move from South to North America, I received my first passport. It was issued in December 1964 by the Republica de Venezuela with the number 146658. According to this passport, my name was Claudia Martina Bauder Holl, and I had Venezuelan nationality: Blue eyes, blond hair.

In keeping with the family tradition, I was also allowed to experience flying and moving at an early age. When I was six months old, I went on my first flight with the airline Pan American. As a six-month-old baby, I was allowed to lie in a basket that was attached to the wall on the plane. Bedded in this way, it must have been such an adorable picture that I attracted the attention of a representative from Gerber, an American baby food manufacturer. He thought I was so pretty that he wanted my face to be the new "Gerber baby". My mother thankfully declined, saying that we were in the middle of moving house, and she didn't have time for that. But the man assured her that he was serious and that she should come to Gerber with me and my face would be on every jar of his baby food across America. But our mother didn't accept the offer.

Pan American Airways flight from Caracas to New York, January 1965

From South America to North America

New York/ N.Y, USA, 1965

In January 1965, we moved to the United States of America. My father worked as the Vice President and Sales Manager for both Willcox and Gibbs, as well as Pfaff, in New York City. At the age of 35, he was responsible for machines and equipment for the sewing industry and for the entire US sales organisation, with 120 people, working in the 6 branches and at headquarters.

We immigrated to the USA as a family of four, as Susanne was still with her grandparents in Germany. Once we arrived in the "land of opportunity", we all received a green card, which was valid for life. My father immediately endeavoured to get permission to bring Susanne from Germany to us in the USA. However, much to his surprise, this authorisation was initially refused. Since Susanne was not with us when we flew from Venezuela to the USA and immigrated, at least according to the reasoning of the American immigration authorities, there was no other child who needed authorisation to enter the country. This news came as a profound shock to our parents, as they had not expected it. They had just left Venezuela, the country where they were used to bureaucratic inflexibility. But they hadn't expected this from a country as modern as the USA. They had a third child and would have to keep trying to bring their child to them. For Susanne, this meant that she had to cope with the bad news and stay in Germany for the time being. Although her parents were confident that they would be able to reunite the family, in the worst-case scenario little Susi had to assume that it would not be possible for her to move in with her family. What a terrible burden that must have been for her! Poor child!

Our new place of residence was to be New York City, where we initially lived in a chic and modern flat hotel on the Upper East Side, close to Central Park. My parents were very happy that my father's aunt, Trudel Pollanetz, and her hus-

23

band Alex, lived in the neighbouring state of New Jersey. Trudel was very happy that one of her nephews and nieces now lived near her, as all the others lived in Europe. So Trudel and Alex travelled back and forth to New York City, sometimes to visit the family and sometimes to look after us children, so that our parents could go off without us, shopping or to a show.

It was the middle of the freezing winter in the New England states. Carin and I, who had lived in tropical Venezuela and were used to light clothing, were in for a big change when it came to clothing. In New York, the climate was the opposite of what we were used to. From then on, we had to wear warm winter clothes: long pants, sweaters, socks, tights and, for going outside, boots, hats, jackets and gloves. Neither of us liked this additional clothing at all and we were constantly fighting with our mother to get dressed and undressed. My mother told a friend that once she had managed to get one of the children dressed, the second one would start undressing. While she was struggling with the second child (which was clearly Carin), the first was already screaming again and would have loved to take everything off again. Once she had managed to get us both dressed and go outside, Carin started undressing again as soon as we were outside. As a result, she constantly caught a cold and regularly infected me. My mother solved the problem to some extent by putting Carin's jackets on backwards so that she couldn't reach the buttons and zips to take them off.

Our parents had to retake their driving tests in the US. Our father had managed to achieve the highest possible score on his test. An African American woman who had heard his result and was supposed to enter the test room after him then said: "Mister, may I touch you?". She explained to him that it would certainly bring her luck in her test if she briefly touched the arm of the man who had passed his driving test with flying colours. Our father agreed to her wish and wished her good luck in her test. Our parents thought this story was funny and so the saying "Mister, may I touch you?" continued to be used in our family. Our father later liked to say to us when we had to pass an exam: "You wanna touch my arm - for luck?".

Bardonia

My parents decided to move outside the city to a house with a garden and so after six months we moved from New York City to a place called Bardonia in the state of New York. In March, Trudel wrote in a letter "I have been babysitting my (great) nieces Carin and Claudia, who are just called Ananita, "little one" in Spanish, or Hermanita, "little sister", several times over the last few months. The baby is cute and looks a lot like Hans, so Alex often refers to the child as "he"."

After 10 years of marriage, my parents bought their first house and lived their version of the American dream. We lived on Joseph Lane, at the top of a slightly sloping dead end street, on which there were about a dozen similar small houses. Our property was unfenced and bordered a forest area at the back. Most of the houses on our street had no fences, so the children ran from one garden to the next, creating a huge playground. What's more, the houses were usually not locked, and the children wandered in and out of them. Such a neighbourhood was ideal for children, as they had the freedom to run around outside and quickly made friends with other children.

Bardonia, New York, our house, Joseph Lane, March 1965.

My father continued trying to get permission for Susanne to come from Germany to live with us. But it was months before this was granted and she was finally able to move in with us in the summer of 1965. After a year, our family was finally happily reunited. In another letter, our great-aunt Trudel wrote in July 1965: "We visited Hansen's once, it was really nice there. Magda went to great lengths to make everything cozy. You would be amazed if you saw all the new acquisitions there. In the house itself, two air conditioning units ensure that it stays cool. In the evening, we had South American-style steaks cooked on the barbecue outside, with salads. It tasted excellent. Susi has settled in well and is fighting with Carin over toys, as is usual amongst children. "My" baby is very cute with her brown curls and mischievous eyes. She now waddles around barefoot in the garden and often lands on his well-padded bottom. The two big one's swim in the pool or take turns playing on the combined swing and slide."

Susanne had left the family living in Venezuela and speaking Spanish. Now she was returning to her family, who now lived in the USA, where English was spoken. She had spent a year in Germany with her grandparents, learnt German and completed the second grade there. Now she was to go to third grade in the USA and suddenly be able to speak English. In September 1965, Trudel describes the situation in our family as follows: "Hans came back from his business trip to Europe on Sunday... Susanne started school here, she is in third grade and is ahead of her classmates in terms of knowledge, as the teacher realised after Magda showed her the exercise books from South America and Germany. So, the transition shouldn't be too difficult, now it's just a matter of learning English. When she thinks she is not being watched, she already speaks whole sentences. Carin also speaks English, she hears it from her playmates, and the baby... looks out into the world quite happily."

Unfortunately, Susi had a shocking experience on her first day at school. The teacher, an American, introduced her to the class and said: "This is Susanne, she's from Germany. The Germans killed millions of people, especially Jews, during the war." That may have been true as a fact, but what could this little girl do about it? Her classmates were horrified by the teacher's statements about Susanne and her origins and initially wanted nothing to do with her and ostracized her, excluding her because of the information they had been given. Susi, on the other hand, was horrified by what had happened to her. Under these circumstances, she was now supposed to learn English and pass the third grade! This incident made her hate the US and she wanted to go back to her grandparents in Heubach, but our parents wouldn't let her go. It was certainly also a very difficult time for our mother, who had missed her child for a year and now saw how much she was suffering from the changes and the judgement of the teacher. As a consolation, however, our parents brought our grandparents over for a visit. Oma and Opa, who had never boarded an aeroplane in their lives, took a long time to be persuaded by my mother, to take an overseas flight. But they did, for Susanne's sake, and it was a happy reunion.

Although we were now living in North America and no longer in South America, our father continued to speak Spanish with Susi, as they were used to doing. Carin also had a small Spanish vocabulary, which she maintained. Whilst Susi was at school, Carin and I stayed at home, where we discovered television and cartoons. We probably watched hours of cartoons every day. Our new "friends" were Mickey and Minnie Mouse, Donald Duck and Goofy. We were fascinated and the TV in the living room was on all day. After all, a television was a status symbol of the time.

We had a heavily built African American woman as our housekeeper. Just as our Spanish housekeeper had previously been instrumental in teaching Susanne Spanish in Uruguay, it was also a housekeeper in Venezuela who spoke Spanish with Carin. In Bardonia, it was once again a housekeeper who kept this tradition of teaching us children the local language, this time English. However, we also had an au pair from Germany called Elke, who was supposed to speak German with us children, but had particularly been brought in for Susanne so that she could speak German with her.

Our neighbours on one side had a German shepherd dog and the neighbours on the other side had a cat. Like the children, the animals in this street also ran around more or less freely. The neighbour's female dog called Lady, took great pleasure in spending time in our garden with the small children, especially with me. Lady was often where I was and was also involved in my learning to walk. She had long hair that I held on to and pulled up until I could stand. So, we walked together, Lady at my side and I held on tight. When I started to walk on my own, I must have been particularly keen to rush into the woods behind our house, because I often headed for them with determination. But Lady wouldn't let me go into the woods. Somehow, she knew that it wasn't a good idea and placed herself between me and the woods and kept pushing me back towards the garden. She was a loyal soul and protected me. I probably awakened her maternal instinct and was her surrogate child. In any case, she laid the foundation for my love of animals.

The neighbours' cat on the other side of our house also liked me. She therefore also wanted to be close to me and I enjoyed stroking this cat. However, the cat didn't always fare as well with me. I sometimes grabbed her like the dog, which she didn't like. But because she was much smaller than the dog, I also tried to sit on the cat, which seemed like a good idea. Sometimes she managed to free herself, but every now and then someone had to rescue the poor little animal meowing for help.

In October 1965, our great-aunt wrote about us: "The baby recently took her first adventurous steps into unknown worlds. Her sister Carin set off with her and they got as far as the last house on the road before they were missed."

My father was one of the many people who worked in New York City but lived outside of the city, which made him one of the many commuters. When the power went out in New York in November 1965 (the big black out), he was one of those stuck in the underground. He later recounted this story with enthusiasm. After the blackout, people in New York asked the question: "Where were you when the lights went out?".

My parents loved their time in New York. They also enjoyed going to Manhattan occasionally for classical music concerts, operas and Broadway musicals. My father had already seen a performance there in 1965 featuring Barbra Streisand. He immediately thought that she was fantastic and raved about her voice from then on. He always said later that he knew straight away that she would become a big star. When her songs were played on the radio, he would later tell me that he had discovered her, so to speak. He bought her records, and I also did, but 20 years later. There were also records from his time in New York by Dean Martin, my father's absolute favourite singer, and of course classics like Bing Crosby with his "White Christmas". From that time on, American music from the late 60s could be heard in our house.

In another letter from our Aunt Trudel from December 1965 it says: "Susi still reads German quite well and hopefully she won't forget it. But I'm not really convinced of that. She already speaks English quite well, it's only her writing that's still a bit of a problem, which is obvious. She is at the top of her class in maths and drawing. As soon as she can speak and write English perfectly, she will have settled in. This will still take a few more months. The two little ones are cute. Claudia is growing up so fast and every time I haven't seen her for a few months, she has learnt so much. Her greatest joy is eating and drinking and as soon as the table is set, she stands there and wants to be lifted into her chair, regardless of whether she has just eaten or not. Then she pushes her empty plate onto the table and demands "more"."

But even though the family had a good life in the USA, my mother was always homesick for Germany, which she also told her hairdresser. He said he had an old book in an old European language, possibly from Germany. He asked her if she wanted to have a look at it. She did and confirmed that it was from Germany. The book was from the year 1596! It was a print of letters by Martin Luther, which was of enormous value to her as a devout Christian and a Protestant. She later told me that she bought it from the hairdresser for 50 US dollars because he no longer wanted it. He said what would he do with a book he couldn't read. For her, as a Lutheran Protestant, it became her most valuable treasure.

My mother was a passionate pianist and was finally able to fulfil her long-standing wish in New York, to buy her own piano. She had had to live without her own piano for ten years, as the family moved regularly and transporting a piano would have been too expensive. As it was quite possible that the family would move again, she had to opt for a small piano. In 1966, she bought a special piano for $3,000, which was smaller than the standard at the time, but it was even suitable for the Metropolitan Opera, so it was of very high quality. She was very happy with her piano, but my father was so shocked by the price, which was equivalent to a new car, that he kept the bill for decades.

Carin started nursery school in fall 1966 at the age of four. Trudel wrote in September 1966: "Carin is now attending a private nursery school because, according to Magda, her exuberance and curiosity need to be channelled. Carin loves it there. Claudia can't believe that both Susi and Carin leave her alone at home for half or full days." In her kindergarten, Carin not only learnt to speak English fluently, which she diligently passed on to her little sister, she also learnt to sing the American anthem and to swear the pledge of allegiance to the American flag. And just like that, a little girl from South America, with German parents, became a naturalised little American.

In our playroom we had children's furniture and a small kitchen with lots of toys that were typical for little girls. For example, we had a small Betty Crocker oven with which we played at cooking and baking, a toy vacuum from Hoover and much more, all small and child friendly. Our dining table and chairs were a copy of the furniture that was fashionable in the USA in the 60s, with a plastic surface and a metal edge that was rounded at the corners. Carin and I not only enjoyed playing at our table, but we also liked dancing on it. One day, however, my sister didn't like having to share the table with me and she pushed me off. I landed with my face on the rounded metal edge and directly on my eye. Blood started to flow, and my mother immediately took me to hospital, where I got stitches. The laceration was a few millimetres to the side and below the eye, so the doctor hoped that there would be no complications and that I wouldn't lose my eye. I was very lucky, and everything healed well.

Substitute grandparents

In a letter in January 1967, Aunt Trudel wrote: "In itself, it would be pleasant to chat with you. However, I'm afraid it won't come to much, because Claudia appears regularly to show me something. Perhaps you know that Magda has been in Germany since mid-December and was finally operated on 4 January. The operation seems to have gone well, and we hope that she will be back on her feet in a few weeks to be able to look after her family. Claudia was with us for 10 days, then Hans brought her home for 10 days as he was still on holiday, and she has been back here since 2 January. ...Carin is with Aunt Liese, and she likes it there, but Carin often has moods like a prima donna, which she wouldn't be allowed to have with me. She's the posh one of the family with her fine little face and good behaviour when she feels like it. Susi goes to school and stays with a neighbouring family."

Friends from the neighbourhood, the Johnsons, had heard about our mother's health problems and offered to let Susi come to their house after school. She stayed there for dinner and our father picked her up late in the evening after work. It wasn't a nice time for Susi because she had to get up very early in the morning, get herself ready and go to school early on her own, while our father made his way to work in the city centre. He wasn't used to looking after the children and had no sympathy for the fact that Susi sometimes took longer to get ready, whereupon he shouted at her. When she woke up one morning with a swollen foot and said she could no longer walk, he had to take her to the doctor. The doctor said it was a spider bite that had caused her foot to swell. There was no question that she could stay at home, as our father would certainly not stay away from work because of a sick child. So, she had to go to school anyway, with one of her mother's shoes on her foot - as her own shoe was too tight - which annoyed her a lot, because on the one hand she was in pain and on the other she was very embarrassed about the shoe thing. But she had no choice, because our father insisted on going to work. So, everything was under control, even though Susi suffered a lot from the pain and embarrassment.

Trudel went on to write: "Once again, my Claudia comes and says, "I did not touch it". In her language this means that she probably touched something that was forbidden to her. Now she's run off in a huff, demonstrating being offended, because I didn't give her any attention". I was in very good hands with my aunt Trudel and my uncle Alex. They both liked me very much, right from the start, and I liked them too. Our "community of three" was always peaceful. Although they didn't have any children of their own, they were exemplary as substitute parents or grandparents. They were incredibly relaxed but also interested and committed. Trudel and I discovered the simplest things together and had a lot of fun eating rice crispies for breakfast every morning. We would sit in front of our bowls and listen to our breakfast make the famous American "snap, crackle, pop" sounds. This kept us occupied for quite a long time and got the day off to a fun start. I didn't know that from home.

Alex went to work as a precision mechanic. Trudel looked after the household in the mornings, and I was allowed to run around freely and touch some things, but not everything. In the afternoons, we either went to the playground or, when Alex had time at the weekends, we went to the seaside and went for a walk along the boardwalk. When I didn't want to walk any more, Alex would proudly carry me up in his arms as if I were his own child and then he would sing me songs. When we were there, his favourite song was "Under the Boardwalk" by The Drifters. It was a wonderful feeling for me to receive so much attention from both and to be loved. We probably seemed like a happy little family and that's what we were, during the times that we were together.

Carin wasn't as lucky with her foster family as I had been. They didn't get on at all and my sister was sort of kicked out. So Trudel and Alex took her in, even though they didn't have much space in their small house and we both had to sleep in the living room. I was happy to have my sister with me and my substitute grandparents. Alex, a trainer clockmaker, couldn't practise his actual profession, but he still made grandfather clocks in his spare time. One of his grandfather clocks, which he was very proud of, stood in the living room. To us children, it was huge, and during the day it had a very nice sound. But at night the sound continued and made it difficult for us to fall asleep. At some point we were so tired that we fell

31

asleep after all. I had difficulties with it at first, but after a while I found the sounds soothing, as being half asleep, I knew that I was with Trudel and Alex. Carin also needed time to get used to it.

When my sister first came to us, she still seemed quite traumatised by her experiences in the foster family, so we had to cheer her up. Through our breakfast ritual, she also started to laugh again. She was soon back to who she really was - she didn't miss a beat, had lots of energy, scurried around, in short, she was quite exhausting. And it wasn't long before she got herself into trouble. After just a few days, she had managed to push her head through the bars of a railing but couldn't get it out again. After Trudel had tried everything possible to free her, she finally had to call the fire brigade for help, who had to weld the child out of the railing! As much as Trudel and Alex loved me and had grown fond of Carin, they were certainly happy when, after a total of two months, our mother returned in mid-February, and they were able to drop us off. I can't remember whether it was difficult for me to leave my mother, but maybe it was. In any case, I was happy to see her again. I don't think it was a good idea to separate us children at first. We should have been allowed to stay together. It would certainly have been better to let us stay at home with an appropriate adult carer. But maybe our mother couldn't find a suitable person at the time. Apart from that, I don't understand why my mother went to Germany for an operation. Surely there were good doctors in New York. She probably wanted to recover with her parents after her operation. In any case, I remember being happy to be able to return to our home, although I was very happy with Tudel and Alex.

No sooner had our mother returned home, than our father had to travel again, in March, this time to San Juan, Puerto Rico, and a month later to Denver, Colorado. She had to cope with us on a day-to-day basis, whether she had recovered and felt strong enough or not.

We had a spacious American kitchen with all the new appliances of the time. This included a large fridge that was as tall as a grown man. The door was difficult to open, and the fridge was always full. We children were allowed to take out whatever we wanted to eat and drink. The top shelf of the fridge was full of drinks and there was always a large glass jug filled with juice or lemonade. Carin liked to be the 'boss' towards me back then, so I usually had to ask her permission first to get something from the fridge. She usually also brought me the heavy glass jug, but the day came when I thought I could take it out myself. My sister was against letting me do it on my own, either because she suspected I wouldn't be able to do it or because it meant she would have to give up her position as the 'drinks boss' if I could manage this task without her help. We were about three and five years old, standing in front of the open fridge and squabbling over the filled glass jug. In the end, I won the fight, but the jug slipped out of my hands and crashed to the floor right in front of my feet. It broke into many pieces and glass flew in all directions, including at my legs. I screamed terribly when I was hit by pieces of glass, some of which cut deep into my skin. Blood flowed down my legs and my mother immediately ran into the kitchen, horrified to see what had happened. She bundled us both into the car and - once again - drove us straight to hospital. My cuts were treated there, and I was given a kind of plaster cast. The doctor gave me a lollipop to calm me down, which certainly distracted me, but the pain remained for the time being. My sister also got a lollipop, but I didn't think she deserved it. After all, I was the injured one! As I sat there and witnessed all the action around my leg, I was convinced that my sister was to blame for everything, just like the last time I had to go to hospital.

In Bardonia, we got to know the four seasons of the American Northeast. This was the normal weather for me, as I came there as an infant, but not for Carin, who had spent her first 2½ years in the tropical north of South America. We both liked the fall best, when the leaves on the trees changed colour and we could see all the transformations the variety of trees, in the forest right behind our house. We collected the different leaves in all shades of green, yellow, orange and red. We also experienced Halloween here. We prepared like the other families by hollowing out a large pumpkin and carving a face into it. My sisters dressed up to go from house to house in the evening with other children and shout "Trick or treat!". I was still a bit too young to go with them and stayed at home. This was also a some-times-scary experience, because the other children in disguises came to our house. Seeking protection - because I had no way of knowing whether there might be a ghost at our door - I stood close behind my mother when she opened the door to give the little children dressed up in scary or creative costumes a sweet as a reward for their successful outfits. At the end of the day, I benefited from the goods which my sisters had collected, because they had to share with me, and I was able to eat lots of sweets for days to come. We didn't think about the consequences for our teeth back then and I don't remember any regular or intensive dental care as a child. Unfortunately, we also experienced that sometimes on Halloween night, the older children simply crushed the beautifully carved pumpkins with their feet, and we then had a huge pumpkin mess in front of the house.

We also loved the snow, which seemed endless. Carin had never experienced it over a longer period before, so she was even more delighted to discover that you could build snowmen out of this mass. After the long winter, spring arrived quite quickly, with an enormous variety and quantity of flowers, so that we were hardly able to stop marvelling. The trees even turned green again, which we would not have thought possible after the long and very cold winter. Spring quickly turned into summer, which was very hot and, to our delight, lasted a very long time. We had our little pool in the garden and jumped into it all the time. We enjoyed the four seasons and made the most of each one. We were completely happy.

In August 1967, at the age of 38, my father applied for a job at Robert Bosch GmbH in Stuttgart. He wrote: "Here in the USA, my main task was to intensify the sales of Pfaff industrial machines. The successes achieved led to my current position as Vice President, responsible for all US sales, not only of Pfaff products, but also of Willcox and Gibbs' own sewing machine line."

As I found out when researching for this book, my father had given the wrong birth years for all three daughters in his application at the time! Instead of 1956, 1962 and 1964, he wrote 1957, 1963 and 1965, perhaps thinking more in terms of relocations or changes of country and associating which child was born in which country. This is how I can explain that he may have thought: "Susi was born, then we moved to South America, so it was 1957. When Carin was born, we moved to Venezuela, so it must have been 1963. Claudia was born when we moved to the USA, so it must have been 1965. Or something like that, I can only guess. I notice that the family moved within a few months of each newborn child. No wonder life was so stressful for my mother.

One day, Inge, a cousin of our mother, came round with her three daughters. It turned out that they had come to pick up our toys because we were moving to Germany, as we would be living there from January. This seemed a bit sudden to us - because we children hadn't known anything about our father's job application - and we hadn't been prepared for these sudden changes. We were faced with a fait accompli, a done deal. These girls were even allowed to take our toy kitchen, which we had all been so proud of, with them. We were horrified! Our mother had said that the things wouldn't work in Germany anyway and that was the end of the

34

matter. We didn't talk about it and certainly didn't discuss it. And the things were gone! We could only wave goodbye to our toys: Bye, bye.

After living in New York for three years, our stay in the USA was coming to an end. I would be experiencing my second overseas move, but certainly for the first time consciously. And I had to say goodbye to my beloved Aunt Trudel and Uncle Alex, my substitute grandparents. I left my first perceived home at the age of three, speaking English. Carin and I had become two little almost-Americans. She left her second perceived home at the age of 5, now also speaking English. My parents went back to their home country, Germany, and Susanne also returned to a country that she was familiar with, having stayed there for longer periods of time and lived there for a year. Susanne had become accustomed to life in the USA in the 2½ years she had lived there. She was in the middle of fifth grade when she consciously left her fourth home country, the US, at the age of 11. A wonderful time and a very pleasant period of life came to an end for the whole family. Now, we were returning to Germany. We would already be spending Christmas 1967 with our grandparents in Heubach.

From North America to Europe I

Heubach/ Wuerttemberg, Germany 1968

In January, my father began his career at Robert Bosch GmbH in Stuttgart, a company founded in 1886. At that time, the company had around 90,000 employees and achieved a worldwide turnover of almost four billion DM, the majority of which was generated abroad. The divisions at the Stuttgart headquarters were automotive equipment, power tools, metal and plastic products, condensers, workshop equipment and manufacturing equipment. In addition, the company was active through subsidiaries and associated companies in the areas of household appliances, radio and television, electronics and photo cinema, packaging machinery, industrial equipment, electrical equipment and plant management.

The Chairman of the Board of Management was Hans L. Merkle, who originally came from the textile, or more specifically clothing industry, but had already been with Bosch for several years. He had also taken over the management of the Liederkranz, a choral society, in Baden-Württemberg from my grandfather Paul Bauder, who was also from the clothing industry. Through stories told by my grandfather, Hans L. Merkle was aware of my father's remarkable international career, at a time when this was very unusual. He was interested in developing Bosch internationally and thus won my father over to Bosch.

As Heubach, our parents' hometown, was only an hour away from Stuttgart, the family moved there. We rented a large, modern house in a street called Weingartshalde. After my parents had lived abroad for 13 years, it was exciting for many in the town, that they were now returning. My father had worked his way up professionally and was just starting his career in one of the most respected traditional companies in the entire Stuttgart region and beyond. My parents also had an international lifestyle, which was very unusual at the time. They dressed extremely elegantly, had experienced a lot of exceptionally interesting things and had a lot to tell. My mother's parents were not the only ones who were very proud of their Magda and, as they always said, "their" Hans. The pride extended beyond the family, and many wanted to share in the aura of the sophisticated and worldly ones. For some people in the town, my parents were local heroes who had "made it". Indeed, they were.

Heubach 1968; Magda, Aunt Klaerle, Uncle Alex,
Sue, Aunt Trudel, Carin und Claudia.

Our parents were often invited to celebrate their return, together with their success. While they went to invitations in the evening, we children stayed at home and were looked after by some of our parents' acquaintances or relatives. These were people whom we children didn't know or hardly knew, and I didn't like being left at home with strangers at all. What's more, we mostly spoke English and didn't understand these strangers very well.

During the years in which my parents enjoyed a better life and better living conditions abroad, they were working on rebuilding Germany. Therefore, for some of their relatives and friends, these extraordinary times that they had experienced outside of Germany and in other countries, may have sounded like a provocation, as if my parents had withdrawn from participating in the work and the task of rebuilding Germany. But they hadn't. They just didn't have to suffer in the coun-

37

try, but they always had to assert themselves abroad, also as the still 'bad' Germans. That wasn't easy, because a large part of the world hated Germany and the Germans after the Second World War. So, it wasn't just about economic interests, but also about international understanding and diplomacy, even without having an official mandate to do so. My parents, and we children too, always had to behave like particularly "good" Germans, being exemplary. That was also exhausting. But it was our family's contribution to "our" country.

In a nutshell, my father's contribution to the rebuilding the German economy was to sell German products. What good are good products if they don't reach the market abroad? How many jobs depended on it? My father had built up distribution networks and managed branches of German companies. That was hugely important! And the others didn't realise how much work he had put into this, or how often my mother had been alone. The success and the financial benefits were seen and often envied. And some will certainly have thought to themselves, that the benefits are what they also wanted. But they probably didn't think about the hard work put into it, or the sacrifices made.

For some, on the other hand, talking about foreign countries and adventures may have come across as boastful. In my opinion, however, it is not boasting if you have achieved something through your own efforts. My parents had self-fulfilled their potential abroad, in many ways. In Germany, the opportunities for this were very limited in the post-war period. People who had stayed in Germany perhaps asked themselves why they hadn't also left to earn money and live abroad? But who would take the risk of leaving their home country? Who wanted to be the "bad German" abroad back then and taking the punches? The visible financial advantage of my father's hard work and the family's international mobility undoubtedly caused blunt envy, without taking the effort into account.

From January, Carin and I went to kindergarten in Heubach. After speaking English in the USA, we learnt to speak Swabian there, the south-western dialect. After Susi had learnt English, she now had to learn German again and finish grade five in German, in the middle of the school year. She went to grammar school and was looking forward to being in the same class with former classmates from her school year in Heubach three years earlier. Unfortunately, the start of the school year in Germany had been changed from spring to fall. As a result of this change, the class she had been in was brought forward by six months, meaning that they had to complete two school years' worth of material in one and a half. This also meant that her former classmates were already in grade six. Susi couldn't understand how this could have happened. She had always studied hard and yet was separated from her former classmates and now had to be in the same class as the "younger ones". The other children assumed that Susi had been bad at school and had repeated a year. She thought it was all unfair and was unhappy about it.

Grandparents and aunts

During this time, we often stayed with Oma and Opa in the Paradiesstrasse (paradise street!). I loved being with them, partly because they made me feel unconditionally loved, if only because I was their daughter's child. Although we were usually dressed well to see them, we didn't have to behave like trained lapdogs when we visited, as we did elsewhere, but were allowed to be children. Hedwig and Eugen Holl seemed more content and relaxed than all the other relatives I met in Germany during this time.

I was fascinated by the house they lived in, a timbered-framed house, which was about 250 years old at the time. It was narrow but deep and three storeys high. There was also an adventurous vaulted cellar made of stone. Our grandparents had a small kitchen - by our North American standards - which was spartan for us, but normal by German standards. When we saw their fridge, which corresponded to the German standard of the time, one door and about 80 cm high, we children asked our parents: "Is it to play with?". We were used to different, larger dimensions in the US and our toy fridge wasn't much smaller than our grandparents' real fridge.

Oma always had a good, warm lunch, served punctually at 12.00 noon. There was usually a soup to start with, then a main course with a salad and after all this food, there was also a dessert. We weren't used to eating warm food at lunchtime, because in the USA, like the rest of the nation, we ate warm food in the evening as a family. At lunchtime there we had sandwiches, sausages or some kind of snack. Here it was the other way round. That was a change that we had to get used to. Despite this change, I enjoyed going to my Oma's for lunch because she was a wonderful cook. But I also liked going to her house just to be near her. She was usually quiet, as if she was thinking about something. She also always managed to keep me occupied with the simplest things. We children also had a lot to explore in her ancient house. And there were still a few of our mother's toys there from her childhood. I was fascinated by the unevenness of this house; the walls in each room had their own angles and some of the floors were uneven. Each room had its own smell and each floor its own sound. The house had character and almost seemed alive to me with its cracking and creaking floors. Even the doors were different and almost every door handle was different. It was the purest conglomeration of a few decades, if not the last two centuries. That fascinated me!

There was a garden behind the house that was laid out as a kitchen garden, with rows and rows of flowers, berries, fruit and vegetables. There was a variety of colours, shapes and smells in a tight density that I had never experienced before. Everything smelled great here, and not like the food from the supermarket. This garden had been necessary to survive in the countryside and, as my grandmother told me, to have food to eat during the war.

Opa smoked cigars, which he was not allowed to do in the house, except in the winter months. Then he was allowed to smoke downstairs in the laundry room. So, he would walk up and down the garden and smoke his cigars with pleasure and with a calmness that was a little infectious. When he puffed his cigar, I liked to be near him, which didn't bother him at all. My grandparents didn't seem to be bothered by us children at all and maybe that's what made them so different from my parents. With my father, I usually felt like I was disturbing him just by being there. Apart from that, I knew that, from his point of view, I wasn't really wanted, as I was the 'wrong' gender. And my mother, as much as she loved me, often didn't have the strength to look after us. Sometimes she was completely absent due to illness. Sometimes she simply seemed disinterested in us children. But she was probably caught up in her illnesses or under the influence of medication that affected her reactions. In contrast, my grandparents were completely different because we didn't bother them - I can't remember being rejected by any of them even once - and they loved us for who we were. My Oma was interested in everything I told her or what I did. Grandma never scolded us, but I never gave her any reason to. I also don't remember my grandparents ever arguing with each other or even speaking badly about each other. They seemed happy to have each other, and they were completely content. This contentment that they radiated was a wonderful feeling for me. Everything in their lives had been organised through their long marriage, both knew the daily routine and their roles and tasks. There was no stress and no hectic pace. The whole house was always tidy from top to bottom, everything had its place, and everything was always clean. As a small child, I found this house an oasis of calm and felt very welcome.

We also visited our grandad Bauder from time to time. He lived in a villa on a hillside, opposite the Triumph site, in a street called "Alte Steige". For me as a small child, the way there was long and steep, and I found it difficult to get there at all. When we finally arrived, this large house awaited us, which seemed quite cool to me. Maybe it was because his wife had already died that I didn't find it warm and therefore didn't like going there. I remember our first visit there after our return from the US very well. We girls were wearing dresses and were dressed to the nines when we were invited in by the housekeeper, who in turn warmly greeted and hugged my father. She beamed at us children as if we had known each other forever, but I had never seen this woman before - at least not consciously. We children then had to be quiet and were led into the study with our father. The way there led through the dining room, which had a very large table, lots of chairs and a very large sideboard. Everything there seemed huge to me. Then I saw an old gentleman sitting in an armchair, not laughing but trying to smile. He had very little hair on his head and was wearing a three-piece grey suit. After he stood up and greeted his son Hans with a handshake, he looked at me with his cold dark eyes and asked in a deep and loud voice: "And who are you?" I froze in fear and couldn't get a sound out. This man was so strong in his presence that I was intimidated at the age of 3½ and tried to hide behind my sister.

Contrary to this, we children were always given a very warm welcome by our aunt Margret. I was particularly receptive to her beaming face when we arrived at her house. She always gave me a big hug and laughed. Margret loved children and especially those of her best friend Magda. Margret had married Siegfried Kelbass, who was a trained gardener, in the early sixties. They had set up their own nursery and specialised in orchids. The greenhouse right next to the house was the most interesting place in Heubach for me. I could stay there for a long time and look at one plant after another. But Margret didn't have much time for us. She had her young son Martin, her husband, her mother, her house and the nursery she had to work for. She also had to take care of the firm's finances. Despite her regular fourteen-hour working days, she was characterised by an unshakeable positivity and had an infectious warmth in her nature that I had never experienced before and that was unique to me.

Kind-hearted people, like my aunt Margret, showed no trace of envy when it came to my parents' professional success. And I could sense this even as a small child. She knew, as Margret later told me, that this success was the result of hard work - by Hans and Magda together. Margret could be happy for her friend Magda that she had experienced an extraordinary life. But she also knew that my mother was the driving force behind Hans, who had his back so that he could go on so many business trips and have a good life at home. Margret knew that my mother did an enormous amount for her husband and her family - and not just in the household. To be able to accompany her husband to business invitations and to take part in the conversation, she always had to keep up to date with economic and political issues on an international level, so she read various foreign newspapers - in different languages. It was also important for her to look good and be well-dressed so that her husband could be proud of her. She succeeded in all of this and brought up three children.

My mother had a few aunts who were born around the turn of the century and had lived through the First World War as teenagers. This war, which Germany started and lost, claimed many victims on all sides. Many young men died as soldiers during the war, which meant that there was a shortage of men after the war. It was therefore often the case that young women were unable to find a husband. These 'manless' aunts of my mother were now in their 60s or 70s, had never married and had no children. Many had lived alone for most of their adult lives and had always worked. Some were now retired. As they had no family of their own, they were even more grateful for visits from Magda and her family. So, when we returned to Germany after many years abroad, we also had to visit these aunts.

That is why I remember many car journeys to small towns, where we got out after one or two or even more hours and went straight to some mostly small, musty-smelling flats. Carin and I usually wore clothes made by our mother, which were usually identical dresses. In preparation for these visits to relatives, we were washed, combed and dressed up nicely before being shown off. We were always told how big we had grown and how pretty and well-behaved we were because we managed to sit still for a very long time like trained lapdogs. I can't remember any of these aunties having any toys for us when we visited, or any other children there, that we could have played with. All in all, these compulsory exercises were terrible for us children. We were always sitting at the table with these aunts, either for lunch or for coffee, sometimes even for both without interruption! Sometimes we went for a walk after lunch, something that was previously not known to us. We thought this was terrible too and would certainly have preferred to be in a playground somewhere. These visits were torture for Carin and me. As if it wasn't enough that we had to visit them, these aunts also came to visit us. But when they came to visit us, we at least had the advantage of being able to run around the house freely, play with our toys and go out into the garden. The supply of aunts and the associated visits seemed to me to be too plentiful.

One of these aunts was called Tilly. She always greeted us very formally with a handshake, which we weren't used from the US and didn't like at all. She stood exceptionally straight, although or perhaps because she seemed to be a little shorter than the other adults, had grey hair pinned up in a tight knot, wore white blouses, buttoned all the way up and wore either grey, dark blue or dark green outfits. She looked more like a general and gave the impression of always acting out of a sense of duty. Accordingly, I looked at her critically and with unease and then tried to stay well clear of her. When Carin was at home, I sought her protection to be on the safe side. I didn't like this woman, and I didn't want her anywhere near me.

Our parents were due to travel to New York for a fortnight in August 1968. They came up with the idea of bringing Aunt Tilly into the house to look after us. Tilly had a commanding vocabulary and, dutiful as she was, she would manage to attend to us, with German discipline and order. I remember her orders to eat, get dressed, tidy up, etc. We had never experienced such a tone from our mother. But the worst thing was her idea of having to play music with us every day. Tilly sat at the piano and played and sang one nursery rhyme after another. We had the task of learning these songs and singing along cheerfully and correctly. I didn't feel cheerful at all. I didn't know many of the songs. Some I didn't like, others I didn't understand. At the age of four, I could barely get past one verse of the lyrics, if at all. Maybe Tilly didn't realise that we had lived in the USA for three years and that we liked singing English songs. Or maybe she was aware of it and planned to teach us German songs. I remember standing at the piano crying and trying to sing. Tilly shouted at me every time I made a mistake. It was the first time in my life that I was scolded and even punished for my lack of language skills and knowledge. She had no inhibitions about slapping us in the face or tormenting us in any other way. When the scolding at the piano got too much for me, I would run away, and Tilly would follow me until she caught me. Then followed a hard slap in the face. If I tried to defend myself, she would grab me and put me over her knee and spank me very painfully. When this happened, I would scream for help and Carin would come to help me. I would scream in rage and pain for my mother, and this would infuriate Tilly even more. Tilly managed to beat me regularly and I

43

remember crying and screaming a lot during this time. It was worse than a nightmare because it was really happening. Our parents had left us for a time that we couldn't assess at that age, and we were defencelessly at the mercy of this so-called aunt. Meanwhile, our parents were enjoying themselves in New York, as my father wrote in a postcard to the Eugen Holl family: "We have arrived here safely. It's quite warm, but we have a very nice room with air conditioning. Yesterday we went to a Broadway show, today we're going to Aunt Trudel's." I was so angry with my parents that they had just left us behind with this bogeyman, or woman.

Heubach 1968, Susanne, Claudia and Carin

After our father had been trained by his new employer and prepared for his first managerial position within the company, he was given his first permanent role within Bosch. Nine months after starting there, he was sent to Bremen in the north of Germany as sales manager. The family had only just settled in Heubach, the house had only just been furnished and we already had to move. Carin had just started school in Heubach after the summer holidays and would have to change her place of residence and school in the first grade. I had just started kindergarten and naturally had to accept the change. Susanne started 6th grade after the summer holidays and had to change schools again, to her 5th school! Just a few days after the move, she would be celebrating her 12th birthday in completely new surround-

44

ings. We children had just gotten used to our schools, the kindergarten and the new children and we already had to say goodbye to them, which was difficult for us.

Although I had grown fond of my maternal grandparents and my aunt Margret, I was glad to be leaving Heubach, despite the other pains of separation. After our lovely, relaxed life in Bardonia, I hadn't felt so comfortable in Heubach. I found that people were much stricter with children than we were used to and that we children were not as welcome as in the US. We missed the open neighbourhood and running around from one house to another. It may not have had anything to do with Heubach as a place, but what bothered me, were the cultural differences, which I did not understand, but distinctly felt.

Bremen, Deutschland, 1968

My father was transferred on 1 October 1968 and, after just one month's training, was appointed sales manager/business manager at the Bosch sales outlet in Bremen.

When we arrived in northern Germany, we girls had to switch from our broad Swabian dialect to correct High German. It wasn't a different language this time, but there was a big difference in pronunciation and sometimes also in vocabulary. So, we said 'Gardedoerle', little garden door in Heubach, and 'Gartenpforte', the garden gate in Bremen. As real Swabians, this linguistic change must not have been easy for my parents either.

We lived in a townhouse with a garden and our neighbourhood bordered a park. On the ground floor of our house there was a kitchen, dining room, living room and a guest toilet. Upstairs were three large bedrooms and a bathroom. Carin and I shared a large room. Susi had her own room, and Carin and I loved nothing more than taking her games out of the cupboard and playing with them. Susanne went to a girls' school that was a bit further away from our house, so she had to cycle there. One morning on her way to school, she was hit by a car and injured. As she didn't like her school anyway and the journey there was too far for her, she expressed the wish to go to a boarding school. As our mother was often ill at the time and couldn't spend much time with her three daughters, she agreed. There was another catch for my mother: Susi also wanted to go to boarding school as close as possible to her beloved grandparents. She also made it very clear that she no longer wanted to change schools, as she had had enough of moving and changing schools. She got her wish for continuity and in the same year went to a girls' boarding school in Korntal, near Stuttgart, where she was able to stay until the end of her school years. Here she started her 6th school but unfortunately had the misfortune of not liking this school either. She was able to stay at her boarding school and change schools within town and was thus now attending her 7th school.

Carin and I were now separated from Susi for the second time. At first, I felt quite guilty because I thought she had left the family because Carin and I kept taking away her games and Susi had finally had enough of her two little sisters. But I had no idea at the time that she was overwhelmed by our parents' lifestyle and the job-related moves. I only know that my mother was very sad about this development because she felt that she had lost her daughter. She could understand her daughter's motives, but my mother felt an obvious sadness when her first child moved away.

Our house was close to a meadow and a forest. I had a friend from my new kindergarten called Harald, who had dark eyes and dark hair and, like me, was quite shy. We played together a lot and spent most of our time outside. That was great and much better than in Heubach, because I could finally run around freely again. We regularly ran through the meadow without a care in the world until I once had the unbelievable misfortune of stepping into a small bees' nest. The pain of the stings was indescribable, and I ran all the way home screaming and crying, where my mother gave me first aid and then took me to hospital. My foot was so swollen that I couldn't walk for days afterwards. The encounter with the bees ended my interest in this meadow, but instead I discovered the forest and the trees. Harald taught me to climb trees and from then on, we regularly sat high up in the tree we had conquered until we got really bored. Carin sometimes had to look for me and tell me that it was time to get down from my tree and come home.

There was always something going on here, visitors coming and going, right from the start. Much to my delight, 'my' beloved Aunt Trudel and Uncle Alex from the USA came to visit us in Bremen in the summer of 1969. As with their visit to Heubach the previous year, this was a particularly joyful reunion for us children. This time, too, I was convinced that they had travelled all the way across the ocean, just to see me. But I wasn't happy about every visitor. Time and again we had visits from men I didn't know and didn't like, but whom we had to address as 'Uncle' this or that. Even if they were relatives or friends of our parents, I didn't know their faces and names. The worst thing for me was when our parents went out, or even went away for a few days and we were then left behind with these people who were strangers to us, who were then supposed to look after us. I was afraid of being at the mercy of strangers and didn't want them around me.

That summer, when our parents wanted to go away again for a longer time and without us, they came up with the idea of taking Carin and me, then aged seven and five, away to be looked after. Perhaps this was the better alternative to bringing Aunt Tilly or some strange 'uncle' into our home. As things hadn't gone well with the uncles either, I thought that anything else would be better than being bullied again in our own home and being at their mercy. And being with other children sounded good too. The whole 'away from home' experience sounded like a fun idea, so we agreed and were taken to a children's home in the Black Forest. Once there, we first realised that we were to sleep in a large room with lots of other children. I didn't like that at all, because I had assumed that Carin and I would have our own room, just like at home. I didn't want to share a room with several other children! What's more, I was also the youngest of the 20 or so children. No other child was as young as me. My parents got the slot for me in the childcare facility, as they assured the management that it would be no problem at all for me to stay there, despite my young age. They said that we children were used to being separated from our parents, which was true. They also said that I had my sister with me, who could look after me, so everything would be fine. So, we were both in this childcare facility. But what they couldn't know, was that whenever we were in an unfamiliar surrounding, I always clung to my sister like a limpet, which my sister didn't like at all and hence she did everything she could to shake me off and get rid of me. She didn't like looking after me at all. And I knew that.

As there weren't enough regular-sized beds for the number of children, as the youngest, I had to sleep in a bed for toddlers, with bars. What an embarrassment! What an injustice! I was shocked and beside myself with anger at this fact, which I simply had to accept as a given and thought the whole thing was mean. I had slept in a regular bed for years and now I was suddenly supposed to sleep behind bars. I was helpless once again. And what was even worse was that I couldn't turn to anyone to complain. I was angry at my parents that they had let me down again. Why hadn't they made sure that I got a regular bed? They had simply left again on the assumption that everything was fine. I had to accept that. But at least I wasn't exposed to the slapping hand of some aunt or any other actions by strangers.

It came as it had to: the sight of a five-year-old child in a bed for small toddlers was very funny for the other children and so they laughed unrestrainedly at me, which offended me deeply. That was the beginning of my very unhappy stay there, where I cried a lot. My sister was the only person who comforted me. During the day, I was really at her heels, which certainly annoyed her, and she tried her best to shake me off. But at night, when I cried for my mother and couldn't calm down, Carin would sneak out of her bed - which was forbidden - and come over to me to comfort me. Once, one of the caregivers came in and scolded her for leaving her bed. But instead of just going back there, seven-year-old Carin stood up to this woman and told her she would stay with her little sister until she calmed down. I was lucky that my sister could be so stubborn, and I was proud of her for it. My sister didn't seem to be afraid of anyone and I was glad that I had her.

I don't have any good memories of this stay. It was back to strict order and German discipline, albeit on a different level to Aunt Tilly's, and I couldn't cope at all with this cold way of dealing with children. Our mother was a warm-hearted woman who treated us lovingly, but there was no sign of love here. I felt pushed away and locked up by my parents, almost punished. Our parents had been away for almost a month, which was an immeasurably long time for us children, the end of which we couldn't foresee. How could I be sure that my parents would come back for us and hadn't separated from us forever? Could I know if they had moved to another country? How was I to know that this would end well and that we would be reunited as a family? This whole situation was terrible for us. When we talk about this time as adults, Carin and I speak of our 'children's prison' in the Black Forest.

Under different circumstances, this stay and the separation from our parents might not have been so difficult for us to cope with. If we had lived in one place and in one house all our lives, we would certainly have had more of a basic trust in our parents and in other people. But we didn't have that. We had already experienced several moves at that age, which always meant a final separation from everything familiar. And we'd had various unfamiliar carers with whom we'd had bad experiences. Overall, there was too much instability and uncertainty for us. My eldest sister had left the family precisely because she needed stability in her life. She had gone to boarding school. And I was already insecure and destabilised at the age of five.

At some point, our parents picked us up again and we went back to Bremen, which I was of course very happy about. But I had lost quite a bit of love and a lot of trust in my parents. I was overwhelmed by the whole situation.

In Bremen, my father had discovered the game of golf for himself and was therefore not only away from home on weekdays, but also increasingly on Saturdays and Sundays to pursue his hobby. In addition to all the other days away from home due to work and travelling, he was now also increasingly absent at weekends. It wasn't that bad for me because I didn't have a particularly close or good relationship with him. I never got rid of the feeling of being unwanted by him and so I didn't like him very much. That's why I remember one day that I spent with my father. My mother said: 'Dad is going to spend the day with you today.' It was unusual for him to spend a day off with his daughters and particularly with only me. That had never happened before. So, I saw this as a special opportunity, perhaps a day that would be quite extraordinary, where he would devote himself solely to me and shower me with attention. Great, I thought, and I was very excited to see what it would look like if the big man spent the day with me. Maybe the two of us would go to the zoo together? Or to the playground? But instead of following my ideas, we followed his and drove to the golf course so that he could play a round of golf. I had to run after him and didn't find the whole thing funny at all. My tall father with his long legs was very fast and I had to keep up. I don't know how many holes later I finally had the courage to tell him how displeased and bored I was with this. How relieved I was when he agreed that all this running after me was probably boring for a child my age and I thought the whole thing would end. Instead, my dad handed me a golf club and a ball and told me I could play with it while he carried on playing. I wasn't keen, but I tried anyway and was annoyed about the long club and the small ball. The trip to the zoo was probably not going to happen and I thought the whole thing was rather stupid. He just pursued his interest and didn't respond to mine. Either he couldn't or he didn't want to get involved with me as a child. My dad and I didn't seem to have the same interests!

My sister Carin and her friends, on the other hand, knew what little girls liked, namely roller skating. Susi had taught Carin and now Carin wanted to teach me as well. I had already tried, but without much success. So, Carin and her friends wanted to help me learn to roller skate together and persuaded me to let them pull me along: Carin on one side and one of her friends on the other. That way, they explained, I would get fast and realise how much fun it was. All right, I thought, let's give it a go. The girls took me by the hand and started to pull me. They got faster and faster and when I realised that I was being pulled towards the garbage cans at the end of the street, I shouted 'stop' in the hope that we would stop quickly. But it was of no use; the girls didn't listen to me because they had no intention of helping me to slow down. They only let go of my hands just before the bins and I thundered right into them, just as they had planned. The girls shrieked with joy at what they had achieved. I was, as expected, infinitely angry! Carin got into a lot of trouble with our mother for this action, the likes of which I had never experienced before. However, she seemed to have factored getting into trouble into the equation, because, overall, she still found the whole thing funny and chalked it up as a huge success for herself.

The following summer I was supposed to learn to ride a bike. However, it wasn't my parents who taught me, but my sisters. I had no reason to be suspicious, after all Carin knew after her reprimand the previous year that she shouldn't hurt me on purpose. I was afraid of riding a bike, but they thought it was time that I learned. Susi was with us for the summer and joined in. I was given a very brief explanation of how to ride a bike and practised carefully once, and then they pushed me, once around the turning area at the end of the dead-end street and then turned me in the other direction. It all worked quite well. Only this time they let go of the bike without our having spoken of this option. They had assured me that they would hold on to me until I managed it on my own! My sisters didn't care that I didn't know how to pedal properly or understand where the brakes were or how they worked. They had already let go of me and simply watched as the bike slowed down and then tipped over due to lack of momentum. Unfortunately, I tipped over with the bike because I hadn't been able to react quickly enough to jump off or catch myself somehow at my shock of realising that they had abandoned me. My sisters laughed their heads off at the whole thing! They thought their little trick of letting me go without any warning worked well. I was hurt and appalled at how mean they had been. From that point on, my trust in my sisters was limited. However, I was pretty sure that Susi had thought the whole thing up and Carin had just gone along with it. But they both obviously enjoyed it. They were both scolded by our mother and I was under the impression that they had understood that they should leave me alone. At least with Susi I had the reassuring knowledge that she would be going back to boarding school after the summer holidays, and I wouldn't have to see her for a while.

School enrollment

I started school in Bremen in August 1970. As is traditional in Germany, I was given a school cone (a German tradition of a big paper funnel, filled with presents, like coloured pencils, eraser, ruler, but also goodies, maybe a bread box) and a school satchel (a big backpack, required to carry books back and forth to school and home every day), on the first day of school. I had chosen a yellow leather satchel, which I thought looked very smart and was proud of, even though it was quite heavy. The children dressed well for our first day at school. I wore a little dress made by my mother, in a red and green checked pattern with a pleated skirt and white collar. I also had matching red leather shoes with a buckle and white socks to match the collar. I thought it was a great event and my friends from nursery school were also excited that day.

We were now elementary school students and would be in the same class together for the next four years. The school enrollment was the first official occasion in my life where I played a role, and I liked that. In addition to my sister Carin, who already attended Horner Heer School, my mother was also there on the day, and she was very proud to experience my big day with me.

Bremen 1970, First day of school. Magda, Claudia.

As I was now also a schoolchild, our mother had given Carin the task of taking me by the hand in the mornings and walking me to school. She didn't particularly like this task as she would have preferred to walk alone or with her friends. I had to put up with her disapproval, even though it wasn't really my fault that my mother had given her this task. I would have preferred to walk to school alone with my mother, but she didn't manage to get up most mornings. One morning when we were halfway across a major road and the pedestrian lights turned

52

from green to red, I stopped in the middle of the road. Carin tried to get me to go on, but I refused as I was afraid, we might get hit by a car. She shouted at me to keep walking, but as the pedestrian lights were red, I assumed she was setting a trap for me, just like with the bins or the bike. I couldn't trust her and so I defied her instructions and even sat down on the road. But as the cars were already starting to drive towards us, she dragged me back in the direction we had come from, and we were lucky not to have gotten run over. Obviously, we were still a bit overwhelmed with the task of walking to school without our mother. After this incident, Carin refused to continue taking me to school in the morning. But our mother didn't want me to walk to school on my own and as she was often ill, she permanently handed over the task of taking me to school to Carin.

School in Germany started in the morning before 8 a.m. and ended at lunchtime, i.e. around 12 noon, six days a week. You could say that as children we were only busy for half a day, and that was in the mornings. Then we all went home to have lunch with our mothers - and in some families also with our dads. This meant that we children were at home in the afternoon and had a day off, after we had finished our homework. Carin not only did her own homework, usually without any help, she also supervised me with mine, which was another of her tasks. Our mother only helped us if we didn't understand something at all or if there was an argument between us. Otherwise, she was often in bed in the afternoons due to her illnesses. When she wasn't feeling well, I was happy to help her and as a first grader, learnt to make tea for her. When I was six years old, the water boiled in a small pot, I climbed onto the kitchen counter, took the teapot from the top cupboard and poured the boiling water into the teabags in the pot. Then I took the teapot, cup and sugar on a tray up the stairs to my mother's bedside.

After I had been in the first class for three months, I received my first report from my class teacher, Mrs. Brandstaetter. It said: "Claudia's quick comprehension makes it easy for her to fulfil the requirements of the lessons. She has no difficulties with reading and her expressions are already quite skilful. She is easygoing and sociable in the classroom." Apparently, I could now speak enough German, and everyone was happy with my linguistic and other developments.

During their time in Bremen, my parents had made new purchases for our home and amongst other things, invested in a new Persian rug for the living room. They usually spent their evenings together in the living room and during this "parents only time", they closed the door between the living room and the hallway. We children knew that we were no longer allowed to disturb them. One evening, they were celebrating downstairs in the living room and toasting with champagne. I had been ill that day and was still feeling poorly that evening. I couldn't sleep and I was getting worse. So, I called for my mother, but she didn't come. Then I got up, went to the stairs and called for her, but she didn't hear me. I went down the stairs and kept shouting "Mommy, I'm sick". But she didn't respond. So, I had to break the rule and open the door to the living room. I cried, looked at my mother and said, "Mommy, I feel so sick." She put her glass down, looked at me and saw that it was serious and came towards me. Before she managed to get to me, I felt even worse and threw up, in the middle of the living room and almost all over my mother, in the middle of the new Persian carpet. My parents' lovely evening ended abruptly. My mother tried to get a grip on me and the chaos, but my dad was stunned by what had just happened. He shouted at me - as if I had done it on purpose - stood up, came towards me and gave me an incredibly strong slap in the face. Now it was me who was stunned! I was sick, had just thrown up and now I was being shouted at and slapped! I no longer understood what was happening, although I had already realised that I had did throw up on the precious carpet. I quickly ran out of the living room, away to the guest toilet and out of sheer fear that my father would come after me, I locked the door. I took the key out of the door lock and threw it in the corner. I cried in fear and pain and screamed. Now, the drama really got going. My mother wanted to come and help me and comfort me. She knelt in front of the door and talked to me for a long time. I didn't believe her when she said that my father wouldn't hurt me if I came out again. In between her warm and loving words for me, she scolded him, went and wiped the carpet clean, came back to me and over time I did believe her that nothing would happen to me if I came out. But now we had the problem that I was so upset that I couldn't manage to put the key in the lock and turn it. I was incredibly tired by now and my eyes were swollen from the crying. Following her instructions, I eventually managed to unlock the door again. I don't remember how the evening ended. I was completely exhausted. But I do know that I couldn't stand my father from that day onwards.

Carin and I had a habit of both running to the front door as soon as the doorbell rang. One day we were racing to the front door at a fast pace again when we tripped over each other, and both fell. To be precise, I fell, but Carin flew over me in a high arc and landed with her head directly on the radiator. The radiator was made of heavy metal and had protruding grooves that resembled thick, blunt knives. She hit one of these grooves with her forehead, making a loud thud and slicing her skin open. Blood poured out of the wound in sheer quantities, she held on to her forehead and screamed. It was horrific and I stood there frozen. Very quickly there was quite a bloodbath, her hands were full of blood and so was her face and I thought that my sister was going to die. For once, our mother was on the spot immediately and had a look of sheer horror on her face. She grabbed Carin and drove her to the hospital. Out of sheer urgency and commotion, she left me alone at home. The two of them stayed in hospital for a few hours, which seemed like an eternity, and I waited in uncertainty as to whether I would ever see my sister again. In those endless minutes and hours, she didn't seem so bad after all, and I couldn't and didn't want to imagine life without her - despite her pranks. The thought of losing her made me very sad, but then, much to my delight and surprise, they both came back on the same day, and I was delighted that my big sister survived this unfortunate incident after all. We had learnt from this and from then on, we no longer ran towards the front door.

Once, in the fall of 1970, we opened the front door for our older sister who was coming home from boarding school. I opened the door, looked at the person standing there and asked her: "Who are you?" I didn't recognise her at first, but that could have been because of her new coat and the fact that she was wearing the hood of her coat on her head, so her face wasn't very visible. Carin enlightened me and said: "That's our sister!" On second glance, I recognised her. Unfortunately, Susi was appalled and upset by my greeting and complained to our mother, crying. This was not how she had imagined being greeted at home! She couldn't believe that her little sister Claudia didn't even recognise her. But that's how it was. We had become increasingly estranged due to the separation due to her boarding school life, which had now lasted two years. She was now a teenager and developing feminine traits. Her whole appearance changed. But apart from her development and our estrangement, the underlying problem was that the age difference between us was so great that we were never at the same stage of development and had no common interests and therefore, had little to do with each other. Apart from that, she just didn't seem to like me. I increasingly had the feeling that I was annoying and stressful for her, instead of her ever having any joy in me. I also don't remember her ever giving me a loving hug, cuddled or comforting me.

This visit, which had started badly for Susi, became even worse for her. Our mother had to tell her that the family would be moving next month and that they were going overseas again, back to America, this time to Canada. Susi had now settled in well at her boarding school and had no intention of leaving. Nor did she have the slightest interest in being separated from her grandparents, as she enjoyed spending most weekends with them. She refused to move again, together with the family and changing countries and insisted on staying at her boarding school in Germany, as planned. She no longer wanted to move with her parents and was determined to finish school where she was.

It really looked like we would be separated across an ocean again. Our stay in Bremen had only lasted two years and we were already moving on. In November 1970, after I had only been in first grade in Germany for a few months, Carin and I were deregistered from school in Bremen.

Before the big move, we travelled to South Tyrol in December. I was a little confused by this trip to Italy, because at first, I thought we had already arrived in our new home country, Canada. After all, we had travelled a very long way and when we arrived in the spa town of Merano, I only partially understood the people. I was told that we would spend Christmas there, together with Susi, and only then would we move to Canada after the holidays. My father's brother, Peter, lived in Italy, which was one of the reasons for travelling there, as my father also wanted to see his brother. And we children should get to know our uncle. And Peter was the godfather of Carin, who should have been named Peter after him, had she been a boy, but that did not happen.

For us children, it was the first time we had been on a winter holiday in the Alps. It was nothing new for our parents, however, as they had already travelled to the mountains to ski as teenagers. But for us, the mountains were new, and skiing was a new sport that we first had to learn. I had the most trouble getting in and out of the small four-person cabins. They simply travelled on without stopping and you had to jump in and out in a sporty manner. My legs were simply still too short for this action and so I was sometimes gently, sometimes roughly lifted in or thrown out. Because of this difficulty, I decided against skiing. Instead, my sister Carin and I went tobogganing the next day. It was meant as a relief for us to slide down the hills, or rather the mountain, on a red plastic sled and have fun instead of fighting the cabins. But our sled wasn't just fast, it was very fast. As always, I found myself in a situation where I had little to say in the matter. Carin was steering the sled, and I was simply her passenger. Pretty soon she no longer had full control of the sled as we travelled down a course and, panicking a little, screamed as our sled had become uncontrollably fast. At the last minute, however, she realised that our run was about to end if she didn't make the turn and that we were going straight down a deep slope. At the very last second, she grabbed hold of me and pulled me off the sled with her and we landed next to the track, right in front of the slope. We then watched as the sled flew down the mountainside in a high arc and say goodbye to us forever. We were quite shocked that we had almost said goodbye forever along with our sled. Being the bossy girl she was, she ordered me without hesitation: "Don't tell our parents!" I was already almost frozen with shock, so her instruction couldn't make the situation any worse, and I nodded in agreement not to tell our parents the truth. We walked in silence a very, very long way back to the village. We were physically pretty much at the end of our strength by the time we got back to our hotel. But once there, we were safe and warm. As for the sled, when our parents asked us where it had gone, we said: "Sled? It's gone." Our parents couldn't believe that we had been so stupid as to have simply 'forgotten' our sled somewhere and we let them believe that we had been that 'stupid'. This version seemed to cause us less trouble than the truth, so we stuck to it. Maybe we should have stuck to skiing after all? That didn't seem quite as dangerous as sledging after all.

In fact, this holiday was our very first real family holiday, as most of our trips together had always been visits to Heubach and we then stayed with our grandparents. It was also the first time we had spent Christmas as a family at a holiday destination, rather than at home or with our grandparents. Apart from the sporting failures, we all had a very nice and very relaxed time, including our sister Susi. The five of us had finally managed to develop a real family feeling. Maybe it was possible for the five of us to live under one roof again? As nice as the thought was, especially for our mother, that we now really felt united as a family, it was even more difficult for everyone to say goodbye to Susi at the end of the holiday. Our mother had hoped that Susi would change her mind and want to stay with us, but her hopes were not fulfilled. It almost broke her heart to leave her eldest daughter behind in Europe to move to North America with her husband and the other children. But Susi remained stubborn and gave her no choice but to move on without her. She was determined to return to her boarding school instead of coming with us. I can't imagine that at her age at the time she realised how difficult this decision must have been for her mother. Nor could our parents - who had grown up in total continuity despite the war - imagine how difficult another move would be for their daughter. Susi would rather accept a second overseas separation from her family, than move to another country and be separated from her friends, school and boarding school. Our mother had to accept this; her daughter could not or would not go through any more changes. She would rather be on another continent without her family. Perhaps Susi had become so resolute in getting her way precisely because she had already had to part with everything so often. And separations and goodbyes are always losses and associated with pain. She was obviously no longer willing or able to accept these losses or pain. So, after this holiday we went our separate ways, Susi to Germany and the rest of the family emigrated to Canada, as a family of four. And now, this was the second time we would be emigrating to North America without her.

By the end of the holiday, I had forgotten that we were moving. I was looking forward to going back home to Bremen, but my mother had to remind me that we had left Bremen and wouldn't be going back. The reminder that there was no going back made me very sad as I now realised that I would never see my friends again.

From Europe to North America

As of January 1971, my father was President of the Bosch company in Canada. The company mainly produced spark plugs, car lamps and VDO instruments. His main task was now to expand sales. In the same year, he also became a member of the "Canadian German Chamber of Industry and Commerce", as part of his professional role. This organisation consisted of members from German and Canadian companies, trading companies and individuals and was tasked with promoting economic links between the two countries.

After our three years in Germany, Carin and I now spoke German and had forgotten our English, when we moved to the English-speaking part of Canada. Initially, we stayed in a hotel called the Valhalla Inn, not far from the airport in Toronto. The city itself is in the province of Ontario, directly bordering onto Lake Ontario, in the south. In our hotel, our parents had their own room and we sisters, aged six and eight at the time, had one right next door, which was connected to our parents' room and the door was usually open, so it was almost like a small flat, but without a kitchen.

We both well remember the very cold outside temperatures of the Canadian winter, which caused us to spend most of our time in the hotel, and in our room. There we rediscovered the television that we were so familiar with from the USA. The many programmes, the many cartoons, what fun that was! We also discovered a drink vending machine in the hotel corridor with soft drinks, from which we always got Sprite, ginger ale and similar drinks. When our cousins Erin and Peter, who were about the same age, visited us for the first time, they were quite speechless about the freedom we enjoyed: watching seemingly endless television and drinking loads of lemonade!

During this time, we also got to know our mother's younger brother, Martin Holl, who was my godfather, with his wife Traudel and their children Sandra, who was about two years younger than me, and Michael, who was still being carried in his mothers' arms as a baby at the time. Although we had already had both of our mother's brothers, Martin and Gustav Holl, with their wives visiting us in the USA, we were too young to remember them three or four years later. They were all very nice to us and noticeably happy that we had now also moved to Canada. My mother was so happy about this move, which was for work reasons, but to have the opportunity to live in the same country as her two brothers, after 20 years apart, and even in the same area! She could hardly believe her luck in this respect, one that was only marred by the separation from her eldest daughter.

Mississauga/ Ontario Kanada 1971

After six weeks, our parents had found a house in a municipality called Mississauga and we were finally able to move out of the hotel. The town borders directly on Toronto in the east and Lake Ontario in the south. When we moved there, Mississauga had a population of about 200,000. As Carin and I had spent most of the day watching TV in the hotel, we had managed to learn some English and brush up on our old skills. My sister had managed to do this much faster than me, which was probably because she had left the USA three years previously speaking fluent English. So, she became my translator, which was important because she could also explain things to me from the television.

Our house was in a purely residential neighbourhood with middle to upper-middle class single-family homes. To the south, our neighbourhood bordered a river, the Credit River. The area down by the river was called "Ravine" and later became part of our playing territory.

The house on Sir Richards Road was on a corner plot that had more of a front garden than a back garden. It was the end of February when we moved in, and we were fascinated by the trees and bushes in front of and behind our house because they were covered in icicles. When the sun shone on them, the whole thing glistened and sparkled like in a fairy tale. We thought this mixture of snow and ice was beautiful and voluntarily went outside to take part in it and play. We had the greatest fun throwing chunks of snow, icicles and whatever else we could find at each other from the slightest distance, and we laughed our heads off. We caught the eye of a couple of "real" Canadian kids who had grown up with all the snow and ice and would never have thought of throwing icicles and the like at each other like we did. They knew immediately that we were immigrants because of our strange behaviour. But somehow, they thought we were funny and approached us.

So, within a few days we made the acquaintance of the first children in the neighbourhood.

In February, we started first and third grade at Hawthorne Elementary Public School, which was about one or two kilometres from our house. I remember my first day of school very well. Although my dad didn't usually take us to school, he did that day. That was strange, because he didn't usually have the time to devote to such tasks. But he had to that day. He took me to my class and introduced me to the new teacher, but I couldn't say anything, because I was quite afraid of my new class. Although I didn't like my father very much, I turned to him and would have preferred to leave with him instead of staying in the new class with all the unfamiliar children. I looked up at him - my tall, slender father in his dark blue cashmere coat - hoping that he would read the fear and despair from my eyes and take me back with him, but he didn't. He left without hesitation, leaving me behind in a room full of strangers.

I could already understand the language a little thanks to weeks of watching TV, but I couldn't speak it yet. I wasn't just a newcomer to the area, I was a foreigner with a language barrier, which was noticeable to me due to the speaking hindrance. The class teacher tried being nice to me, but I didn't understand much of what she said. Her vocabulary was different from that of the cartoon characters. She appointed me to a desk, and I sat down. It was easy to sense the 20 or so pairs of eyes staring at me from all directions. I felt uncomfortable and could only hope that this discomfort would end as soon as possible. Much to my surprise, I was then allowed to paint with watercolours on an easel at the back of the class while the other children were learning something. The first word I learnt properly was "paint". My teacher asked me several times: "Do you want to paint?". I didn't understand anything at first. She literally had to take me by the hand and lead me to the easel until I finally realised what she was asking me. Of course, instructing the "alien", as I felt to be, was observed by the whole class, which made me feel even more uncomfortable. I then stood behind my easel so that the children could no longer see me, and I could finally breathe a sigh of relief.

As we were accustomed to, Carin would have to walk with me to school and back home. On the first day after school - I have no idea where our mother was - we walked and walked and walked along the main road as we had been instructed to do, but we didn't get anywhere. With my little legs, the path certainly seemed several kilometres long, but it wasn't. The problem was that neither of us could remember which street we lived on, or where we were supposed to turn off. I still remember how we stopped at the street corners and asked each other: Is this our street? Then she read the street signs and asked each other if that was the name of our street, because we couldn't even remember exactly. Luckily, Carin eventually recognised the house next to ours and we knew the search had been worth it. And so, we got lost for a few days until it finally worked, and we found our way home straight away.

As it was still considerably cold - a lot colder than we were used to in Germany - our mother sometimes drove us to school or picked us up if it hadn't warmed up by the afternoon. She wasn't much better off than us at first. At least she knew where we lived, but driving a car on snow-covered roads, which often still had a layer of ice underneath the snow, gave her a lot of trouble. The "Queensway", the road we mainly walked or drove along, had a ditch on the right-hand side, about half a metre or a metre deep and just as wide. Later, we children had great fun riding our bikes along or across this ditch. But that day we had our first real encounter with one of them. Our mother was driving our father's Mercedes safely along the road until she realised that she had to turn off into our street. She braked hard and pulled the steering wheel to the right. However, the car did not react as planned and instead simply continued to slide straight ahead along the icy carriageway until the wheels could grip again. Then the car promptly reacted as it should and drove in the direction in which the steering wheel had turned, to the right. Unfortunately, by this time we had already passed the road we were supposed to turn into and we drove straight into the ditch and ended up half on the right-hand side. We were startled for a moment! Our car was stranded. But even the nicest and newest Mercedes at the time was no use if it was lying on a slope, so we all got out on the other side with some difficulty. Our mother then had to walk with us the rest of the way and finally realised that it's very cold when you're on foot. Shortly after this incident, she got her own car, a second-hand Pontiac.

Although we children gave the impression that we would cope with this move to another country without any problems, I didn't sleep well at first. I often woke up the wrong way around in my bed in the morning and, at the age of six, I looked pretty worn out, like some young adults after a night of drinking. I also started sleepwalking. Sometimes I had nightmares and didn't know where I was. My mother tried to comfort me as best she could about my restlessness and temporary confusion, but we never investigated the actual reason for it. It was simply accepted as a fact that I was often restless at night and sometimes had nightmares. Perhaps the changes were more stressful for me, than others could imagine.

School in Canada was different from school in Germany in many ways. It started in the morning just before 9.00 am and went on all day until just before 4.00 pm. In the morning, at least back then, the Canadian national anthem "O Canada" was played over the loudspeaker system in every classroom in Canada. The children learnt the words as early as first grade. They stood up during the anthem and sometimes sang along loudly and often passionately. During the lunch break, we usually stayed at school. We took a lunch box, with sandwiches for the lunch break and everything else we needed to get through the day nutritionally: Apple or banana, something to drink and other little things like raisins or nuts. We children usually ate together in the classroom. Sometimes they compared who had what with them and then exchanged food. Carin quickly realised the importance of bartering and packed something in the morning that she could use for trading. These were her first successes as a businesswoman, or girl! After lunch, we went out to play in the school playground. We liked this daily rhythm straight away and had no problem with the change from being at school for around 4 to 5 hours to 7 hours a day. On the contrary. We loved the new school system immediately! After all, we had a lot of fun at our new school, and it was nice to spend the day with other children, instead of being at home in the afternoon. Overall, it was different at school than in Germany because you were allowed to laugh more and play outside a lot more during the breaks. Because we were at school all day, we didn't have any homework. We learnt the new material during lessons, and everyone did the corresponding exercises together in the classroom. We were also taught more practical subjects, sport, music and art than we were used to having in Germany. There was more movement and variety in this school system. It was very appealing for us children and certainly easier for immigrant children to cope with. Especially in the practical subjects, it was very easy to get by without knowing the language. In the other subjects, you were mainly helped by your classmates, who had time during lessons to help you understand things. There were no grades in the first and second classes, so that even an immigrant child is not completely demotivated from the start of school due to poor performance.

There were still significant differences to the school in Germany. A picture of Queen Elizabeth II hung at the front of every classroom. Canada is part of the Commonwealth, whose head the Queen of England was. And I thought it was nice to see this very likeable face hanging on the wall. Apart from the crown on her head, the photo of the Queen almost looked like a photo of a family member who lived far away. There was something comforting about it and I liked it straight away. Some mornings, we sang 'God save the Queen'. It was also different that the Canadian flag was flying on the flagpole in front of our school, which was a very nice welcome. With its red maple leaf, it flew clearly and was easily recognisable, even for six-year-old children. What a wonderful country and school system: fun at school, the friendly Queen on the wall, the proud national anthem and that lovely flag. I was thrilled all round!

At that time, I didn't know what the German flag looked like, and I can't remember consciously seeing it at any point during our three years in Germany. I had never heard the national anthem either. But the Canadian flag was unmistakably memorised. It was not only in front of the school, but could be seen on flag-poles in many places, even at private houses. Even as a child, you could sense that the people who lived here were proud of their flag and their country. And it was a great feeling to be part of it.

Although I had been proud of my school bag in Germany, it became redundant, thanks to the Canadian school system. The children had a classroom that they went to every day and each child had a fixed seat. The desks opened from the top and there was a generous space inside, about ten centimetres deep. The desk looked like a large wooden shoe box. You could leave pens, exercise books and books in your desk and you didn't have to lug them home all the time and bring them back to school the next day. We found that a very pleasant change.

One month after we started school in Canada, we received an interim report in March. But we didn't get any grades yet. This report said, among other things: Claudia will have the greatest difficulty coping with the new vocabulary. In June, just four months after we went to school in Canada and learnt English, we received our final reports for the school year. Now we would find out whether we had learnt enough in the short time to be assessed at all and whether we would be promoted to the next grade. But we both made it and were advanced. My report said: "I am very pleased with Claudia's progress... she has made friends, and the children all like her." It certainly helped me and my sister that we had lived in the USA for three years before living in Germany and spoke English there. Otherwise, I don't know if we would have made the connection so quickly.

Our Canadian relatives, the families of our mother's brothers, visited us at Easter. My mother's brother, Gustav Holl, emigrated to Canada in 1951 at the age of 22 after completing an apprenticeship as a radio mechanic in Germany. Their brother Martin followed him a year later at the age of 19, after training as an industrial clerk at Spiesshofer and Braun. It was a hard blow for their parents to see both sons move abroad. My mother was the only one of the three Holl children to stay in Germany. But she also moved abroad after her marriage in 1954. But now, 20 years after the first of they had left Germany, the three were reunited and living in the same country.

It was a wonderful celebration, probably especially for our mother. Carin and I liked our two aunts because they were both very nice. Our uncles were both quite lively and laughed loudly, which we weren't used to. They were different than the uncles and aunts in the Bauder family who were rather more reserved in their refined mannerisms, characterised by their parents' classical upbringing, and they were also quite emotionally distant. But the Holl's we met in Canada were completely different. They were warm-hearted and I enjoyed spending time with them much more. Our cousin Erin and our cousin Peter were also very nice. I especially liked having a younger cousin, Sandra, because I didn't have a younger sister or a younger brother, but I had always wanted one. I loved playing with Sandra and with the baby, Michael. This Easter was the start of a tradition of celebrating Easter and Christmas with our mother's family. I had never seen my mother as relaxed as she was here. It would become more beautiful with every celebration over the years, and we had plenty to eat every time. My mother and her brother Gustav both loved to cook, which was good because we all loved to eat! Here in Canada, I got to know colourful and cheerful family celebrations, which were wonderful.

A Chinese family with the surname Ma lived in the house across the street. This was the first time we had Asian children in the neighbourhood who could become our playmates. The parents were both doctors and worked. I can't remember how many children they had at the beginning. At some point there were five or six children, all with black hair and they all looked similar, at least to us. We were fascinated by the constant bustle of these small children, because one of them was always on the move. There was a lot of movement in the whole neighbourhood. There was a family with two to four children living in almost every house. We younger children all played together, moving from one house to another

65

- as we were accustomed to from the US - sometimes in hordes of five to ten children. Origin, religion or skin colour were not relevant, at least not at our age.

Our house, like many others, had a fence at the back of the garden that demarcated the property from the next one. However, there was no fence in front of the houses and the houses were usually not locked, even when nobody was at home. This meant that children had free range of movement throughout the neighbourhood. Some people didn't even lock their houses at night, which was quite common there. You rang the doorbell and waited to be let in before entering a house, but it wasn't usually locked and you could have just walked in, which nobody did, except sometimes us kids. We usually didn't lock our house either, even at night at first. At some point, however, our father realised that the house was hardly ever locked and from then on, he insisted that we at least lock it at night so that we couldn't be attacked or robbed in our sleep. But his fears were of European origin and had been influenced by South America. Here in this area, and in this country, the clocks ticked differently. People didn't attack each other and weren't afraid of being robbed. At least not back then. I also don't remember any houses in our neighbourhood being broken into or anything stolen in the three years we lived there. The people here seemed to be extremely peaceful and content, without any noticeable aggression. How marvellous! What's more, everyone we met was simply friendly and very nice. I sensed a positive difference in the people here compared to what I knew from Germany. The whole family felt at home here straight away and we children were welcome everywhere, just like back in the USA.

The only thing that some of these friendly and peace-loving little Canadians didn't seem to like very much were Americans. You were immediately welcome in Canada, no matter where you had travelled or moved from, but there seemed to be a skeptical reserve, or even rejection, perhaps even necessary, towards our own neighbouring country, the USA. At least that's what the other children taught me. We mostly played outside either in the garden behind the houses or in the front gardens. In spring and summer, we had great fun jumping through the sprinklers in the front garden and moving from one house to another to get wet by as many sprinklers as possible. I remember the first time I saw a car with an American licence plate drive through our street. One of the older children immediately recognised it as such and shouted after the car: "Yankee, go home!" And the other children joined in. I asked my friends what they had against Americans, because this aversion was strange to me. Not only that, but we had also lived there and liked it, which meant that we had also belonged to "the Americans" a few years earlier. I didn't necessarily want to tell them that because I didn't have the courage. It was now explained to me clearly and unmistakably: "The Americans leave their garbage everywhere, they are dirty. Americans don't learn as much at school as we do, they're dumb. Americans steal; they are thieves." Well, if that's really the case, as the children said, I thought, they must be bad, these Americans. I couldn't remember any Americans like that, but maybe I'd just been lucky not to have met any. It now seemed to me that I was lucky to be living in the better of the two North American countries. As I liked and trusted my new friends, from then on, whenever a car with an American licence plate was in our neighbourhood, I would shout along with them: "Yankee, go home!"

Susi comes to Canada

Our house was a white bungalow with three garages, which stood at right angles to the house, in an L-shape, to match the shape of the plot. Our garden was full of birch trees, which we had never seen before. We had four bedrooms and two bathrooms on the ground floor. There was also a living room with an open-plan dining room and, of course, the kitchen with an additional seating area.

Our sister from Germany had announced a visit us for the summer holidays. Now our mother was hoping to persuade Susi to move to Canada after all, once she got to know the country and our family life there. The fourth bedroom, which had previously been empty and looked deserted, was now furnished for her with a lot of love and effort. Everything had to be perfect for when Susi came to visit us. Originally, she didn't even want to come to us during the holidays, which was a huge blow for our mother. She was afraid of losing her daughter completely. But then she came up with the idea of inviting her to Canada with her best friend from boarding school, Henny. It was only intended to be a visit for the girls and the return journey to Germany would be guaranteed for both. That is how she managed to get them to come Canada, after all. My mother spent the whole summer exerting herself to make life in Canada as palatable as possible for the two 14-year-old girls. She took them to all the sights and probably fulfilled their every wish. My poor mother! But her efforts had paid off and by the end of the summer she had managed to convince Susi to stay in Canada and live with us. And so, the family was reunited, and Henny flew back to Germany alone.

From then on, the five of us lived under one roof and Susi seemed to like it very much in our new home. After the summer holidays, she went to Kennedy High School in Mississauga and started ninth grade. At first, she had the fourth bedroom, next to Carin's, but this may have been too close to us for her. Or it was too small for her. She soon moved into a small flat in the basement that our mother had prepared for her. Susi had her own entrance, her own bathroom, her own living room with kitchenette and, of course, her own bedroom. This area was originally intended for our visitors, such as Aunt Trudel and Uncle Alex. But it was also intended for Susi to become an integrated part of the family again. Perhaps the separation had been too long, and it was simply no longer possible to be close to the rest of the family. My eldest sister's needs always took priority in our house and so she was given her own separate living area.

In my second year at school, I got a new class teacher. Her name was Mrs. Pillay, who had a slightly different skin colour and dressed strikingly differently. She came from India. As I was still learning English as a foreigner myself, I didn't notice that my class teacher had an accent in her English pronunciation. Mrs. Pillay was friendly, calm, warm-hearted and always confident. I don't remember her ever scolding me. And she was very understanding and patient with me and my linguistic endeavours, as she herself was a foreigner who had only lived in Canada for a few years. As she was though fluent in English, she became my role model and motivated me to improve myself through her skills.

Soon Carin and I experienced our first Canadian fall. The leaves on the trees turned orange and red and we thought the blaze of colour was beautiful. It was just like we had once experienced in New York, which we had initially forgotten about, due to our years in Germany. We also got to know the downside of fall, namely that the leaves eventually fell from the trees and landed in the garden. We learnt very quickly how to rake leaves. Basically, raking was fun, even though it was quite strenuous. The children in the neighbourhood taught us how to gather the leaves into a huge pile, then take a running start from a few metres away and with a big leap, jump into the pile of leaves. It was great fun! You landed softly, deep in the pile of leaves and could see the whirling leaves flying around above your head. We didn't know anything like that in Germany. This country seemed to be full of little surprises and the Canadian children seemed to enjoy everything. It was wonderful to always have fun everywhere.

One fall day, however, my fun in our garden was spoilt by a heated argument with my sister Susi. At some point, she ordered me to put the pile of leaves in bin bags for disposal. I refused, partly because this pile of leaves was part of my new play inventory, but also because I was supposed to do the work on my own. Susi was so upset that I didn't obey her that she shouted at me that I was spoilt and lazy. I'm sure she hadn't expected me to fight back, verbally at first. The verbal exchange turned directly into an exchange of blows. The argument ended with her winning, which she only managed to do by dragging me back to the house by my hair. It hurt like hell, and I screamed as loud as I could. Our mother came to this scene, which she must have found unbearable, and scolded us both as if we had lost our minds. Probably rightly so. From that day on, to me, my sister Susi was no longer welcome. I hadn't liked her much since her return. Everything seemed to revolve around her and her special requests. She could have gone back to Germany to her boarding school, where she had lived separated from us for the last two and a half years, for all I cared. I hadn't missed her either. After this incident, I didn't want her in the family anymore and I let her know that at every opportunity. I did not need her.

That year, I was often ill and stayed away from school. I suddenly had a high temperature and nobody, neither the doctor nor my mother, knew what was wrong. I just stayed at home on those days. By the end of the year, I had missed 30 days of second grade. As it was no use going to the doctor, I was given aspirin to bring the fever down and was allowed to lie in my mother's bed and watch TV during the day. I watched game shows like "Wheel of Fortune". I loved staying at home and watching TV and was never in a hurry to go back to school. My mother brought me tea from time to time and soup at lunchtime. And I just had to wait for my fever to go away. What's more, my sisters were out of the house, and I had my mother to myself all day. Oh, I loved all of it! I couldn't imagine anything better back then and was happy every time I got sick.

Unfortunately, I also fell ill during the Christmas holidays. We had just gotten a new leather couch for our living room, in black with rosewood on the back and sides. We had the couch made and were even able to watch it being made, which we all found very interesting. The precious piece was delivered just before Christmas and now I was lying on it, ill, for several days. It was so nice for me because I could look at the Christmas decorations in the living room and I wasn't alone in my room all day long. My father, however, was annoyed by the fact that I was laying on his new couch, which he also wanted to sit on, and so he kept asking my mother whether "this sick child" really needed to lie on his couch. His words and the way he spoke about me really hurt my feelings.

Our father had the idea of having Bosch Canada sponsor a snowmobile race in winter. This was his way of drawing attention to the performance of Bosch spark plugs in the cold Canadian winter, which he succeeded in doing. The race in question was the "Canadian Snowmobile Races", a sport of snowmobile racing that had only recently been launched at the time. The Canadians knew how to have fun in the winter as well, depending on the weather, and the atmosphere at these races was accordingly great! We children were allowed to take part in the races, which were still quite manageable in the first year. Our father had yellow sports jackets made with the Bosch logo and a huge spark plug sewn on the back as a promotional item. Sue got a jacket, and Carin and I got the same in children's sizes. We thought we looked irresistibly sporty in them. Perhaps because of the jackets, but perhaps also because we were the boss's daughters, we enjoyed a lot of attention at these events. We were even allowed to sit on a snowmobile and drive around the course. That would certainly have been a lot of fun if I hadn't almost got cold shock for one thing and almost wet my trousers from sheer fear of the speed on the other! I was very happy to get off the bike again and pretended that I had really enjoyed it. In my cool jacket, I couldn't "out" myself as a frozen scaredy-cat.

My report card at the end of the school year in June 1972 said: "Claudia is working well in all areas of the curriculum. She is making good progress in reading. She understands what she reads and shows a good command of English. Her maths performance is also good. However, there is a lack of pace as she is slow to complete her tasks." This would certainly have been a good report, except for the observation that I work slowly. My mother didn't mind, but my father did. He did not think that the criticism was okay and urged me to work faster. My sisters found the criticism quite funny and as Sue, as my sister Susi was now called, and I were in an open battle against each other anyway, she took every opportunity to make fun of me from then on by calling me "slow" in everything I did, and she incited Carin into joining in. I didn't find the whole thing funny at all. Carin managed the school year without any trouble. Her reports contained no criticism. Being in her shadow and always doing slightly worse than her made life difficult for me, even then. Sue wouldn't let me look at her report card, but pretended it was fine.

Up North

At the beginning of the summer of 1972, we travelled "up North" by car. That was the name given to the area that started about two hours outside the city, where one was in pure nature. Here, where there were also numerous lakes, was the beginning of the recreation area for people from the city and the suburbs. At one of these lakes near Huntsville, Kirkland Lake, distant relatives of ours, Uncle Harry and Aunt Inge, had a so-called "cottage resort", a kind of cabin complex. Back then, it wasn't a luxurious "resort" with comfortable weekend homes. What we encountered were about a dozen small wooden cabins with a front room that served as the entire living area, equipped with a kitchenette, small dining table and a few chairs. Behind it, separated by a very thin wall and curtained doors, were one or two bedrooms. Basically, these huts were not much bigger than a comfortable caravan. But what they didn't have was a toilet. Things weren't that modern back then, or there. Instead, at the edge of the forest, perhaps 50 metres away from us, each hut had its own outhouse. Each one was a different colour, ours was pink, which was appropriate, for a family with three girls. As our wooden hut was designed for several people, our outhouse even had two seats! However, these were right next to each other and not separated by a wall. In an emergency, it was probably designed so that you could do your "business", sitting next to each other. We found this idea incredibly funny and talked about the "love seat", the two-seater for couples who didn't want to separate, but we all preferred to use it individually.

We had to chop our own wood to heat our oven, so we girls were taught to chop wood at the ages of eight, ten and fifteen. We were told that real Canadian girls could chop wood, so we did our best to learn the skill. Sue missed once and the axe landed on her foot. Luckily, she was wearing work boots called Grubbs, with a metal cap over the toes. Otherwise, she might have chopped off her toes or suffered other serious injury.

From the very first day I made a friend, a dog called Hobo, which is synonymous for tramp. He was a large black poodle and belonged to a young couple from the US who were travelling through Canada and were staying at the same "resort" as us for a week. Hobo and I became great friends and could hardly be separated during this time. I also found his dog mom and dad quite nice, even though since they were American, and my friends had warned me about them. Had my friends perhaps been mistaken and were the Americans all right after all? It seemed like it. At least these two didn't give me the impression of being dirty, dumb, or thieves.

1972, Claudia and Hobo

We also learned to fish on our adventure holiday and that included spearing worms or small fish on fishing hooks. I found the worms disgusting, but I had to go through with it if I wanted to learn to fish. And since that also seemed to be part of the "Canadian way of life", I wanted to do it too. We also learnt how to canoe and paddle. All in all, we learnt real Canadian leisure behaviour. What was great fun was taking a running jump into the lake from the pier. However, swimming in the lake was only fun until one day a leech docked on my leg. Not only did it hurt, but it was also super disgusting to have this slippery thing that couldn't be brushed off, stuck to me. I ran to the hut with the reception to get help. Our aunt immediately saw what the problem was and reacted very calmly. She took the saltshaker that was always next to the cash register and, much to my surprise, poured salt on my leg and over this thing. Lo and behold, after about a second it fell off my leg! My aunt smiled, pleased with the result and I had to accept that I had just been sprinkled with salt like a breakfast egg. But as the result was good, I also accepted the remedy and now understood why there had been a saltshaker next to the cash register, which I had been wondering about all along. From this point on, I was no longer as much interested in swimming in the lake and switched to fishing from the shore.

There were also real North American black bears in this area. When we arrived, we were advised not to leave anything edible lying around in the hut at night, otherwise the bears might try to get the food, which they would probably succeed in doing. That's when I realised why we had so many tin cans full of food with us. Food was to be put in a bag and hung up on a rope outside the hut, in the evening. I was really scared about the bears, but I was assured: "No bear has eaten a child here yet." "Oh, yeah?" I thought to myself, how reassuring! We realised that the bear issue was serious when we were briefly instructed on how to behave correctly should we encounter a bear. The first thing we were told was that if a bear was chasing you, there was no point in running away. The bear is always faster. Well, great. What a prospect! Not running away seemed to go against every survival instinct. Instead of running away, we were told, we should throw ourselves on the ground and play dead. Play dead when a bear wants to attack you? How would that work? I was assured that the bear might no longer be interested in you if you were dead. It would then sniff at you but would probably move on uninterested. Possibly? And sniffing? What a prospect! We were also told that a mother bear and her cub were currently in the area, and that one should not disturb them or get too close to them under any circumstances, because mother bears are the most aggressive bears when they think their babies are in danger. Great.

One morning, our father had the brilliant idea of setting off early in a canoe to possibly see bears in the water somewhere. This adventure was certainly not for me, but Carin was absolutely thrilled at the idea of experiencing real bears in nature. So, the two of them set off to look for bears, even though my mother was against it. I watched the action from the shore and was sure that the two "crazies" would be attacked by a bear. They were paddling their motorless boat and we could see two black figures in the lake from the shore. They were the heads of mom and baby bear, who were just out in the lake, not far from the canoe that Carin and my dad were sitting in. I think that any normal person would have paddled back towards the shore at this point at the latest, to get to safety. But not these two. They paddled slowly and carefully after the bears and, as they told us later, found the whole experience rather exciting!

After ten days, we had completed our introduction to real Canadian life with wood chopping, outhouses, leeches, canoes and black bears, and headed back towards civilisation. We were a few experiences richer, and we were all still alive. And we certainly all felt a bit more Canadian.

Back at home, I pestered my parents with the desire to have a dog of my own and started to get books about dog breeds and dog care from the library and read them. Thanks to my experiences with Hobo, I was sure that I understood enough about dogs to be able to look after one myself. It was my greatest wish to have a dog, but my father flatly refused. The reason he gave was that Sue had once been bitten on the face by a dog, and he had no desire to go through that again. He also said that it would be unfair to Sue to get a dog, as she was afraid of dogs because of the attack at the time. Somehow it seemed to me that my father was almost happy to have a reason to deny me my wish and to have used this story for practical reasons. What could I do about the fact that some little dog had bitten my sister at some point? Why did I have to forego something now because of it? I found this argument quite unfair because I couldn't argue against it. The matter wasn't even discussed. After all, it was possible or even likely that "our" dog wouldn't bite Sue if he had known her from the start. The other dog was probably just startled and bit her by mistake. Or maybe my sister had even annoyed this little dog, as she sometimes annoyed me, and was possibly to blame herself? Secretly, I was sure that this little dog had only defended itself and that my sister certainly deserved it. Good dog, I thought to myself. But all the arguments were useless, because the case wasn't discussed any further. So, if Sue wasn't here with us in Canada, but still at her boarding school in Germany, could I possibly have had a dog after all? This thought alone was another reason to wish my sister would disappear back to her boarding school. I would have preferred to have a dog back then than this sister. Maybe I could get her to go back after all?

Sue and Ed

After the summer holidays, Carin went into fifth grade, and I went into third grade. From my level onwards, grades would be given for the first time. The interesting thing about this school system is that all subjects are counted equally and not just the "academic" subjects, English and maths, as in Germany, at least in primary school. I felt very lucky to have my cherished class teacher Mrs. Pillay again.

74

Sue was in 10th grade and 16 years old when she met Edward Fujarczuk, a boy from her school who was a year older than her, in the fall of 1972. He was born in Canada to a Polish father named Stanley and a mother named Stella, who was born in Canada but had Italian and Polish parents. Ed was soon in and out of our home, as was Sue with the Fujarczuk family, known as Fay. The two became inseparable within a very short time.

In the fall, Sue got her driving licence at 16. Ed could already drive and was driving a car like we had never seen before. It was an American Chrysler car, a Dodge Challenger, a two-seater with a long hood. It was bright orange and had a white roof! It seemed to be the ultimate car for young men at the time. My parents, who were a bit more conservative, were not fond of this car. They themselves had a white Mercedes and a gold-coloured American mid-range car. But Ed was a nice guy and seemed to be all right and was allowed to stay, despite the car.

That fall, our parents wanted to travel to Europe for three weeks. In their usual manner, they planned to bring some relative into the house to look after us. But Sue didn't agree to this. She now had her driver's licence and felt quite grown up. She managed to convince my parents that we girls, then eight, ten and sixteen, would manage perfectly well without supervision while they were overseas. Our parents agreed to her wish not to bring anyone into the house and instead put her in charge of us, and of the house. Unbelievable! Susanne got the car and credit cards from our mother so that she could drive us around and do the shopping. If she wanted to pay for something by credit card, she was supposed to sign "M." Bauder instead of "S." Bauder. It couldn't be that difficult, so our mother and Susi practised the perfect signature forgery at the kitchen table, and I enthusiastically joined in. I didn't manage the forgery, but Sue did, and from then on, she was nicknamed "Musanne" in our family.

Before we left, our father, who was now known as 'Dad', asked us what we would like to eat because he wanted to buy supplies for us. I said: "Ravioli and spaghetti." He did a bulk shopping at the supermarket, which he liked to do anyway. This time he was focussed on a three-week supply for three girls. He bought can after can, almost countless cans. The whole trunk of his car was full of heavy shopping bags and boxes. For me, there was a tin of ravioli or spaghetti in single-dish sizes for every day and the whole thing in large tins for two people, in case someone else wanted to eat with us. For breakfast we asked for "Pop-Tarts", which you warmed up in the toaster. We had boxes of Pop-Tarts, cans and TV dinners. TV dinners were very fashionable at the time. It was a pre-cooked meal consisting of a main course, meat or chicken in one part of the aluminium container, then mashed potatoes or rice in the second part, vegetables in the third part and sometimes a fourth section of stewed apples for dessert. The "TV dinner" was frozen and we just had to heat it up in the oven. My parents seemed to have prepared everything for their absence. There were also stacks of Coca-Cola, Sprite and ginger ale in crates in the cellar, so we had plenty to drink. They had apparently thought of everything. Sue had cash, a driving licence and the car, food and drink had been bought, in addition she also had credit cards in case she ran out of cash. In an absolute emergency, we could have called our uncles Martin or Gustav, who also lived in Mississauga, and then they our parents were gone. I wasn't entirely comfortable with this, and I didn't really want my parents to leave me in Sue's hands. But my sisters loved the idea of being without adults for three weeks and put pressure on me not to leave our parents in any doubt before they, left that the whole thing wasn't so great after all.

While our parents were away, the three of us went about our usual daily routine. If I had made myself a sandwich to eat in the morning and brought it to school, I stayed at school to eat. But sometimes I didn't have enough time, or I didn't feel like packing myself anything and I went home at lunchtime. I would then climb onto the kitchen counter and choose my lunch can from the hanging cupboard. I opened it with our electric can opener and poured the delicious food into a small pot to heat up on the stove. After the meal, everything went into the dishwasher and that was it. Then I went back to school.

Ed was already together with Sue at the time. He was sometimes nice to me, sometimes not so much. One day he gave Carin and me a nice little surprise. Ed was a cool guy anyway, with his "super cool" car, wearing a leather jacket and plateau shoes. This combination was simply unrivalled at the time. Ed wasn't just fashionable. There was a relatively new restaurant in Mississauga at the time that we had heard of, but not yet visited: it was called McDonalds. Ed drove Carin and me there to eat and invited us in, which really impressed us. A hamburger cost around 10 cents back then. As a novelty, McDonalds was very 'in' and if you could say at school that you had been there, you could brag about it. After that day, I thought Ed was rather okay. The self-catering thing worked quite well and if I pretended to obey Sue, there were no incidents between Sue and me.

The only incident the three of us had, was an accident. I was in the house and watched from my window as Carin, aged ten, tried to ride down the road on a bike that was sized for an older and bigger child. She must have felt quite big and strong until the moment this big bike took control and Carin crash landed. She landed very roughly with her face on the road. There was a huge scream and a lot of blood. Carin had hit one of her teeth and broken it in half and, of course, her lip was split open. Luckily for Carin, Sue had just gotten home and was able to pack her into the car and take her to hospital. I was left alone at home, just like last time when Carin had to go to hospital in Bremen as an emergency. This time too, my sister survived the accident and was back home after a short time. Our uncle Martin came round every now and then to see if everything was OK. Each time we said: "Yes, everything is fine." This one time we had to say that Carin had broken half of a tooth. I don't know what effect this story had on him, but he asked anxiously whether we would really be able to manage on our own. Inwardly, we were probably glad that an adult kept coming round to check on us, but we never would have admitted, that it was reassuring for us. And we probably never would have admitted it if we couldn't cope. For my part, I was overwhelmed, but I wasn't allowed to say anything.

It wasn't long after our parents left that some of Sue's friends, aged between 16 and 18, came round in the evening. They stayed partly in the flat downstairs and partly in our recreation room next to it, as there was a stereo system there as well, where they wanted to listen to music and have their own little parties. Everything was quite harmless for the first few days as everyone was still reserved. Carin and I were also allowed to join in briefly, but at 9pm we were told to go to bed as usual. At the beginning, Sue or one of her friends had wished us "good night". Then we lay in our beds upstairs and they continued partying right below us. The music started moderately with Cat Stevens, who we also liked, went on to Pink Floyd, Deep Purple and ended somewhere with Alice Cooper. So, we lay upstairs in our beds and tried to sleep, while downstairs it went from "Father and son" to more lively music and finally to "Dead Babies". I didn't have the heart to go downstairs and say that we couldn't sleep like that while they were shouting: "Dead babies, can't take things off the shelves..." I was no longer a baby, but as loudly and aggressively as they sang the words, I could only hope that they would stay down. How relieved I was when our parents were back! Of course, Sue made me promise not to mention anything about their parties.

Our neighbours next door was a retired couple with a cute little Shih Tzu dog. As Carin was taking private guitar lessons with them, I sometimes came along and played with their dog. As my wish to have my own dog had not yet been fulfilled, I thought I could learn how to handle dogs in the meantime. I still had hope of having a dog one day after all and thought to myself that at the latest, when my sister finally moved out of the house, the excuse my father used would no longer be valid. I had to wait a few more years until then, but I had to accept that. I presented my case to the neighbours and was then allowed to take their little dog for a walk. I also played with him and learnt how to look after and train him. They found it a relief not to have to go out with their dog as often and wanted to pay me to take their dog for a walk every day. My interest turned into my first job. As a big chocolate lover, I had the rare fortune of being able to combine two of my biggest interests. My neighbour used to work for the Sara Lee company, which also made chocolate and pralines, and he still received boxes of them from the company as samples. So, I was allowed to spend my time working with an animal and was even rewarded with a box of chocolate every time. That was simply brilliant for me back then! I couldn't imagine a better job and I had the feeling that I was very lucky and very successful. However, I felt that my sisters were envious of my success. They seemed to begrudge me it. Nice as I was, I still generously shared my chocolate, my first salary, with them.

Carin and I felt very comfortable in our neighbourhood. There were lots of children and usually five to ten of us went from one house to another to play. One of the neighbours had a daughter called Lisa, with whom Carin spent a lot of time. When the play Peter Pan was performed at our school, Lisa was given the role of Peter Pan and Carin the role of Wendy. They were both very talented, but they seemed more like overachievers to me. Under pressure from my mother, I also took part in the rehearsals for the play, although I knew even then that I certainly didn't have a particularly good singing voice. My talent ended up just enough for a role as one of the "Lost Boys".

There was a boy in the neighbourhood called Rupert, who I thought was incredibly cute with his blond hair, but many other girls thought so too. One family had a daughter called Caroline, but she was called Missy. Her father worked for a Californian wine producer. At the time, the company had a television advert about this wine, so we children usually sang this song as a greeting when we saw Missy. It really annoyed her, but that didn't stop us from singing it anyway. Her mother, as Missy showed me, had once been on a cover of the American fashion magazine Vogue, which I found impressive. I had never been to a former model's house before.

Our parents also got on well with an Austrian family. We often went to play at their house as well. Sue also had a girl from her class called Pam living diagonally opposite of us, with whom she became friends. The whole family made friends. We children also often played baseball in the fields. In the summer months, we would stay outside and play in someone's backyard, sometimes until it got dark at 10pm. Life seemed perfect in our new home. It was a carefree and wonderful time for all of us.

Mississauga, Carin and Claudia, Halloween

My report card after third grade was surprisingly good. I only got the grades "G" for good and "O" for outstanding, so there was nothing to criticize. There was also no weak point that my sisters could have used against me again. Surprisingly, I had "only" missed 18 days of school that year, which was less than compared to the previous one. My health seemed to have improved.

Despite the Bauder girls' good and very good reports, the teachers asked my mother to come to school for a chat. They had written to her nicely to say that they would like to invite Carin and Claudia's parents to a meeting to get to know them and discuss a "concern" about Carin. Our mother drove to the parents' meeting in the car. Both parents now had a Mercedes, one blue and one white, although cars like this were still quite expensive and rarely seen in our neighbourhood at that time. Our mother drove the Mercedes into the schoolyard, parked and got out. Wearing one of her colourful European dresses and striking gold jewellery, she introduced herself to the astonished teachers in the schoolyard with the words: "I am Magda Bauder, Carin's mother." During the interview with the school principal, she realised why the teachers were so amazed. The particular "concern" they wanted to discuss with her related to her middle daughter's appearance. What had completely escaped our mother, but not the teachers, was that Carin regularly came to school in dirty clothes, wore scuffed sneakers with holes in them, combed her hair irregularly and gave the impression that she didn't wash herself very often. The headmaster thought that Carin came from a poor family who couldn't afford new clothes for their child and wasn't very concerned about hygiene. Although my mother knew that we both showered regularly, she assumed that the worn clothes were fashionable because we hadn't said anything to the contrary. My mother was very embarrassed and promised to take care of Carin's appearance. She took us both to the hairdresser and then went shopping for new clothes.

Visit to Germany, travelling by ship

In July 1973, we travelled to Europe again. This time, however, on a cruise ship instead of flying. And what a ship it was! Our parents had decided to travel on the SS France, at the time the longest cruise ship in the world at 315 metres. We flew from Toronto to New York. By taxi, we were driven through New York, and I remember thinking that the city stank beyond description. After a few days in New York, we embarked onto the journey. When we arrived at the harbour, we boarded this huge black ship with its two red chimneys'. We kids didn't realise that the ship, built in 1960, was one of the most elegant passenger ships in the world.

We had two adjoining outside cabins with sea views through the round hatches, one cabin for the parents and one for us girls. We met for breakfast in a huge dining room at the table that was allocated to us for the duration of the trip. After breakfast, we went our separate ways, only to meet up again in time for lunch. I can't remember any explicit programme for children or young people. Maybe there was back then, but I don't think so. In the absence of any recognisable activities, I followed my sister - as I had done all my life in unfamiliar surroundings - on the assumption that she would find something to do somewhere. There was something like a reception desk on each floor, and this became my constant port of call for the seven days of the crossing to Le Havre, France. As I usually stuck to Carin, it sometimes became too much for her to have her little sister in tow all the time, so she kept shaking me off. Sometimes, just for fun. But without her, I usually didn't know where I was, so I would walk down some seemingly endless corridor until I arrived at a reception. There I just had to say my name and they already knew (although there were no computers back then) how far I was from my room, or they showed me the way to another destination.

One had to dress properly for dinner on the ship. On some days there was also a proper gala dinner, where the women dressed even more elegantly than usual. In hindsight, it's a mystery to me how we managed to take enough clothes with us for all kinds of occasions. Our mother had bought new suitcases for the trip and we each only got one. Mine was the smallest, which I thought was unfair. But my mother said that everyone had to be able to carry their own suitcase and that's why I only got a small one. There was a certain logic behind it, because my father couldn't carry the suitcases for all of us. What's more, five of us were always supposed to fit into one car and have all our luggage with us, which is why there was only one suitcase per person. The fact that we were able to cope with this restriction was certainly because it was summer, and we could manage with bikinis, T-shirts, shorts and light cotton dresses for the evening.

On the S.S. France, July 1973, the family.

There was a lot to discover on board and what I liked best was a room with slot machines, and playing pinball immediately became my new passion. There was also the opportunity to shoot at targets on other machines, which I also really enjoyed. We discovered that, at almost nine years old, I was incredibly good at aiming and hitting targets, better than the rest of the family. At last, I had a talent too, no matter how insignificant it seemed! What a great feeling!

To exercise, we initially went to a gym, but training with weights didn't seem quite right for us girls and we decided to go to the swimming pool. The first time we went there, our dad was there too. We took a running start and jumped into the deep part of the pool with vigour, like the way we jumped into the lake the previous year. I was sure there were no leeches here, but didn't expect there to be any other surprise. The boat had its natural movements on the high seas, and we didn't think that the water in the pool might also have its own movements, like a gentle wave and I had foolishly jumped in before I realised these movements. I jumped in at the deep end just as the water started to move slightly in the opposite direction. This meant that the deep end wasn't as deep when I jumped in, and I was quickly at the bottom of the pool. The water then moved back towards the deep end, and I felt as if I was being swept over by a wave. I had to hold my breath for far too long until the wave was over. When I finally came up for air, I took a big gulp of water to make matters worse. I realised that the water in the pool was filled with seawater, and I had the taste of salt water in my mouth. I found that incredibly disgusting! I thought I was going to throw up. My father came to my rescue in this situation because he realised that I couldn't cope with the situation, jumped in and pulled me out of the water. He may have saved my life because I wasn't a particularly good swimmer, and I was out of my depth at that moment. After my father rescued me from the water, he was really caring in a way I hadn't known him before. I was amazed at what my father was capable of! And what's more, he wasn't angry with me, which I had expected. He didn't scold me and instead took care of me with great affection. That was a side of my father that I had never seen before.

After my encounter with the salt water and the wave, I refused to swim in this pool again. My father was exceptionally understanding and enquired about a solution to this problem. There was, but only for in the first class on the ship, but we were second class passengers. My father sometimes lived by the motto: "What doesn't hurt, doesn't hurt". He thought it wouldn't do the first-class passengers any harm if we used their swimming pool from time to time. And so, our father, Carin and I snuck unobtrusively into the first-class swimming pool and behaved as much as possible like first class passengers. There we were able to swim in normal fresh water, which took away my nausea. And we also learned how to deal with the waves.

There was also a room on the ship where stage performances took place in the evenings. Some of these were performed by the passengers themselves and our sister Sue was chosen to take part in a dance piece about the Moulin Rouge. She practised the "can-can" with other young women, practised kicking her legs in the air and then lifting her skirt at the end. On the evening of the performance, we children were also allowed to watch, and we simply loved the whole show! We were also excited to see our sister on stage.

I also loved the clique that Sue was travelling with on the ship. They were young people around 18 who were discovering the nightlife. They had discovered that one could see the sunset at one end of the ship and a few hours later, the sunrise at the other end. So, she spent some nights out with her friends, watching the sunset and a little later the sunrise at the other end of the ship.

S.S. France, Carin, Sue, Magda, Claudia.

The ship also had its own cinema (Note: there were no TVs in the rooms back then). Usually, children's programmes were playing in the afternoon, so Carin and I sometimes went there when we weren't spending the afternoon sunbathing on deck. Our parents were outside most of the time during the day, and in the evening, after putting Carin and me to bed or at least in our cabin, they liked to go to one of the restaurants, bars or shows. One evening, Carin said that the two of us should break out of our room and go to the cinema. In principle, I was not in favour of breaking the rule that we were not allowed to leave our room alone or without adults in the evening, but my sister was determined to go and only gave me the choice of coming with her or staying in the cabin alone. Staying alone didn't seem like a good alternative and so I followed her. When we arrived at the cinema, we saw a sign on a small board that read: "Adults only". This was a clear indication for me to go back to our room, but Carin assured me that this wouldn't apply to us. She could also explain anything I didn't understand. I wasn't thrilled, but at least I believed her that she could explain things to me. So, we snuck into the cinema after all and were very quiet so as not to attract attention. I didn't like the film straight away because it was kind of creepy and the music was scary. It was Alfred Hitchcock's film "Psycho", which was considered a ground-breaking shocker in the early 60s, but we weren't aware of it. After just a few minutes, I was quite scared by the music alone and just wanted to leave, but my sister kept telling me to stay. She said that if we got up and left now, the others in the cinema would notice that we were children and then, if they caught us, we would get into real trouble. That seemed logical to me, so I stayed seated so as not to attract attention. But then came the famous scene with the knife in the shower, which terrified me! I ran out of the cinema in complete horror and my sister ran after me. There was a race to our cabin, during which she kept telling me to come back. But I had been so shocked by the shower and knife scene, that I couldn't calm down at all and locked myself in the bathroom, but also to escape my sister. She tried for a long time to calm me down through the locked door, but it didn't help. She finally had to get our mother, who thought her two younger children had been fast asleep for some time, out of her lovely evening. On the one hand she tried to talk to me, on the other she scolded Carin about what had happened. She scolded and scolded and eventually I opened the door. My mother had to stay with me that night and Carin probably got into a lot of trouble.

When we arrived in France, we travelled to Paris for a few days. We stayed at the Grand Hotel (later known as the Intercontinental), right next to the Old Opera. We were particularly impressed by the fact that you could see the Opera from above, from the bathtub, with its various statues, one of which even resembled the Statue of Liberty in New York. After a week of exquisite food, we children finally wanted something hearty to eat again and so our father took us out to look for hamburgers in Paris. After a long search, he found them in a hotel and said afterwards that they were the most expensive hamburgers he had ever bought in his life. At that time, there was no McDonalds or anything similar, to be found. In Paris, we were presented with culture in concentrated form. We visited all the famous museums. At the age of ten, Carin already had a great interest in Leonardo da Vinci and my mother had to give her a book about this great artist. Now at eleven, she told our parents she had to see da Vinci's Mona Lisa, so we visited the Louvre and Carin got to see it. As well as the Eiffel Tower, we also visited the Palace of Versailles. I still remember how we had to put slippers on our shoes to protect the precious floor of the palace and that really impressed me. But I could hardly keep up in the Palace of Versailles for sheer amazement: How high the ceilings were, how sumptuously the rooms were furnished, with all the decorations, colours and glittering gold elements, I had never seen anything like it before. And the fact that someone had lived there was unbelievable to me.

After Paris, Carin and I spent a few weeks with our grandparents in Heubach, which was quite boring for us. The contrast could hardly have been greater, in many ways, not only because we had just come from a world metropolis and were now in a small rural town. We were already used to the generosity of the Canadian lifestyle. As children, we were allowed to be loud and run around outside, we moved around a lot, and when we wanted to take a break, there were a few channels on television in Canada that also offered something for children, even if it was just comics. All in all, the people in our new homeland were friendlier than in Germany, and as a child in Canada you felt welcome and taken seriously. In Germany, however, we neither felt welcome nor taken seriously. Children always had to be quiet and were not allowed to attract attention or cause a disturbance. The difference was so extreme that we could make jokes about it and sometimes even snuck around the house, almost as a parody. However, there was little on offer for the children in the neighbourhood.

What we couldn't realise was that a terrible war had ended in Germany some 30 years earlier. Many people, including civilians, had suffered terrible things during and after the war, and they had to come to terms with it. The difference between the oppressive worries here and the carefree attitude we had learnt in North America could hardly have been greater. We were happy and financially privileged children, bursting with a zest for life. We certainly got into trouble here and there and were happy to leave Germany again and head home across the ocean on our "steamer".

Oakville/ Ontario, Canada 1974

Back in Canada, our mother developed a penchant for driving around the neighbourhood on Sundays looking for nice houses with "For Sale" signs. She felt the need for a bigger and nicer house, and in a better neighbourhood. From then on, we often drove for hours with our parents north and west of Mississauga to explore the possibilities. At the end of these trips, we usually got an ice cream as a reward. We had been living in our house in Mississauga for three years, which was a long time for our family. Then my mother decided that after 18 years of marriage and seven countries, she had moved around the world enough with her husband. She also realised that this was enough moving for her daughters, and she liked living in Canada the best. She had decided to grow old here and that this would be the country where her children could stay for good. She had also had enough of living in houses that other people had built and customised to her taste. She decided to build her own house and looked for a suitable neighbourhood where she could finally settle down with her family.

Economically, it was a time of enormous growth in and around Toronto, it was booming. In 1973, a shopping centre called Square One was built in Mississauga, which was huge by the standards of the time. It broke all the records of the time and coincidentally opened on Sue's birthday. It was the most modern, most beautiful and largest shopping centre in Canada with 165 shops, and a symbol of the economic growth of the time.

Continuing her search for a suitable place to live, my mother discovered the town of Oakville to the west of Mississauga, which immediately appealed to her the most. There she found a building project called "Paradise Homes", which she was very interested in. New, large, detached houses were to be built in a very

86

beautiful neighbourhood. She convinced our father of the merits of the project and so they got involved in the construction phase at an early stage. They were able to choose a model, design the interior and choose the colour of the house and the shape and colour of the roof. My mother, who was 43 at the time, realised her dream home. I was often allowed to accompany her to the building site. At first, Carin still came with me, but supervising a building project turned into time-consuming work and she soon stopped enjoying it. But I did, I couldn't get enough of our building site and always travelled with her. I found it incredibly exciting to witness the progress of the house construction. We constantly had to make decisions about materials, colours and shapes. We always had samples with us, first for the outside of the house, bricks in different colours, roof coverings and panels.

While the house was still being built, we had a two-fold visit in Mississauga. A great-aunt, Klara Reichle, called "Klaerle" (Swabian for little Klara), had travelled from Germany. She was the youngest sister of our grandmother, Emma Bauder, who died in 1964, and also the sister of Trudel Pollanetz, who had arrived for a visit at the same time. So, we girls had a double visit from our great-aunts. Although the ladies were now around 70 years old, they still behaved like two sisters who loved each other but they had little in common. Klaerle had worked at the post office in Germany all her working life and had never changed her place of residence. She was almost a head shorter than Trudel and a little sturdier. She was a very jovial person and loved to laugh. She also had amazing stamina when it came to drinking and Sue and Dad tried to keep up with her. Trudel, on the other hand, was tall, slim and always elegant. She was worldly and annoyed by her clumsy sister.

Oakville, construction of the house, Sue, Aunt Klaerle, Aunt Trudel,
Claudia in the chimney.

We three sisters, Sue, Carin and I, found the whole thing very interesting and amusing to watch and couldn't imagine having to deal with sisterly differences one day in our "old age". We took them, as we did all our visitors, to the usual sights including Niagara Falls. And they also came with us to the construction site. While Trudel was happy with and for us about the house, our "Klaerle" was a little overwhelmed by the size of the project. In Germany at that time, housing was much more expensive than in Canada and there was less space available for a building plot. Klaerle had never married and had always lived alone in a small two room flat. She couldn't understand why we needed so much space. We may not have needed it, but in Canada the dream that many Europeans have of spacious living on a large property came true for us.

Later came the even more exciting part of interior design of our new house. We visited furniture stores and took heavy folders with samples of carpets, wallpaper, wall colours and floors. We took a long, hard look at the selection and I enjoyed the preparations immensely. When the house was finished, my mother told me that we had spent 30% on the interior of the house and the construction of the swimming pool, compared to what the property and the construction of the whole house had cost. That seemed like a lot of money to me. She agreed, but explained

88

to me that this house would ultimately remain our home for many years and that the higher investment was therefore worth it.

When our large house in Albion Avenue was ready for occupancy in the spring of 1974, we were finally able to move in. On the moving day, we packed the portable TV from the old house, along with some blankets and cleaning materials, into our car and drove ahead of the moving truck to our new place of happiness. On the way there, we bought our very first meal that we would enjoy in our new home, at McDonalds. When we got there with our fast food, the furniture wasn't there yet, so we sat on the floor in the family room and ate our burgers and fries, feeling, as Carin recalls, "like God in France", meaning in the lap of luxury, despite the lack of furniture. We all felt as if we had finally arrived at the destination we had always wanted to go to after a very long journey - and by that, I mean years of moving around. We had arrived in our own house, our home. It was the first move in our lives that was at our mother's request and not at our dad's request or due to his work. That made this move very special. It wasn't a "must", but happened because our mother wanted it that way, a "want" so to speak. She wanted to have her own house built and have a nicer environment for herself and all of us. She succeeded, because that was exactly what we now had.

We were now about an hour's drive west of Toronto. Although we had felt comfortable in Mississauga, everything was a bit nicer in Oakville. The town with a population of around 70,000 at the time had a lot of nature to offer. There were more trees and, above all, old trees. The streets were nicer, and the houses were mostly on larger plots of land. In general, there were mainly detached houses and few office blocks or industry. I can't remember there being any apartment buildings in our area at the time, but there might have been in the town centre, downtown, which was a few kilometres away from us. On the outskirts of the town to the north was an assembly plant of the car manufacturer Ford. However, it was far enough away from the residential areas that we didn't notice it. At the southern end of the town was Lake Ontario. In between, our residential area, which was located between Maple Grove Drive and Wedgewood Drive, was very conveniently situated, as we were only one kilometre away from the lake. And at the end of our street, very practically situated, was the primary school Carin and I would attend, Maple Grove Public School, a beautiful little red brick building, which looked like it was straight out of a children's book.

There were also larger older houses in Oakville, but they could no longer be described as houses. They were huge mansions with mostly very large plots of land belonging to rich families, some of whom worked in Toronto but appreciated the spacious and comfortable life in the smaller town of Oakville. To enjoy this advantage, they commuted back and forth between home and work every day. Alternatively, some owners were very wealthy, established industrial or political families who were rarely or almost never seen, as they travelled a lot, or they owned the villas in Oakville as an investment, or as a second home. One of the large villas, which was always empty, was allegedly owned by the Kennedy family, who had bought an additional home in Canada as a precaution, after the murders of family members in the 1960s. The children told these and other stories to each other, but it was never found out whether they were true, or not. With the large mansions and the stories that went with them, it is not surprising that the town of Oakville has repeatedly been a place with the highest per capita income in Canada throughout its history. Oakville itself was bought and founded by an English colonel at the beginning of the 19th century. It soon became the first private harbour in Upper Canada and in the middle of the 19th century Oakville became a town. In the old part of town, called "Old Oakville", several houses from the founding period can be seen, which is not a given in North America. The English influence of this early period can still be seen everywhere.

Our neighbourhood was not full of tradition and history compared to the older part of Oakville, but on the contrary, it was modern and full of life. It was an exciting time of change, as an entire neighbourhood had been developed! However, at the very beginning, our neighbourhood still looked a bit like a desert landscape, where houses had been built out of nowhere, this there was still a lack of grass, plants and trees. There was also no grass around our house at the time of its completion. The desert landscape particularly amused our father. He bought a sign in a DIY shop that read "Please keep off the grass!" and attached the sign to a post and put it up in front of our house, where it stayed for a few months until the lawn could finally be laid.

The plot of land my parents had chosen bordered a nature reserve, part of which consisted of a tree nursery. At the time, my father had enquired about what was to become of the area behind our house, as it was important to him that it remained undeveloped. He was assured by the town planning department that it would remain that way, which was the decisive factor in choosing in favour of this plot.

The house had central heating and air conditioning in the summer. So, we didn't have to worry about anything to keep the house at the perfect temperature all year round. We also had a newly invented device installed, a central vacuum cleaner, which was an extraction system with pipes running behind the walls through the whole house. A hose with a suction device was supplied and all you had to do was take this hose into each room, connect it to a plug and start vacuuming. All the dirt disappeared into this tube system and ended up in the basement in a kind of giant vacuum machine. The days of the classic vacuuming were over for us.

Oakville 1974, our house, Albion Avenue.

Not only was everything in our kitchen completely new, but we also got a new, huge double-door fridge and freezer, a side-by-side. The freezer side had a built-in water dispenser and the option of dispensing ice cubes in one piece or crushed into the glass at the touch of a button. This was relatively new at the time, and we thought this technical innovation was great. The reason we decided in favour of the water dispenser was that Carin only drank water and nothing but water, no milk and no juice. She could now always get her water at the perfect temperature from the fridge. The kitchen was an eat-in kitchen with its own dining area for everyday use.

I was nine years old and making my sixth move after New York City, New York State, Heubach, Bremen and Mississauga. My mother had realised her dream of building her own house. She had built a beautiful house and had a real concrete swimming pool installed in the garden. My parents both liked to swim laps and therefore had the pool built a little slimmer and longer at 18 by 44 feet instead of the usual 20 by 40 feet, about 6 by 12 meters.

My mother assured me that this would be our last move. She had explained to me in detail that she had discussed with our father that she had finally had enough of moving and wanted to settle down and stay. Sometimes they had been in a country for just one year, the longest ever was for four years at a time. Especially in the early years, when my father had built up distribution networks in Europe and South America and was therefore travelling a lot on business, she was often left alone, sometimes for weeks at a time. Most of the time, she didn't speak the local language and had to work hard to learn it. In the early years, she had to cope with her first child alone and in a foreign country, and later with three children. She had never been able to build up long-term friendships anywhere. She couldn't work when we children were small either, as she had to look after us and was often ill. But she wouldn't have been able to get a work permit in foreign countries either. She had always travelled to the respective countries as a member of the family, a so-called dependant of her husband. He alone got the work permit, and she did not. Together with my father, she enjoyed the opportunity to get to know countries and cultures and to go on many interesting trips. But now she had reached her saturation point in terms of variety and adventure. In Canada, she finally felt that she had arrived in the country where she wanted to stay. She also had her two brothers and their families living nearby and, for the first time in her married life, developed a sense of stability. Now her dream home was complete, and she had no intention of ever leaving, as she told me. And she also intended, as she explained to me, to finally give us children a home that would remain our home for as long as we wanted to live in it. Our for-ever home. It was a wonderful feeling for me to know that the moving had come to an end. She wanted to give us the opportunity to finally live and grow up in peace after so many moves and so many changes. That was her plan, and I thought it was great and for the first time in my life, I felt like I had arrived and was no longer just passing through.

Originally, the house had six bedrooms upstairs and two bathrooms. However, my parents had a wall removed so that their bedroom was double the size and had room for an entire sofa set. They also had a small balcony with a view over the garden. Their bedroom had a walk-in closet and a large bathroom with an extra-large shower for our father and a bathtub for our mother. It was all unusually spacious for the time.

Each of us girls had our own room and the three of us shared a bathroom. Sue had majestically declared one sink as 'hers' and Carin and I had to share the second one. Finally, there was a guest room upstairs, which also served as our mother's sewing room.

Our house was one of the few in the neighbourhood with a double door entrance. As impressive as these doors were, they had the disadvantage that our stairwell was very dark. The doors took up so much space that no additional window could be installed in the entrance area. As a result, we usually had the light on in our entrance area all day long.

We had a circular staircase to the upper floor. Our father had his own study on the ground floor, which we children were not allowed to enter. There was a large living room on the ground floor for our parents and their visitors, with was open to the dining room, which we used for formal occasions. My mother had discovered her love of rosewood and bought rosewood furniture for the living room and dining room. She had chosen a very large rectangular dining table and ordered eight chairs to go with it. She explained why she had ordered eight chairs: "They are for my family. Sue already has a steady partner, and you two little ones (meaning Carin and me) will also have steady boyfriends and later husbands. We need the eight chairs so that we can all sit together at one table." I liked that idea.

The family room was for us children and our friends, it was the TV room, and it had a fireplace. We bought a brand-new white Zenith television, which was very large for the time, mounted on a white stand and equipped with a completely modern remote control. In terms of fashion, this television was the absolute hit of the 70s. Back then, the remote control only had four buttons, and the volume could only be adjusted in four different levels. You still had to press the large silver protruding buttons quite firmly and the remote control made a loud click every time you pressed it. But it was the most modern model and would be much admired by visitors to our house in the years to come. There was also a laundry room on the ground floor with a washer and dryer, and this room had its own entrance from the garden side. This meant that when we children were dirty or wet, which was especially the case in the fall and the long winter, we could use the side entrance and leave our dirty or wet clothes there instead of carrying the dirt and wetness through the house. Everything seemed to have been thought of in this house. Our parents hadn't had the basement developed but left it as a space for the heating and as a storage area. Everything we needed was already upstairs. Due to this, we were later able to use the cellar occasionally for our teen parties.

Through the family room, we went out through the sliding glass doors over a small terrace into the garden. In the summer months, this became the path to the swimming pool at the end of the yard. When we moved in, however, the swimming pool had not yet been completed. I remember the surprising sight of a concrete mixer in our garden, pouring concrete into the swimming pool pit. There were also pallets of bricks in the garden at the beginning. These were left over from the actual construction of the house, and we were still thinking about how we could use them, whether we needed them at all, whether we should store them in the cellar or what should be done with them. For me, they provided an additional something to play with for the time being. I literally had building blocks with which I could build objects in the garden, which I really enjoyed. We had a small terrace right next to the house, where we often sat outside to eat in the summer months, as well as a terrace by the swimming pool, which was also suitable for eating at. So, we had two dining tables and chairs in the yard. The house had a double garage and a circular driveway to the house, which was unique in the area. My mother had a small hill built in the middle of it. Sue and Ed conjured up an enormous stone from somewhere, which was placed in the centre of the little mound and a tree was planted there.

Our schools

Sue attended her school in Mississauga for the first few months and transferred to Perdue High School in Oakville after the summer holidays. However, as she didn't like it there, she transferred to Oakville Trafalgar High School, or O.T. for short. At the age of 17, she went to grade 12, making her change of schools for the last time, to her eleventh school!

Carin and I were enrolled at Maple Grove Public School, right at the end of our street. It was a primary school that went from kindergarten to sixth grade. We transferred again in the middle of the school year. I was in the middle of 4th grade and Carin was in the middle of 6th grade when we moved. Fortunately, my fear of a new class was unnecessary, as I was warmly welcomed by both the teacher and the children, who I immediately liked. Somehow the people in this neighbourhood seemed even friendlier than those in Mississauga. Perhaps the change was easier for me this time because I didn't have to change languages and in addition, could say that we were from Mississauga. We were from the town bordering Oakville and not from abroad, so I didn't feel like a foreigner! Overall, it was very easy to make friends there as a newcomer, as the real locals were very nice, and the many newcomers were welcome. Some of the new families came from the US and some even from Europe.

The first girl I spoke to in my new class was one who, like me, was half a head taller than most of the other children. Her name was Kirsten, and she was American. Her family had recently moved to Canada from the USA, and they didn't live in our neighbourhood, but in a very nice big house on Lakeshore Road, which ran right along Lake Ontario. Her father was Norwegian, which I thought was nice because she also had a European father and not just me. Interestingly, her mother was working, which most other mothers were not. She was a lawyer and that really impressed me. Until then, I hadn't met many women who had studied, apart from the teachers I had. But the fact that a woman could even be a lawyer was groundbreaking for me. My friend Kirsten had two sisters. The older sister, who was incredibly beautiful, was in the same class as Carin, and so contacts and friendships developed very quickly all around.

Iin addition to my new American friend, there were two girls who were originally from Oakville, Janet and Jacquie. Janet lived in a modest neighbourhood on Duncan Road, on the northern edge of Oakville. She had a sister and two brothers. One of them also went to class with Carin. Her father worked in Toronto and commuted back and forth every day. Jacquie lived with her mother and three siblings on the other side of Maple Grove Drive, not far away on Pinehurst Drive. Her father seemed to have moved out at some point and so her mother had to cope with four children on her own. She was the first single mother I met, and I wondered how it was possible to manage without a man in the family, who earned the money. As much as I disliked my father at times, at least he had always earned the money to provide for the family. But apparently life was also possible without a father. Lots of new impressions! I would have to see how that worked, I thought to myself at the time. The four of us girls very quickly became a regular group of friends. It was the first time in my life that I was part of a clique, and I really liked that. But there were also boys in the class that I became friends with. Matt and Chris were also from Oakville and both very nice.

During this time, Carin and I started doing gymnastics at our school. We already had physical education, also known as PE, four times a week as part of our school curriculum. There were also meetings for kids interested in gymnastics after school. There were lots of nice and some very athletic girls there, the likes of which I had never seen before. I was totally impressed by everything that Kirsten and Janet could already do. They were both incredibly flexible and had a lot of strength. I was just starting gymnastics and felt a bit out of place, because the girls there could already do so much. It was Janet who encouraged me to keep going and not give up. Her positive nature was infectious, and her kindness was genuine, something I had never experienced before. She was a good person at heart, and one would be lucky to have her as a friend. It wasn't her fault that she was about a head shorter than us tall girls. She was so small and petite that her family nicknamed her 'Bean', which we all adopted. She even seemed to accept this lovingly, which impressed me even more.

Another girl in my new class was Suzanne and I liked her straight away. She was very pretty and the eldest of three children. Her mother was from Germany and her father from Holland. The family also lived in our new neighbourhood on the other side of the nature reserve behind our house, in Durham Street.

One day in June, I had just come back from the shops with my mother. We were unloading things from the car when we saw a girl standing there, who looked like she was my age. My mother told me to go over and have a chat with her. But I was too shy to just talk to someone. So, my mother approached the girl for me, asked her what her name was and how old she was. Her name was Shelli, she was also nine years old and lived in one of the new houses two streets away. At my mother's invitation, Shelli simply came to our house to play and so I made another friend in the new neighbourhood. The family were American and lived in Dolphin Court. Her father worked in research. Shelli had three brothers, one of whom went to the same class as Carin. By the summer holidays, just a few months after our move, I already had five new friends. The six of us girls met up often and did lots of things together. For the first time, I had my own circle of friends, which I really liked. And two of them were very nice Americans, so I was finally able to put aside my prejudices against this people.

However, my first report card from the new school in Oakville was not very good. In almost all subjects I had only managed to get a "satisfactory" grade, which is a C, equivalent to the German three, and it was noted that I had missed some of the lessons and was particularly slow in reading. It seemed to me that the level of schooling here was higher than I was used to. As usual, Carin achieved A grades in all subjects, how could it be otherwise!

In the summer of 1974, I turned ten years old, which I was particularly excited about because it meant that I would finally be in double digits instead of just single digits. At least that was how I imagined I would get a little closer to my sisters and be less and less "the little one". My dear Aunt Trudel came to visit us in July and, as she secretly confided to me, had travelled from New Jersey especially for my 10th birthday. On the night of my birthday, I was so excited that I could hardly sleep. In the morning, Trudel was already in my room to congratulate me and give me a present. I was so happy.

From my room, I could hear my sisters moving around uneasily. They were doing something mysterious in the hallway and I thought they might be preparing a surprise. But then my mother came into my room to congratulate me. I couldn't have wished for anything better than to be with the two people I loved most in the whole world: my mother and my great-aunt Trudel! I then got ready and went downstairs for breakfast. As I hadn't met my sisters upstairs yet, I thought they might be waiting for me downstairs, with their surprise. And so, it was. The surprise was that they weren't even there. When I asked where they were, my mom replied: "I sent them to go shopping." They came back after a while, both with a birthday present in their hands. At that moment, I realised that they had both forgotten my birthday, which really disappointed me.

After the summer holidays, I was in the 5th grade, Carin in the seventh. As primary school in Canada ended after grade six, she had to transfer to a secondary school, a junior high school. Unlike in Germany, the pupils were not separated after primary school (which only went to include grade four) but continued to attend school together. Junior high, 7th and 8th grade, prepared students for high school, which ran from ninth to thirteenth grade. Carin went to E. J. James Junior High School a few streets away on Cairncroft Road. I stayed back in Maple Grove, without my sister. I quite liked not having her with me when I entered the 5th grade. She always had better grades than me, so my father had a comparison between us. He wasn't usually happy with my results. I was never as successful as she was at school and that always led to discussions at home. Much to my delight, I was rid of her for the time being and hoped to be able to tell my father a story about the teacher being too strict or that the subject had become more difficult, as reasons for lower grades, because of the lack of direct comparison.

With all her talents, Carin could hardly have ended up at a better school. The regular school programme offered a lot of everything. In addition to the traditional subjects such as English, French, maths, physics and geography, there was also art, music, sport and home economics, which would later become my favourite subject. In addition to these subjects, there were also some after-school sports and music. Within a few months, Carin developed a keen interest in music and started playing the flute. After a short time, she was already in the school orchestra. She owed her rapid success with the new instrument to the support of her music teacher, Mr. Mugford, who was affectionately referred to as "Muggy" by his best students. He gave her lessons both in a small group and as part of the school orchestra. She was at school two to three times a week after classes to practise and to rehearse. But she also owed her rapid progress to the fact that she practised at home every day. Although our house was very large, nowhere was safe from her new hobby. One could hear the beautiful and the off-key sounds of her flute throughout the whole house. But Carin was so enthusiastic about this instrument that she practised and practised and practised. Our mother, a passionate pianist, shared Carin's enthusiasm for music, so she also managed to defend Carin from the comments and complaints of the rest of the family. The rest of us, who were less musically gifted, simply had to accept that we were living under the same roof as someone who was suddenly obsessed with music.

Perhaps my sister and my mother encouraged each other to practise their musical skills. Since the purchase of the piano in New York, we were used to our mother playing the piano regularly. Sometimes she would bring very dramatic pieces by composers such as Beethoven, Bach, Chopin, Schumann or Schubert to life through her piano, with vigour and passion. One could also say that she hammered away at her piano, but incredibly well. Our house was the only one in my circle of friends where you could sometimes hear someone playing the piano, whilst on the driveway. Only a very good stereo system could have competed with that volume.

At home, we slowly got used to Carin being there for dinner most of the time, but sometimes not, as she was pursuing her musical passion at the age of twelve. She also went to gymnastics three times a week after school. One day, however, we saw her being escorted home by another musician, and when he gave her a tender kiss on the cheek, we slowly began to understand where her strong musical interest might have come from. Her interest was named Doug, was a year older than her, tall and blonde and played the trumpet. Now we had something to tease her about and we did.

For a while, my two sisters, our mother and I had piano lessons at home once a week. Apart from our mother, however, nobody practised regularly and so there was always a scramble for the piano just before the lesson started. At some point, our mother had to admit to herself that her three daughters weren't particularly interested in learning their favourite instrument or that they now had other priorities, and she cancelled our piano lessons at home. But she asked me to keep trying, so I agreed to go to a very good music school in downtown Oakville for lessons. Having already had a year of unsuccessful piano lessons in Mississauga, I was sure my mother understood that I had no aptitude for the instrument. But she would not be dissuaded from her plan to educate us all-round, which included mastering at least one musical instrument. So, week after week, I travelled into town on the bus with my piano book under my arm in the hope that my music teacher would be ill. This was usually not the case, and we had to struggle through another lesson together. I can't say who the lesson hurt more, the teacher or me. But each time we were both glad when it was over. Even the music school's comment to my mother that her daughter wasn't that talented didn't dissuade her from her plan to have me trained musically. The lessons continued. The two years I spent there were almost certainly my mother's biggest unprofitable investment.

Our neighbours

One day, there was a white VW bus in the driveway of our neighbour's house. As it didn't fit in with our neighbourhood at all, we thought that it was probably the car of men who were still working there. A young man was occasionally to be seen, very slim and tall with long, tousled black hair. He looked just like a young workman, we thought. One of our other neighbours in Albion Avenue, Mrs. Francis, told us that the house had now been sold. We were eagerly waiting to see when the new family would move in. But she told us that the new owner had already moved in, had we not seen him yet? No, we had only seen a workman so far, we thought. But not so, she explained: the young man we saw occasionally wasn't a workman, he was a student. All right. We thought this student must have parents and we would soon get to know them. He did indeed have parents, but in Italy. As it turned out, Mario had come to Canada without his parents with the task of buying a house there. He was very nice and when he wasn't trying out how loud he could turn up his stereo at night, he didn't really stand out. I remember that his parents came to visit after a short time. Presumably they not only wanted to see their son, but also the house he had bought. My mother invited them to come and visit us. At the end of the visit, Mario's mother told mine how reassured she was now that she knew Mario had such a nice European family as neighbours. And she would worry less now that such a nice mother lived next door. My mom knew the worries of having a child far away. But Mario seemed to be old enough by now to go his own way. For a while, he was with us sometimes. We all liked him, although it was hard to understand him at first because his English pronunciation was still very Italian. Sue and Ed also looked after him and became friends. Personally, I found Mario quite attractive and charming and was therefore particularly pleased when he dropped by.

Our neighbours on the other side of the house were the Morrisons, who I also liked. The parents were incredibly laid back, much like my friend Janet's parents. I liked that straight away because they seemed so stress-free. They even smoked in their house, which I had never experienced before but thought was cool. They had a son my age called Cam. He and I didn't really have much in common, but we were neighbours and so we visited each other every now and then. Cam had a considerable record collection and his own record player, which I didn't have. So, we usually listened to one record after another by Donny and Marie Osmond, the Beatles or Elvis Presley. We also had no inhibitions about singing along quite loudly, even though it certainly didn't sound that good. Cam loved music and it wasn't long before he had his own drum set. After he lost interest in it a few years later, I bought it from him for $50 Can and it ended up in our basement.

The Morrisons had a dog and a cat, which I really envied because I wasn't allowed to have any pets. George the cat and I got on well straight away. George would greet me when I walked up the street from school. Over time, however, he no longer waited for me outside his front door, but first in front of our house and not much later, when I came home from school, he sat right outside our front door. I liked that very much because it was almost as if I had my own pet. However, my father didn't like the fact that the cat was on our doorstep and from then on, he forbade me to let him onto our property. I was quite stunned by this ban, and I couldn't understand how my father could be so mean to me. But he was and I had to chase George off our property.

During the Easter holidays in 1975, my parents took Carin and me "over" to the USA, our former home country. The border from Canada to the USA was only an hour's drive away from where we lived. It wasn't just any border, but the one at Niagara Falls, which I found to be unique. We planned to visit Trudel and Alex in New Jersey and then drive to Washington D.C. Carin had chosen the trip and wished for it. From her point of view, it was very important for our general knowledge and education, to have visited the capital of the USA once, which was of course the right thing to do, so we did. She had the youth edition of the Encyclopedia Britanica in her room at the time. The encyclopaedia had information spread over about twenty thick, heavy books. It was exactly the kind of thing that a straight-A pupil had to have in her room so that she wouldn't get bored. At the age of twelve, she got the idea for this trip from there, and she kindly informed us about everything we needed to see there.

We sometimes travelled long distances at a time, which was not easy for us as young people, who were used to moving around a lot. My father was therefore instructed by us to always park where there was a meadow, or a field, or some other possibility so that we could let off steam after sitting for a long time. He did the same as usual, when we arrived in Washington D.C. He parked and we got out, walked across the lawn and did handstands and cartwheels and had a great time. Our parents were very amused, and our father took pictures of us, which we also enjoyed. Then he said: "Girls, you're doing gymnastics on the lawn in front of the Capitol." We hadn't even realised we had gotten there! We only had eyes for the lawn. We asked if we were even allowed to do what we were doing. Our father was quite calm and said that if our gymnastics disturbed anyone, they would come and tell us. But nobody came and so we continued.

The Capitol, Claudia   *The White House*
Washington D.C.

Religion and leisure activities

In the spring of 1975, my friend Shelli told me that she had started horseback riding. Her mother had driven her to a farm, where one could sit on a rather old horse and just ride off. Good, I thought, I'd like to try that too. We were ten years old when we managed to take it in turns to persuade our mothers to take us to the horses. The first time there, they showed me how to ride, in a fenced-off area. But then I wanted to go out into the field with Shelli. I couldn't ride properly yet, but that didn't matter to me. We were usually led by someone at the start of the ride out and then had to follow them along the trail. That worked well, without any further riding lessons. We paid one dollar for about an hour of riding.

Our house, with its relatively large yard and swimming pool, had not only brought joy and relaxation, but also work, as everything had to be looked after. So, it was quickly decided that Carin and I, aged ten and twelve, would be responsible for the garden and swimming pool. It was important to our mother that we didn't have all the comforts laid at our feet, but that we also did our bit, so that we could appreciate things more. She didn't want us to be spoiled too much, because she didn't like spoiled children. She also believed that bearing responsibility made children more mature and sensible. I thought she was right in her reasoning. On the one hand, it was good to be given a real task and therefore also a responsibility, because I did feel more mature and taken a bit more seriously. On the other hand, our tasks were quite strenuous because they involved real physical labour, which we found difficult in the first year. But we helped each other and taught ourselves how to mow the lawn and clean a swimming pool. Everything was done without having been given instructions and our procedures were developed through trial and error. Outdoor maintenance became our Saturday task. After a few weeks, we decided that our work should also be remunerated and approached our father with demands. He listened to our concerns and agreed to our demands. Carin and I divided up the work so that each of us had a fixed task, and it was immediately recognisable who had completed their task and could therefore collect their pay, and who had not. My sister had decided that she would take care of the pool. I was then left to look after the lawn mowing and maintaining the garden. So, after my dog walking job in Mississauga, I already had my next job. In the first year in our new house, we were paid 50 cents each time we completed our work. After two weeks I could already afford my riding out sessions.

Our father used the swimming pool almost every day for his morning exercise. He got up, went for a swim, then got ready and went to work. He did this not only throughout the summer and fall, but also, much to our amazement, in the spring, even though it was still so bitterly cold in the morning that there was water vapor over the swimming pool. He would run through the garden in his bathrobe as soon as the winter cover was removed, and the pool had warmed up a bit and jump into the water, without any hesitation. In the summer, he would come home after work, put on his swimming trunks and go for a swim before getting ready for dinner. It was very practical to have your own swimming pool!

Carin had already developed an interest in the Bible and at the age of 11, even wanting to have her own as a Christmas present, which she received. So, she had another common interest in her relationship with Doug. His family were devout Christians and went to a Baptist church in Oakville most Sundays. Doug also went to a church in Mississauga called the "Re-Organised Church of Jesus Christ and Latter-Day Saints", or "RLDS" for short. RLDS had an active programme for young people, which probably made the church attractive to many young people at the time. And it worked. Bible class, which is not available in schools in Canada as it is in Germany, so Doug went to the Baptist church in Oakville for that. Carin started to accompany him to RLDS as well as there and at some point, I also joined in occasionally. The people there were all very nice and the classes were interesting. My mother welcomed the Bible lessons and supported us in our interest. Carin was now reading her Bible every evening. It wasn't long before she started having discussions about the newly learned word from the Bible. Strongly influenced by both churches, but somewhat more radically by RLDS, she began to develop her own idea of what was good and what was bad during this time. She relatively quickly formed a picture of what people should and should not do. For her, alcohol became something terrible, and she even criticized our parents when they drank alcohol. She even started quoting from the Bible in some situations. She became increasingly straightforward and strict in her views. She always had to be brought back from her ideal world into the real world, out of her somewhat fanatical beliefs. She was quite exhausting for the other family members during this time. I, on the other hand, had discovered the Ten Commandments for myself and was enthusiastic about them. I found them good and logical and tried to live by them in my everyday life, but it wasn't as easy as I imagined. Apart from that, I wasn't as influenced or radicalised as she were.

My sister wasn't just exhausting, she also had good ideas. During this time, she began to work on our parents - about our needing sailing lessons. After all, we lived just a few minutes away from Lake Ontario, so there was a certain logic to her argument, that we could learn to sail there. So, we made our way to the Oakville Club. My father enquired about opportunities for us as a family to become members. After some consideration, our parents concluded that we didn't have the time to sail, or to join a club. Our father often worked and travelled, played golf on the weekends and was already a member of a golf club. When he wasn't at work or playing golf, he liked to be at home. So, the only choice our mother had was to join the Oakville Club with us girls, without her husband, and she decided against it. Her reasoning was that if we did that, we wouldn't see each other at all as a family. Sue was mostly with Ed; I was mostly horseback riding, and our dad was mostly golfing in his spare time. Carin had a lot of interests, music, gymnastics and her churches. Why, she asked, did we even have a nice home if there was hardly anyone in it? Somehow, she was right, there really wasn't much time left for anything else like sailing and it would have been a real shame for the beautiful house if we had spent even less time there.

After grade five, I had an all-round good report card and there was nothing to complain about. I had the pleasure of having had a very nice teacher, Miss Pattison, and she had managed to get me up to speed in all subjects. Miss Pattison was quite a self-confident woman. She had even incorporated yoga into our class programme. She was also the first teacher to realise that I couldn't read properly and that I was cheating more than reading. I had memorised the texts up to that point and was repeating what was written on the respective pages, from memory and with the help of the illustrations, instead of reading correctly. She put an end to my cheating by giving me her own texts, without pictures. I had to read the stories and tell her about them. But she did this in such a nice way that I didn't feel punished or marginalised. I understood that she wanted to help me overcome my weaknesses. We managed to do that quite well. So, I was able to go into the summer holidays feeling relaxed.

At the beginning of the summer holidays, I went "up north" with my friend Shelli and her family. They had a small weekend cottage on a lake, about 2 hours north of Toronto in a place called Katrine, near Huntsville, where they went to regularly. Shelli asked me if I would like to go with them. She had three brothers and wanted to take a friend with her so that she didn't always have to put up with boys around her. The "cottage programme" with water skiing, swimming in the lake, fishing and making a campfire sounded very exciting and as Shelli was my best friend, I went along for ten days. The only concern I had was that I would miss my mother. I still loved being around her and often felt a sense of loss when I couldn't be with her, which was almost certainly due to the many long separations in my childhood. My mother told me that I was now 10 years old and would be able to manage 10 days without her. I had to accept that, so I went with her.

The cottage did have a telephone, but it was a so-called "party line", which means that several houses share the same line. So, you didn't know if anyone else was on the line and possibly listening in. As I always wanted to have undisturbed phone calls with my mother, I called her from a phone booth in the village, when we went shopping. At first, I still cried when I called, because I missed her so much. My mother and I were both surprised at how hard it was for me to be away from her. But Shelli's mother was understanding and very patient with me, even when I suddenly fell ill with stomach pains. I was back on my feet after a few days. I was in the kitchen that day of all days when Shelli's father was preparing a fish he had caught. He was completely absorbed in his task, asked me if I was all right again and took out one of the fish he had caught. I looked at this beautiful fish, at the colours on the surface of its skin, I looked at the fish's eyes and watched it gasp for air. It was very beautiful, and I thought that we should throw it back into the water. I was just starting to talk to Shelli's father about that, when at the same second, he raised his arm, then coming down and hitting the fish hard on the head with a wooden hammer, to stun it. Then he asked, "What did you want to say?" The whole fish twitched and wiggled. It was horrible. I was so startled by this, also because I was about to suggest throwing that fish back in the water, but it was too late now, so I just replied, "Nothing". I didn't want to eat any more fish after that. Surely the point of fishing was to catch a fish to eat. But since I had taken this fish to my heart, I didn't want to eat it, or its friends. Apart from that incident, I had a lot of fun being in the countryside and thought it would be great if we had a cottage as well. My parents weren't in favour of the rough life, they were more into the finer things, so I didn't even need to tell them about my idea of buying a cottage.

Trip to Germany, vacation in Austria

In the summer of 1975, we flew to Germany again. We were supposed to pay another visit to our parents' home country. We children had completely lost interest in Germany due to our many wonderful years in Canada and nothing drew us there anymore. Carin and I would have gladly done without the trip, because we had been Canadians at heart for a long time and now belonged to Oakville. We had almost nothing to do with Germany anymore and we didn't miss it. Like most of our friends, we wanted to spend the summer at home and saw no reason why we should keep flying to visit our relatives. We couldn't understand why they couldn't come to us if it was so important for them to see us. If they made the journey to visit us, we wouldn't have to miss out on our friends and our interests for the whole summer. But our parents felt the need to travel to their homeland, which I could understand. They wanted to "go home" and see their parents too. My mom couldn't be persuaded to go without us. So, our father scheduled his business trip to the Bosch headquarters in Stuttgart during the summer holidays so that our mother and us children could make the "home visit" together and we could see our relatives, as a family. My father's employer paid for a "trip home" for the whole family every other year. This meant that we didn't really have a good argument for my mother to go without us. We had to go with her.

As we really had everything we could wish for at home, we didn't even want to go away. Above all, we didn't want to go somewhere where we were offered much less than at home. Compared to our happy and varied life in Oakville, the simple life that our grandparents led in a small town like Heubach with a few thousand inhabitants and in a rural area was completely uninteresting for us. We had no school friends there, no swimming pool in the backyard, no lake, no varied leisure programme, we had nothing but our relatives. And they all spoke German! And we hardly understood them at all. We couldn't recognise any similarities either. But that was precisely our mother's argument for why we had to go: to maintain the connection to our roots. Our roots? Her roots! Her problem, I thought. Carin and I didn't find this seemingly grey life in what we considered to be a monotonous and small place to be a profitable experience. We called the constant coffee drinking with all the aunts and other people to whom we were or were not related "looking at relatives", which we had hated even as small children! We had neither the age nor the maturity nor the empathy to understand our parents' emotional ties to these people and to this place that seemed old-fashioned to us. Apart from that, it would have been a good idea to fly to some foreign country to give us a change, to further our general education or to broaden our horizons! Or it would also have been nice to just go on a nice, lazy sun and beach holiday as a family, relaxing and having fun together! It would have been obvious to go on holiday to Mexico. But we didn't do that.

For Sue, these trips to our parents' hometown were also partly a journey back to her homeland. She had travelled there repeatedly in her life and was connected to our grandparents and the place. There may have been places or areas in Germany, such as the North Sea, the mountains or Berlin, that would have shown us a more interesting picture of Germany, but we didn't visit these places. We always travelled to the same destination, to a place where we had little emotional attachment to and didn't experience much. The strict Protestant-Puritan daily routine at our grandparents with saying grace, modesty and gratitude had a rather oppressive effect on us and we couldn't empathise with this whole attitude of humility at all. We didn't know any bad times, no war and no hardship. How were we supposed to feel gratitude for daily bread when we had always had plenty? We didn't know about the famine and had no real empathy for the suffering our grandparents had endured. There was no global TV at the time, to see war elsewhere.

107

To counteract our boredom at our grandparents' house, we spent hours there listening to Beatles records, which were all the rage in Germany at the time. The English lyrics meant a piece of home to us and although the music was no longer as modern for us, it was better than what was usually heard there at the time. We thought the music fashion in Germany and the German lyrics were simply awful! But even listening to modern music seemed to be offensive to our grandma. It wasn't easy for us to put up with so much piety because we had learnt to enjoy life.

The monotony in Heubach was interrupted this summer by a ten-day holiday in Austria. We took a hire car to Lake Woerthersee in Carinthia in the south of Austria. I remember the long, long journey in the car because it was summer and hot and, as always, I had to sit in the back between my sisters and the car had no air conditioning. So, the journey was cramped, hot and uncomfortable for me. Luckily for me, we also travelled part of the way by car train, which I found much more comfortable than just driving on the motorway. When you weren't travelling through a kilometre-long tunnel through a mountain, you had a fantastic view of the mountains. Shortly before we reached our destination, I was fed up with the long journey and asked my father why he didn't just drive faster? He explained to me that one must be patient, especially on a long journey. He said that you get careless when you've been driving for a long time, and it could be easier to have an accident. He concluded his explanation with the words: "Better late than dead". Just as I was wondering whether he was dramatizing something, we got into a long traffic jam. And sure enough, there had been a terrible accident. As we passed the spot, we saw a family car and the attached trailer lying upside down in a meadow. I now realised what my father had just explained to me and made his saying "Better late than dead" one of my mottos.

When we arrived at our destination of Velden am Woerthersee, we saw our hotel and were speechless at first. It was no ordinary hotel, but "Schloss Velden am Woerthersee", built around 1600. The beautiful castle with its warm and friendly yellow colour and dark green shutters was very inviting despite its impressive size. There were lush flowerbeds in the inner courtyard. The castle was located directly on the shores of Lake Woerthersee, separated from the lake only by a road. I could hardly believe that we would be staying in a real castle. My sisters were just as excited as I was. Our parents had really come up with something very special.

We girls were given a large double room and once again the discussion started about who would sleep in which of the fixed beds and who had to sleep on the extra bed. As always, Sue defended her position as the eldest almost majestically. Of course, it was out of the question that she would sleep in the additional bed. Carin adopted her reasoning for herself; to have priority according to age. According to the motto that I was lucky to have been born at all, I was allowed to sleep in the extra bed, as I always did when travelling. Our parents had treated themselves the luxury and fun of staying in one of the hexagonal tower rooms. We had never seen anything like it before! A hexagonal room that looked round from the inside. We were all absolutely thrilled, and my father was very happy to fulfil his wish to stay in a tower room.

The holiday was fantastic. We swam in the lake every day, which was very warm, much to our surprise, and took water skiing lessons there. The town of Velden itself was picture-perfect and after lunch and before coffee we enjoyed strolling through the little shops looking for things we thought we absolutely needed. In contrast to the Germans, I found the Austrians to be very friendly and warm-hearted people, who also liked children. What a pleasant change that was!

After dinner, we sat on the terrace right by the lake with the other hotel guests and let the evening gradually come to an end. On one of these evenings, we were approached by a young man sitting at the next table. We could tell from his English pronunciation that he was also from North America. The young man, about the same age as Sue, told us that he was from New York and was travelling through Europe with his backpack. He asked if he could join our family for a bit as he had no one else to speak English with. As Joshua knew how to behave and was also likeable, my parents included him in our family. Sue was particularly happy to be able to talk to someone about the same age in English instead of having to put up with us "little ones".

It was a wonderfully relaxed and, for the adults, probably romantic atmosphere in the evenings by the lake. For the entertainment, a small band played and managed to get us singing and dancing. The hit of the summer this year was "La Paloma Blanca". This song was played several times during the evening and our father enjoyed singing along at the top of his voice. It became his favourite song and from then on, much to my regret, he sang this song, which would outlast all other souvenirs from this holiday, whenever and wherever he felt like it. But it wasn't just our father who liked the song, Carin did too. Back at home, she would learn to play it on the flute. Another souvenir from our holiday was our friendship with Joshua, the nice young man with the good manners. That same summer we received a visit from him and his mother, who were travelling through Ontario.

After the summer holidays, I started grade 6 in fall 1975, at the age of eleven. That was a great feeling for me, because our school went up to sixth grade and so we were now the big kids at school. We got a new class teacher, with whom I unfortunately didn't get on with from the start, which dampened my high spirits. Things were important to this teacher that weren't important to me. In my opinion, she gave us too much homework and I usually didn't do it either. We had French lessons that year, which I really liked, firstly because I wanted to learn the language. In addition, French lessons with a different teacher to our class teacher, which I was very grateful for. At that time, people of Canada realised that they had two official languages. So, it was decided that from that year on, children should learn the other language as of grade one, instead of only offering it as an optional subject as of grade nine.

At Maple Grove School, there was a dance evening once a month on Fridays from 6 to 9 p.m. for pupils in grades 6 to 8, including those from the nearby junior high school. For us younger children, it was an exciting and sometimes embarrassing matter to go there. Many pupils from 6th to 8th grade were there and so the gymnasium filled up. One made their first attempts at dancing in front of one's classmates and of course, there was a risk of being the object of ridicule. If so, you probably wouldn't have dared to go back onto the dance floor any time soon. It wasn't just the boys who dared to ask the girls to dance together, we girls also asked the boys if they wanted to dance with us. So, with equality, there was still the possibility of being left behind without being asked. It was Matt who realised that we girls were all afraid of being the only ones not asked to dance. Matt was a head taller than most of us and had thick blonde hair that he wore a little longer, making him look quite cool. He had a lovely inviting smile that was hard to resist. He was a classic alpha male, slightly taller, stronger and more intelligent than the other boys, but still reserved and friendly. All the girls seemed to like him or even have a crush on him, the boys looked up to him and he seemed to have a natural talent for leadership. He suggested on our first dance night that we should do the following: Every boy in our clique had to ask every girl to dance at least once. It was a very good idea, and all the boys followed his suggestion. No girl was left out and the evening was saved for all of us, because we were all asked to dance. It was also the ideal solution for the boys, as they could use this excuse to

110

ask us all out and keep their little secret about which of the girls, they liked the most.

When the evening was over, some boys dared to ask a girl if they could walk her home. That was quite courageous, especially as everyone else was whispering about whether he would try to kiss her on the way home. Nobody asked me, as everyone knew that I was walking home with Cam, as he lived in the house next door and was my safe escort home, at my mom's request. It was normal for everyone to walk home or ride their bikes, each on their own, even though it was usually already dark. Back then, it wasn't considered dangerous for us to walk alone in the dark, even though we were only between eleven and thirteen years old. The neighbourhood was safe.

From that year onwards my mother thought I needed to learn German. During the summer holidays, she realised that I could barely speak German and understood very little and under no circumstances did she want me not to speak her language. In her opinion, otherwise I would completely lose access to her background. She complained that we children were "only" living the Canadian life and were no longer interested in anything else. And that was true! What did we care about the "old" world, which we experienced as rigid, joyless and monotonous, when we were happy and content in the "new" world, in the here and now? But that wasn't good enough for our mother and from then on, she would emphasise: "We are Europeans" and probably meant that this obliged us to cherish our origins. And she would enforce it.

As German lessons were not offered at the school, she had to look for an alternative solution for our lessons and unfortunately found one. She had found a school in Toronto where German was taught on Saturdays, as she confidently told us. On Saturdays? Excuse me? On our day off from school? Like all children in Canada, we went to school all day Monday to Friday. We had seven lessons on five days, so a weekly workload of 35 hours. That had to be enough. The weekend was for relaxing and having fun. How could she have come up with the idea of sending us to school on top of that? But even though we couldn't see the point of going to school on Saturday mornings for something we weren't interested in, we couldn't argue with her decision to go through with it. She was convinced that it was right and necessary to make us learn her language.

Not only did we not fancy a ruined Saturday morning or German lessons, we also simply had no interest in Germany. But we couldn't tell our mother that

111

directly, because she was attached to her home country. We had to pretend to have a little bit of interest. The whole thing was difficult for us children. And it was the first time that I had a conflict of interest with my mother, which made me very uncomfortable. I tried to make her realise that her background had no place in my life without hurting her feelings too much, but I didn't really succeed. And although we tried giving logical arguments as to why her idea was doomed to failure, she won, and we had to bend to her will. Despite our demonstrated reluctance, she remained stubborn and travelled into the city with us almost every Saturday. So, unlike my classmates, I not only had to learn two foreign languages instead of one, but I also had to go to school on Saturday mornings. I found both things extremely unfair and my resentment towards my parents' background grew accordingly. We certainly shared the fate of many children from immigrant families who lived here in their new home country, but whose parents could not or did not want to separate themselves from their countries of origin and expected the same from their children.

First, we had survived this boring holiday in our parents' home country, now we were supposed to take extra lessons to learn the language of these people. We were so annoyed! Our mother soon had to bribe us to go with her to Toronto for lessons on Saturdays. She often offered us the chance to go shopping with her to the Sherway Gardens shopping centre in Mississauga after class or to go to a restaurant for lunch. Sometimes our motivation was so poor that both lunch and shopping were necessary.

Swimming, riding and sailing

As of late fall, the pool needed to be prepared for the winter. To do this, the water was first partially drained and then the pool was covered with a thick plastic sheet. The pool cover was then weighted down all around with large stones to prevent it from flying away. However, both the cover and the heavy stones were too heavy for us girls to lift. As the pool was part of the household chores in my parents' division of responsibility, it was our mother's responsibility to take care of it. This meant that she had to make sure that everything was in working order here, and she could do whatever she thought was the right choice to have things done: do it herself, mobilise her daughters, get and pay specialist staff or anything else. Our father's job was to earn the money, he played golf in his spare time and was not available for such manual labour in and around the house. Some chores were carried out by Heinz, one of my father's employees at Bosch, who liked to be at our house and help with whatever needed to be done. Or craftsmen or skilled workers came to the house. We simply needed muscle power for certain chores. In the first year, it was Ed who kindly took care of this task for us with his friends Jeff, Stefan and Andy. The following year, however, they were all studying or working and no longer had time for such things. Our mom came up with the idea of asking Carin if some of the many male friends she had from the school orchestra, church and gymnastics could come over and lend a hand. That was an idea that I really liked! Carin asked her friends and some of them came to help us. From my point of view, they were the nicest and most handsome boys Oakville had to offer in this age group. Besides Doug and his brother Brad, Steve, John, Scott and Richard also came. For me it was a parade of beautiful boys, and I was even more pleased that they not only offered their help once, but were so happy to be at our house, that they agreed to do the same work in the spring, in reverse order of course. And so, over time, covering and uncovering the swimming pool became a ritual that I particularly enjoyed. One by one, they arrived at our house to help, the young men were so well behaved, and I was able to see them all up close in our house. I was particularly impressed when they lifted those heavy stones and you could see the tense muscles in their arms, which were particularly well developed in the boys who did gymnastics. Unfortunately, I was not allowed to be outside with the boys because I had to help my mom in the kitchen to prepare things for our helpers to eat and drink. So, I stared at the beautiful young men from afar through the kitchen window!

One year, the boys thought that they just had to jump into the water one last time, at the end of the season, end of October. So, they did, albeit clothed. One of our gymnasts, Scott, took an elegant run-up and somersaulted into the water. The others imitated him as best they could. The whole thing was hilarious, and the boys had a lot of fun. The mood was so good and contagious that our mother, who was usually formal and not very sporty, got swept away by the fun, that she also jumped into the water fully clothed! The boys were speechless. It was great fun all round and all the boys were back in the spring when it was time to cover the pool again and open the swimming season. The only thing was, that they wanted to start where they had left off. One of them jumped fully clothed into the water that had just thawed, initiating a real Canadian test of courage. I realised that I didn't want to take part in this dare. As if they had read my mind, they grabbed me by all fours and threw me into the water. I got a real shock and could hardly move in the ice-cold water. My mother gave the boys a good scolding and ordered them to fish me out immediately, which they did. Despite this incident, the event became a tradition. In the end, my mother even drove the soaked boy's home! Their parents must have thought they were all crazy! And they probably were.

My report card said "Excellent" for my ability to learn French and at the end of grade six I was rated an "Above average ability". I was very proud of that. And I was able to bring this home to my father, with my head held high.

In the spring of 1976, Shelli and I went riding again. We had already ridden for a whole season and were now looking for a farm where we would be allowed to ride on our own, and we found what we were looking for. So, at the age of 11, without ever having had proper riding lessons, without helmets or any other protection and in the days when there was no mobile phone, we simply rode out into the countryside. Amazingly, nothing ever happened, even though we loved galloping across open fields with our horses. I loved riding so much that I wanted to have my own farm with horses. I was passionate about riding and was sure that it would always stay that way. Until then, I had never had anything in my life that I enjoyed as much and that I mastered straight away, as riding. Finally, I also had a talent.

In the meantime, my friend Suzanne had also started riding and, as my mother told me, was taking riding lessons. My mother believed, unlike me, that my friend would learn to ride "properly", namely in the so-called English style, whilst I "only" rode in the Western style. I could live with that, because I quite liked "only" riding Western, and so this little attempt by my mother to convince me that I should see that my Canadian riding style worse than it was, was useless. And I stuck with western riding.

Then Suzanne told me that she was going to a riding camp for two weeks in the summer. I was immediately thrilled by the idea and begged my mother that I could also go. She understood my enthusiasm for riding because she had also learned to ride in Uruguay. So basically, we had no problem. But there was still another issue. As Europeans, my mother said, we should ride "properly". I already suspected where this discussion would lead. This meant that instead of riding western like a proud Canadian, I should switch to "English", in the truest sense of the word. She was happy to sign me up for riding lessons with a "proper" riding instructor. There it was again, the "being European", which did lead to a longer discussion. I couldn't see anything wrong with my riding style and I really enjoyed riding the way I did. But it just wasn't good enough for her. So, I bowed to her will and promised to retrain. I also had no choice if I wanted to go to the riding camp. I agreed to learn the fine English way of riding in future. In return, I was allowed to take part in the riding camp, if I took a horse that was trained in the English riding style. It was a deal. So, I started my English-style riding lessons in the spring. But that wasn't as easy for me as I had imagined. Now I always had to sit up straight, which I found completely unnatural. I found this riding and the associated exercises terribly stiff. But the worst thing was when my riding instructor told me after a few weeks that there was also a side saddle and that I should learn to sit sideways on a horse. Oh man, that was a test of my patience! What did I care about riding side-saddle? Real cowboys and girls didn't need either and I was more inclined to be a cowgirl than a lady. But well, for my mother's sake, I gave sitting sideways a go. And I promptly fell off the horse backwards and landed with my head or also my face in the sand, and not just once. Luckily for me, I was quite flexible at the time due to gymnastics, which certainly helped me to avoid serious injury.

The property on which I trained bordered the same nature reserve as our house. The house where my riding instructor lived and the yard that went with it, which was more like a small farm. They had horses, dogs, cats, rabbits and other animals there. Anita used to ride her horse where our neighbourhood is now and wasn't particularly happy about the new housing development, because it restricted her riding opportunities. On the one hand, as a resident of one of the new houses, I represented the decline of a piece of nature. On the other hand, I also brought her revenue as a customer. I recognised this immediately and so my guilty conscience towards her and nature was moderate. Building projects don't just take away land, ideally, they also generate income for the area. And sometimes nice people too! In any case, it was not allowed to ride directly behind our house as trees were planted there. But once I did, because I wanted to wave to my mother, sitting atop of the horse, and looking over the garden fence.

I reached my goal quite quickly and was now also able to ride in the English style, which meant that I was allowed to go to the riding camp after all. I was proud of myself and very happy about my success. On the day of departure, I was excited. I would be able to devote the whole day to riding and the smelly horses at this riding camp, how heavenly for a riding fanatic. In the morning, I hurriedly

115

packed the last of my things and my mother was already yelling for me to come, because we had to leave. I grabbed my bag and made an athletic leap towards the door of my room, when I caught my toe on the footpost of my bed. I felt a crack in my little toe and howled in pain. The situation was serious. As our mother was used to doing, without hesitation she put me into the car and drove me straight to hospital. The x-rays showed that my toe was broken, and the doctor said that I should probably cancel my riding camp. I was given a bandage that was so big that I could no longer fit into my sneakers.

Back at home, I tried to convince my mother that the injury wasn't as bad as it looked and that there was no problem, so I could now leave for my riding camp. But my mother wasn't quite as blind as she sometimes pretended to be. She had seen the injury and my pain-stricken face, and my riding camp was again up for negotiation, until we reached a compromise. I was to rest for the rest of the day and stay in bed, and if I could get up the next day and walk around without any problems, she would take me there. As for the shoes, she said: "Why don't you go and look through your sisters' things for a bigger pair of shoes?" I was happy to do so, because with her permission I was allowed to rummage through my sisters' wardrobes, which was otherwise forbidden. I found what I was looking for, in Sue's wardrobe and opted for the steel-toed work boots. But I didn't really want to put them on because the thought of pressing my foot into something was very unpleasant. For the time being I didn't have to, because I could stay at home. Basically, I was very happy about the prescribed bed rest because I was really in pain. But I did not want to miss out on my riding camp for anything in the world, I was sure of that. That evening, I had to have a foot bath, then took my medication and went to bed, disappointed that I was still here and not at my riding camp.

The next morning, still lying in bed, I could feel how excruciating the pain was. But I got up, walked straight up to my mother and said that we could leave now. The pain when I walked was enormous, which I tried to hide. My mother pretended not to notice how much I was suffering. She knew I wanted to go riding and so she took me there, without asking any more questions. I played everything down and when I finally arrived at my destination, my joy was so great that the pain subsided.

Unfortunately, I had another accident, on the second day. Because I had to bandage my foot in the morning and couldn't walk well, I was late everywhere. Even for the ride. I gave my horse a proper slap on the belly, to let out the pent-up air in his belly, swung the saddle onto him, tightened it and galloped off after the others. Unfortunately, the slap on the belly didn't impress my horse at all and didn't have any effect at all, and he only deflated when he galloped. As a result, the saddle became loose and before I could stop, along with the saddle, I slipped to the side and then flew off the horse in a high arc. The landing was even more awkward than the fall itself, because I hit my head on something hard and was quite dazed. So, I lay on the ground for a while. But other girls arrived straight away and helped me up, forcing me to get back on my horse, even though I was thinking about everything else at that moment but that. They said that a rider must get straight back on his horse after an accident, otherwise he might not be able to do it again, for fear of the next accident. They made a quick process of it, and I was on the horse, and escorted back. A quick medical examination revealed that I had a slight concussion and should stay in bed for at least a day. Great, I thought; another day lost. Getting up the next day was bad, as I was quite stiff in my shoulders and neck. The extra pain was horrible. I took the extra medication I had been given and carried on despite everything. I felt like quite an idiot, having arrived injured and then injuring myself again. I was a wreck. At the same time, I thought, that accidents do happen when one does a dangerous sport. Despite my fall and the inconvenience with my foot, I still ended up having a lot of fun on my riding camp, even though I missed the first half of it more than I took part and had to ride in work boots.

Claudia 1976, riding camp

117

After this riding holiday, I would have loved to have had my own horse, so when I got back home, I tried to convince my parents. Yet, my efforts were in vain. At first, they said it was too expensive, and that was no longer possible. Then, too much responsibility, I was still too young. Finally, my mother argued, I would only be with the horse and less at home. Aha, I thought to myself, she doesn't want me to be at home even less and that was the point. There was something to all the arguments, but the main concern was that my mother didn't want to let me go, however much she otherwise supported our interests. I had the strong feeling that it didn't do her any good at all that her three daughters were getting older and needed her less. At least she had the impression that we needed her less as we were at home less. She was often alone in her big dream home. But who wants to enjoy a dream alone? As far as my horse was concerned, I had to give up the idea. Then, I tried to persuade my parents to say "yes" to a smaller animal. After all, I had wanted a dog for years and I could keep one at home. What's more, a dog wouldn't be expensive and wouldn't be as big a responsibility as a horse. But my father told me that neither a dog nor a cat would be in our house! It was very frustrating for me to always be fobbed off with a "no" when it came to my desire to have an animal of my own. No animals in the house, no animals anywhere else, was there any possibility at all? I didn't understand. At Shelli's house, everything seemed to be allowed. They had a dog that we children had all grown fond of. Her brother Scott had several animals in his room, which is why we referred to it as his zoo. I envied her parents' calmness regarding the matter. After a visit to a pet shop, I came up with the idea of getting rabbits and keeping them outside in the garden. It was a huge fall from a horse to a dog, to a cat, and finally to a rabbit. But I wanted my own animal and wasn't going to let my father deny me all my wishes. He had to be able to say "yes" at some point, right? After tough negotiations, he finally had to agree, and I was at least allowed to keep rabbits. My father couldn't help but comment: "At least one can eat them." Great, I thought!

Heinz built a rather large rabbit cage for me in his spare time. He was something like the caretaker and the good soul at Bosch and took my father's car to the car wash every week. He was one of many immigrants in Canada who had also come from Germany. As he had no family of his own, he was always very grateful when my mother asked him if he could do something for us. That way he could come home to us, instead of being on his own. He was just happy to have a connection to a family from his home country. He seemed so incredibly lonely and deeply hurt inside. He never talked about it, what made him seem so sad. I can only surmise in hindsight that it might have something to do with his experiences during the war. He just loved being together with us. I was impressed by how empathetic my mother was towards him and other people. She had no reserves or prejudice, but took people as they were, listened to them and tried to help them. Heinz told me that my mother was a very special person. I thought so too. And once, Heinz even helped me with my physics homework. I was very impressed that he understood what I was supposed to be learning. It also made me realise that my father had never done homework with me. When my customised rabbit hutch was ready, I went to Anita's and got two rabbits. I finally had pets too, even if they lived in the garden. It was a long journey and a modest victory, far from the horse that I wanted to have, but I had won.

In June 1976, the "Canadian National Tower", or C.N. Tower for short, was completed in the city of Toronto. At 553 metres, it was the tallest free-standing tower in the world at the time. The whole area was proud of the achievements of the Canadian engineers and construction companies who had created this incredible structure. People felt as if they were part of this huge success and were happy to be able to live in this wonderful area and in this country. The overall spirit in the country was positive and infectious, and people were proud to be Canadian, even if they didn't have a Canadian passport. There was an economic boom everywhere and this tower symbolised it. Around the same time, there was an advertising campaign which, as far as I remember, was intended to help overcome the inferiority complex towards our big neighbour, the USA, which was simply: "Proud to be Canadian". Incidentally, you still hear this slogan there today, no longer as an advertising campaign, but from the Canadians.

That summer, Carin and I attended sailing school at the Oakville Yacht Squadron, or OYS for short, to get our first sailing licence. Our father had agreed that we could and should learn to sail, if he didn't have to buy a boat or become a member of the yacht club. As this course cost much less than we thought, we were allowed to join. The course lasted four weeks, Monday to Friday from 9am to 4pm. This meant we were away from home all day, just like at school. There could hardly have been a better activity for young people our age. We had theory lessons mostly in the clubhouse, but sometimes also outside. There was so much to learn about sailing. We had to learn the rules of sailing, everything about the boat, the wind and the water. Then you had to combine everything and try to move this thing called a sailing boat. It also involved looking after the boat and the sails, so we also learnt how to clean a boat, wash the sails and fold them up properly. But we also had to practise following instruction and moving on a boat so that we knew how to deal with the situation when someone shouted: "Watch the boom", which meant that this metal pole which is attached to the mast, swung at head height from one side of the boat to the other at quite a speed and if you didn't duck very quickly, you could get a good blow to the head. Once you were caught by the boom, you were lucky if it only hurt terribly. But a blow to the head had the power to knock you unconscious and throw you out of the boat, which is why the whole thing was so dangerous! We also had to learn how to turn a capsized boat around again, which was difficult if you hadn't fixed the otherwise removable keel beforehand so that it wouldn't fall out of its holder during the exercise. Because without a keel, you can't turn a capsized boat round again. But the worst thing for me was the knot-tying lesson. It was a bad thing right from the start, and I immediately recognised that I had no talent for it. Me and tying knots didn't work.

We also had to learn to swim far out into the lake, dressed in long jeans, and do survival drills on the water. Doug was one of our instructors, and when I sometimes swam or did survival exercises in Lake Ontario, I was sure that as a good friend of the family, he would spare me a long ordeal and get me out of the cold water early and back into the boat. But that wasn't the case, he remained totally strict and said he couldn't justify not forcing me to do the exercises. What would happen if the worst came to the worst, and I had to stay in the water for quite a long time to save my own life? I had to realise that he was right, because it really was a survival exercise. I also had to keep to the required times, which took an enormous amount of mental and physical strength. I was proud of myself when I managed it. Despite all the fun, sailing can be a strenuous and dangerous sport. I hadn't realised that before.

Some days there was no wind for sailing, and it was too hot to learn. Sometimes, out of boredom, someone was thrown into the water from the dock, with the explanation: "Emergency simulation, man overboard!" You could only be glad if you didn't have to take part in this exercise too often. This was also because the others didn't make much of an effort to help you get out of the water again but instead watched calmly as you tried to pull yourself up the dock.

I favoured another exercise that could certainly be used while sailing, namely sunbathing. It was not uncommon to find me lying on the quay with suntan lotion on my body and me in a bikini top and shorts, conducting my favourite pastime. At the end of the course, there was a farewell party where we were all presented with our sailing licences and other hard-earned prizes. We were all proud of our success, especially me, as the "knotting" almost cost me my licence. But every year there was also a so-called "dummy" prize. This was in recognition of an achievement that was outstanding but had nothing to do with sailing. I won this award for what was described as the most loyal sunbather of the year, the "Sunbather of the Year Award", kindly presented by Doug.

After our father was elected to the board of the German Canadian Chamber of Industry and Commerce in 1973, he became vice-president of the chamber in 1976. For him it was an honour, also a recognition, but one that we children really didn't understand. But he and my mother were proud of this appointment and very happy about it.

Junior High School

In the fall, I started junior high school. It was a step in my academic development that I was very happy about at the age of 12. However, the teachers at my new school usually greeted me with enthusiasm in their voices with the words: "Carin's little sister!", which I didn't like hearing at all. Sometime added comments like: "Surely you're going to join the school orchestra, aren't you?". I always waved them off and tried to explain to these teachers who were used to success, that I was indeed Carin's little sister, but unfortunately only a "B" student and not an "A" student like her. I lived in the shadow of her success, which really got on my nerves. I also couldn't understand why people didn't just accept me as I was, as a B student. My family and teachers should be quite happy with that. But instead, they always made me feel like I wasn't good enough and they weren't satisfied.

Carin went to Oakville Trafalgar high school, called O.T., which went from grade nine to 13. That was great for me because again, we would not be at the same school at the same time. There she could let off steam with all her talents in peace and quiet, far away from me.

Sue started studying at the University of Toronto that fall, at the Mississauga Campus, where Ed was already going to. Now she was back in Mississauga and back with her Ed. I was proud of Sue for going to university and decided that I would follow her lead and study at the University of Toronto.

One day she came home with one of her heavy books under her arm and, as so often, with Ed in tow. I was very impressed by the size of these thick and heavy university books, just carrying these books made a student look smart! My sister held one of these massive books in front of me and asked me to read the title out loud. I tried my best; ps, no psi, no pssi, no, pssik, no, pssikko. But I gave up because I couldn't read the word. Sue burst out laughing and said to Ed, "I knew she couldn't read the word 'psychology'! She can barely read." That hurt. But I tried to pretend to be slightly amused, even though she had once again hurt me deeply. The open secret in the family, that I was a poor reader, she not only said, but she also made fun of me for my lack of ability, and that in front of her boyfriend. The fact that I suffered from mild dyslexia had not been considered at the time. My father and sisters simply thought that I was stupid and said so all the time. It hurt every time, because what could I do about my reading difficulties? They were all so mean.

Although I often didn't like her and she could be downright mean to me, I still thought my sister Sue was exemplary except for this one point. She had had a steady boyfriend for years and had now also become a university student, after successfully finishing school. She and Ed showed me the way I wanted to go. They were both straightforward, determined and scandal-free. Now I was in junior high school, then high school and then university. If I was lucky, I might even have a boyfriend in a few years and possibly go to the same university with him. I thought that was an exciting prospect and was looking forward to it.

For now, I was only in grade seven and still had a long way to go before I could go to university. Our class teacher introduced herself to us as "Ms." White. We asked her why she wasn't called "Miss White" or "Mrs. White" and what the "Ms." was all about? She explained to us that this form of address had come about through the women's movement to give women the same neutral status as men, who use the abbreviation "Mr.", which gave no indication of marital status. It should not be possible to recognise whether a woman or a man was married or not, by the form of address. After all, men were not differentiated according to whether they were married or not. That made sense. Nevertheless, we children laughed heartily at this supposed form of liberation from male oppression. It sounded unusual and therefore somewhat absurd. However, we girls talked it through and after about a week of silliness we understood and accepted the deeper meaning and then apologised to Ms. White for our silliness. We were also grateful to her, because she had laid the foundation for our interest in gender equality issues. She was a pioneer for us, and we thought that was brave and great.

There were four parallel classes in grade seven. For us, coming from Maple Grove, that meant lots of new classmates. My friends Shelli, Janet, Jacquie, Suzanne, Kirsten and I were now 12 years old and going through puberty at the beginning of seventh grade. New words came into our vocabulary such as lip gloss, mascara, make-up, higher heels on our shoes, tighter jeans, lower necklines on our T-shirts and, above all, boys. How convenient it was for us to suddenly experience a huge increase in the number of boys we had never met before. How practical it was that most of us were allowed to organise a birthday party in the basement at home. Of course, we could not only invite the boys and girls we knew from grade six, but also our new friends. The whole thing was exciting as we were at the age when the first couples were forming, and the first couples dared to kiss each other. We played a lot of music at our parties and always played a slow piece to which we could dance closely together. The Beatles' "Hey Jude" was best suited for this purpose.

I was completely happy during this time, except for one thing. My mother's high expectations of our upbringing, which were always justified by the European standard, gradually got on my nerves. I talked to Shelli about how I wanted to be like everyone else and not be any different. I simply wanted to be a teenager growing up in Oakville, nothing more and nothing less. Shelli explained to me that our family was very different; my parents both had a strong German accent in their English, they both drove Mercedes, which was quite unusual for the time because these cars were not only German but also very expensive, my mother often wore printed dresses and I remember her preference for the Lanvin brand, a French fashion house, and they both loved to wear shoes from the Swiss leather goods manufacturer "Bally". Most parents, however, wore jeans, polo shirts and sneakers. I began to realise that we were different and wished my parents were more like my friends' parents, casual, relaxed and Canadian.

Our interior design, the furniture and decorative objects, was also completely different to that of all my friend's families' and, as a complete work of art, resembled an ethnological museum. In our dining room, there were antique vases from China on the sideboard from Brazil, above which hung a painting of a local woman from Uruguay in traditional dress with her baby tied to her back. The display cabinet opposite was from Denmark and full of souvenirs from various travelled countries, including a Buddha from a trip to Asia and an antique vase from

South America. In the living room hung a picture of the Easter Islands, a painting of a harbour scene somewhere in South America, next to it a painting of Montmartre in Paris. There were vases and plates from my mother's Rosenthal collection everywhere. On her American piano was a wooden Madonna figurine from Germany. Our carpets were Persian rugs. These were all objects that my parents had brought back from one of their trips that they went on together. And we incorporated everything into our daily lives. These were objects to be used, not just looked at. We had a handcrafted brass dinner gong in the kitchen, I believe from Middle America, which we would hit with a mallet so that everyone in the house knew that dinner was ready. This was perfectly normal to us. Since we lived in Canada, my father also collected Eskimo art, mostly soapstone figures, that stood here and there and didn't stand out in our multi-cultural home. In fact, my parents were already different from the other parents. They had an international lifestyle, whereas many of my Canadian friends' parents had either never left the country or never left the North American continent. And I had to learn to accept the advantages and disadvantages of being different.

Church, culture and homeland

It was also in this fall that Carin came home one day and, at the age of 14, told our parents that she wanted to become a member of the "Re-Organised Church of Jesus Christ and Latter-Day Saints" (RLDS). She liked it in the church and their community and now wanted to become a full member. My parents told her that this wasn't possible because she was already a member of the Protestant church and that you don't just leave your church. Our parents didn't seem to have realised what had happened to Carin over the last few years. She had developed a strong interest in religion, which was encouraged by a church other than ours. In specific terms, this meant that our parents' church and "being Protestant" meant practically nothing to us, as we only visited our church a few times a year, but there was no community anywhere near us, that we could have become a part of. Hence, the lack of identification. It may be that our mother had brought us up according to her Christian faith and the protestant convictions. However, we had no connection to her church, it was simply not local and had not captivated us as teenagers. There was a Protestant church in Toronto, and we went there as a family every year at Christmas and sometimes at Easter. We found going to church as such terribly boring, also because we hardly understood any German, and the service was so serious and almost depressing. The whole thing was also held in German, the language that we had rejected for years, but which we were confronted with time and again. This made going to church a double punishment for us and the ultimate test of our patience. But we had to go, and our presence there made our mother visibly happy. However, we couldn't really empathise with how our parents felt when they went to "their" Protestant church to listen to a service in "their" German language. Our worlds were already too far apart in this respect. Carin had found a religious congregation that suited her at the time and where she felt she was in good hands, and I couldn't see what was so bad about it. RLDS offered us young people a lot and we had even been to a Billy Graham sermon together in Toronto once, which was much more appealing to me, than what I was hearing here in the protestant church. What Billy Graham said was so easy to understand, so logical and full of positive energy. It really captivated our attention. But the services at RLDS were also lively and full of positivity, like the Baptist church. I also felt comfortable at RLDS, but didn't yet have the desire to become a member, as my sister did. I was more inclined towards the Baptists. But it was not yet my time to make decisions in this direction. I could still live with just going along with her, so to speak, for the ride.

Carin's desire to change churches led to a discussion in our house that had never happened before in this dimension. My father, whose favourite child was obviously his straight A daughter, and this very favourite child as the main characters, argued as fiercely as I would never have thought possible. It was the first time I had ever seen my father get loud with Carin. She was the model pupil who had never disappointed or annoyed him until that day. My mother and I were the side characters in this discussion, each trying to support the other. My mother wanted to help my father, and I wanted to help my sister. It was a discussion that went much further than 'just' about the church. Once again, it was about the old world versus the new world. It was about the values our parents had brought with them from their home country and which they were now trying to pass on to us children as the measure of all things or even impose on us. They had not succeeded in familiarising us with "their" church. Now they couldn't accept that we were drifting in a different direction, which we couldn't understand at all, because after all we had stuck with the religion, Christianity. So, what was the real problem?

My father made terrible accusations against my mother, saying that she had allowed us to hang around with a 'cult'. It was terrible to see him vigorously attack her with these accusations. He became loud and shouted at her, accusing her

125

of failing in her parenting and neglecting her duties in bringing up her children. She firmly rejected the accusations and said that she had made enquiries and that this church was not a sect. She also told him that she had gotten to know the people there and found them nice. She also welcomed the Bible lessons, as there were no religion lessons in Canadian schools. She also said that he couldn't expect her to teach us everything herself, let alone Bible lessons. I was under the impression that my father had no idea what our mother was already doing for us and where the actual limits of her support lay.

Perhaps they were really convinced about their church and wanted to share this conviction with us, but they didn't succeed. Our needs were not met by the church from our parents' old home country and the service in German. And it wasn't local either. What could my mother do about the fact that there wasn't a Protestant church in every town, as she might have wished? The discussion about changing churches ended with a strict "no" from our father to Carin, who forbade her from ever coming up with such an idea again. She, in turn, was so deeply disappointed and hurt that she left the living room crying. My mother was also deeply hurt by my father's behaviour, and I was under the impression that there had been a tear in her feelings towards him. Yes, I could really feel it. And indeed, after this incident, she was more reserved, more restrained, cooler towards him.

That evening, however, my parents were jointly criticized for not having convinced us of their church and that we couldn't really do anything with it. So, from then on, our mother made it her job to teach us about church and religion. We were now "allowed" to go with her to the German Protestant church in Toronto more often. She also planned to send Carin to confirmation classes the following spring and me the following year. We were supposed to learn more about our church in confirmation classes and our parents decided it was high time for Carin.

At the same time, my mother told me that I was old enough to continue my cultural education. Until then, she had sometimes gone to classical concerts or the ballet in Toronto with our father, Sue and Carin. Now, at the age of 12, I was allowed to come along with them once a month. The cultural aspect sounded interesting. We saw Nureyev and Baryshnikov dance in the ballet, heard the Vienna Boys' Choir sing Christmas carols just before Christmas, saw Tchaikovsky's Swan Lake and the Nutcracker at Christmas. For the first time, I was happy about my parents' cultural knowledge and interest and began to appreciate the art of music and dance. Our cultural programme was also rounded off with visits to museums, where my mother tried to give me an understanding of painting. All in all, it was very nice and interesting to broaden my horizons with cultural knowledge. I considered myself lucky to have such an educated and culturally interested mother. In contrast, I heard nothing about cultural education from my friends of the same age.

The journeys from Oakville to Toronto on the motorway called "Queen Elisabeth Way", or QEW for short, were fun. Unfortunately, as always, I sat in the back of the car in the middle between my sisters. Just before reaching the city, however, there was a small event that made up for sitting between my sisters every time. There was a kind of wave in the road that our father declared to be a ramp, over which he thought he had to let his car speed. At a certain point, he started to slow down a little to create some distance between our car and the one in front of us. Then he started to accelerate his Mercedes, and we could clearly feel that our car had power. We shot towards the "ramp" and flew over it. Each time we laughed with delight and debated whether the wheels were off the ground or not and if so, for how many seconds or fractions of a second. My father loved this little challenge, and we all enjoyed it when he made the car fly.

In addition to our cultural excursions, in the winter, we sometimes started going to brunch on Sundays, after church. For us as a family, it was a time when there were many new things to see and experience. Much to our benefit, there were huge building developments in the city during this time. The spirit in and around Toronto was characterised by an economic boom. There was construction everywhere and although I didn't understand much about it at my age, I had a positive feeling that the future would bring a lot of good things. We discovered a restaurant in Toronto that revolved, on top of the hotel called "Harbour Castle". From there you had a fantastic view of Toronto and Lake Ontario while you ate. It was always wonderful to sit up there, a real privilege. I don't know whether my parents had really made up after the argument about the "cult", whether my mother had forgiven my father, or whether my father had apologised to her. But our whole family life seemed to have changed for the better. All our trips were also, as my father didn't hide from us, quite expensive.

At the same time, I started with my next job. I had discovered the market for babysitters in the neighbourhood, because there were young families everywhere. We were already one of the families with "older" children. So, I drew up notes with a brief description of myself, my phone number and address and the offer to look after the little ones on Friday and Saturday evenings, while the parents went out. I had no experience in this area, apart from the occasional visits from my younger cousin. But I liked small children and was sure I could manage. If necessary, I could call my mom and ask for advice. My new customers had no problem with my lack of knowledge and explained to me what to do. It was as simple as that. My little side hustle flourished within a few months, and it got to the point where I was working almost every Friday and Saturday night. I think I was earning a dollar an hour at the time, and it quickly added up to quite a lot for my circumstances at the time. I enjoyed the whole thing, but it soon became too much for my mother. I couldn't miss our cultural evenings anyway, but my job meant that I wasn't at home enough for her. We came to an agreement that I would only be allowed to babysit once a week in the evenings. Shelli had also started babysitting. If I couldn't take a job, I recommended Shelli and vice versa. As a result, the two of us took it in turns to look after the same children in pretty much every house in the neighbourhood and were known to most families. With the money we earned ourselves, we bought our first tickets to a rock concert and went to see the Bay City Rollers, the most successful boy band of the seventies, after the Beatles.

Wonderful Christmastime

As every year, Christmas was a big event for us. In addition to attending services at the German Lutheran church in Toronto, we had our own additional customs that began before the first Sunday of Advent, when our mother put up an Advent wreath. Much to our surprise, every year she placed it in a large silver bowl that otherwise stood decoratively in our living room. When I once asked her if it was such a good idea to put the wreath with the candles on top in a silver bowl, which seemed very valuable to me, she simply said: "I can do that, the bowl is mine." Of course, I thought to myself, who is going to scold her for dirtying her own bowl? No one. She was right. This Advent wreath was usually tied by her herself, and any of us girls who wanted could join in. I realised that my mother - in stark contrast to most other mothers - was very skilled at handicrafts. She could create wonderful decorations herself, she had made vases, painted pictures and she could sew very well, she prepared fantastic festive meals, baked her own Christmas cookies (from scratch) and could even make her own candles! She was a real all-rounder, and I realised that most other mothers didn't know how to do these things.

128

It was nicer and more personal when the candles were made by your own mom, and the cookies didn't taste like ready-made dough. The work she did for us and our household simply made our home a little nicer, more personal and cozier.

On each of the four Sundays before Christmas, an additional candle was lit on our Advent wreath, and we sang German Christmas carols. For once, this was something from her home country, that I really liked. In Canada, Advent and the Advent wreath were not a common custom. To me, this tradition was very beautiful, because the candles on the Advent wreath made the winter days a little warmer and brighter. It brought light into the darkness. I also liked the fact that it was a way to prepare for Christmas, week by week. My Canadian friends thought it was all very nice and envied us for the custom.

Every year at the first Advent we received a parcel from my father's employer, Bosch, in Germany. These parcels were unmistakably recognisable by the fact that they were made of an extremely robust, unmarked grey cardboard box, which could not be surpassed in its sobriety and ugliness, as if it would normally contain screws or car parts. However, when we opened the box, we were presented with the full range of things that are traditionally part of the Advent season for a German family. There were candles and Christmas stollen (a dried cake with winter fruits), Christmas cookies, small presents, Christmas decorations and every time, there was also a small fir branch. The whole thing smelled of Christmas. There was also an Advent and Christmas greetings card with best wishes and love to the whole family. Every year I was a little overwhelmed by this gift from the Bosch company in Stuttgart. It was almost like receiving greetings from close relatives and it really made me feel a bit like part of the big Bosch family.

One of our rituals was that we would buy and wrap pretty much everything that everyone in the family needed or wanted, bit by bit, and then put it under the Christmas tree day by day. This started a good two weeks before Christmas when we would get our tree and then all together, decorate it, which I loved every year. In contrast to many families in the US and Canada, it was not customary for us to decorate the Christmas tree as colourfully as possible. Instead, we kept it modest in a Protestant way and limited ourselves to the basic colours of red and gold. Our mother didn't tolerate much more than baubles and carved wooden figures. No kitsch, nothing modern, nothing colourful. I liked the result, because despite the size of our tree and the enormous pile of presents underneath it, it still looked contemplative and cozy. Every year it invited us to sit down and admire it. My Canadian friends also thought our Christmas trees were beautiful.

According to German custom, we celebrated Christmas Eve on 24 December. After church and before the meal, which each year consisted of lentils, sausages and spaetzle, my father would devoutly read the Christmas story from the Bible. He always looked confident in his dark blue blazer and beige-coloured turtleneck jumper and, with his deep voice, seemed to take the Christmas story seriously. You couldn't help but listen with rapt attention every year. Afterwards, we sang a few more Christmas carols and then it was on to the presents. My mother always got a bottle of champagne from her favourite brand, Mumm Cordon Rouge, which my father opened, and they both enjoyed throughout the evening. Our mother wore a new elegant evening dress every year, which she usually made herself, and we girls wore our best dresses. Of course, I never wore a new one, but the used hand-me-downs from my sisters. But I was used to that. The celebration was fantastic and all the arguments that we had had within the family over the year, seemed to magically and finally disappear on that evening, every year. And so, it was always a wonderful celebration.

Canadian and American families celebrated Christmas on the morning of December 25th, which was about opening presents early in the morning. This certainly had its charm and if you were used to it as a tradition, it was probably the right way to celebrate. But I couldn't imagine it being as nice as our version of celebrating in the evening, when it's dark outside and the candles are lit in the living room. There was something almost heavenly about it. But the evening was just the beginning and so on December 25th we had a lavish Christmas celebration with an elaborate feast. The best Rosenthal chinaware and heavy crystal glasses were laid out to match the sumptuous menu. The food was served on silver platters and in crystal bowls. We children were even allowed to take a sip of real wine from the heavy, colourful crystal glasses that our parents had received for their wedding, to underline the festive atmosphere. At this feast, I said to my father that I thought alcohol was forbidden for children. He replied: "No government in the world is going to tell me what to do in my own house. We're celebrating Christmas and you can have a glass of wine." On the one hand, I was impressed by my father's independent attitude of standing by what he thought was right. On the other hand, I thought to myself: these laws have a purpose, don't they? Maybe they were also meant to protect us children? I didn't feel quite so comfortable drinking the wine after all, and I only sipped a little and then immediately put it down again in the hope that nobody would notice that I wasn't really drinking along. But I didn't dare say anything to my father. He wasn't very open to critical questions regarding himself and his views, and I didn't want to start a fundamental discussion on this wonderful evening that my mother had put so much love and work into.

The Christmas celebrations continued with a family celebration the following day, alternating each year between one of my uncles and our homes. It was also nice to celebrate with the whole Holl family, with aunts, uncles, cousins. After all the festivities - three days of celebration and far too much food - we children still had a good ten days before school started again. Our family never travelled during the Christmas holidays, with the one exception of Merano, because our holidays were always in the summer. I liked it that way, though, because it meant that we could spend the days around the New Year at home in a cozy and lazy way. As almost all my friends weren't travelling, we were able to visit each other, try out the new games or keep ourselves busy with whatever else we had received for Christmas. It was wonderful to be able to stay at home in the freezing Canadian winter. The fireplace was always on in the evenings and as there was snow outside in the yard, it was incredibly cozy in our house. I couldn't have imagined or wished for a more beautiful home in my dreams. To me, ours was perfect.

In the spring of 1977, our mother became increasingly ill and stayed at home even more often than usual. She was in more and more pain and went to doctors' appointments increasingly often. She seemed to be able to cope with very little. Her plans to take Carin to confirmation classes could not be realised for health reasons. At the same time, her visual acuity began to deteriorate and, at the age of 46, she was given glasses, which she couldn't really cope with. As a result, she was often frustrated, angry and depressed. Nothing seemed to be functioning for her anymore. My father made the joke about the glasses that my mother was just starting to get older, but that he still loved her, even with the signs of wear and tear. No doctor could really help her, and she became increasingly weaker in her physical condition and mentally unhappy. At the same time, my father was travelling to Germany on business. Our parents thought it might be good for her to go with him to get her mind off the subject of health and illness. So, she flew with him.

Back from the journey, my mother made a very tired and rather sad impression. I had expected the opposite and asked her if something had happened to make her so sad. She explained to me that, on the one hand, the journey had been very exhausting for her as she felt quite weak. Secondly, she said that she had had arguments with my father and that she was seriously considering separating from him. I found this partly surprising and partly not. After the arguments last year, I had already noticed how she felt so hurt by him that she had distanced herself from him emotionally. Even the perfect Christmas had probably not healed her scars. My poor mother! But now I was very upset about my father, that he had obviously hurt her again, even though she was already in such a bad way. And I really wanted to know what exactly the argument was about this time. She didn't want to tell me specifically, nor did she want to tell me everything. The main thing was though, that he was flirting with another woman and that my mother was no longer prepared to go along with it. I was surprised. On the one hand, I learnt that he was flirting around, but on the other, that it had probably happened before. My mother was so hurt and so angry. Now it was me who was angry with this man! Why was he doing this to her? What surprised me the most - apart from the fact that she was talking to me about it at all - was that this time she was even talking about a separation. That had never happened before. A separation was not a solution for a woman like her. She was convinced that a marriage was meant to last a lifetime, just like with her parents. But inwardly, she seemed to have decided and her sadness about it was apparent. I told her that we would manage, should she decide to do it.

The third thing she told me was that she cried terribly when she said goodbye to her parents. She knew that she would never see them again. Of all three things, the last one bothered her the most. We talked about the fact that her parents were now in their late 70s, and it was therefore quite possible that one of them would die in the next few years. She was aware of all this, but she said that when she said goodbye, she could clearly feel that it would be the last time she would see her parents! My poor mother was completely sad, and I felt so sorry for her. I also didn't see how I could help her or what I could do for her other than be with her.

For our father, life went on as normal, and he seemed unaffected by the events of the trip. He didn't work too long in the evenings on a regular working day, but he also had a lot of other jobs, including through the Chamber of Industry and Commerce. This meant that he always had various events or appointments in the evenings. Sue was at the university and usually spent a lot of time with Ed. As usual, Carin was rarely at home and went her own way. After the argument about the church, she was angry with our parents and stayed away from home more than before. Here, too, the perfect Christmas had only helped temporarily. I didn't share her disappointment that our parents hadn't given her complete freedom in everything she did. Nor did I share her anger at our parents for refusing her something specific. During this time, it was often just my mother and me at home, even on the weekends. I liked being home alone with her, without my father and without my sisters, all of whom I had always found exhausting.

In the meantime, I usually not only did the lawn mowing, but also cleaned the swimming pool for Carin. I also helped around the house even more than usual, as my mother could do increasingly less. We did have a cleaning lady who came once a week and cleaned the house from top to bottom. But a lot had to be done in between so that everything was always clean and tidy. So, I took on most of these jobs, like getting the kitchen ready or doing the laundry. All in all, I already had a lot of work to do with our garden and now the house on top of that. On the one hand, I enjoyed supporting my mother and making her at least a little bit happier. On the other hand, it was also exhausting, and I knew that none of my friends did as much at home as I did.

From time to time, however, I was lucky enough to have the son of the house opposite ours, who was about four years older than me, mowing the lawn at the same time as me. He was very athletic and had a very good physique. In the summer, it got too hot for him to mow the lawn, so he worked wearing nothing but his work boots and a pair of ripped short jeans. Although I was only 12 years old, I took great pleasure in the sight of this very masculine-looking body, which almost seemed to me to be a reward for my own labour. One day, while I was mowing the lawn and watching my neighbour out of the corner of my eye, my lawnmower suddenly cocked out. Now I was standing there trying to get it going again. This dream body from across the street came to my rescue! He inspected my lawnmower and, after a few checks on my lawnmower, said very expertly and calmly: "Try some gas." What, gas? How could something like that happen to me? I had forgotten to check the gas because I was so busy staring at him. How could I have forgotten? Oh boy, was I embarrassed! I must have turned red with embarrassment. And he must have thought to himself: "She's stupid!" And yet I had secretly hoped that he might find me cute or attractive. Now I had embarrassed myself so much that I would have loved to sink into the ground, but I had to refuel my stupid lawnmower and do my job - right in front of him. I think his friends were amused.

Another time, when I was mowing the lawn in front of the house again, a girl from my school rode past on her bike. She recognised me, stopped briefly and said: "Man, that's a big house." And I replied "Yes". She went straight on, "That guy must be really rich, does he pay well?" and I replied, "I get a dollar." Then she said goodbye and drove on. I didn't even get round to telling her that "the guy" was my father and that I lived in the big house.

Together with her gardener, my mother had started planting the flowers in the garden, as she did every year. I was always happy to help, because I enjoyed gardening, as did my mother. This year, however, she could hardly bend down and sitting on her stool caused her problems and pain. So, I did her part of the work too. I never minded working outside. But one day on a Saturday when I'd really had enough after finishing my work, I wanted to visit my friend Shelli and was about to leave. My mother got really upset about it and snapped at me "Go on, leave me all alone!" To emphasise her anger, she kicked me in the bum. But she had hit me so hard that it threw me forwards onto the ground. I was completely perplexed and didn't know what this was all about when I snapped at her: "Are you crazy? Have you gone mad kicking me?" At that moment, we were both taken aback. My mother had never been physically violent towards me before and I had never shouted or sworn at my mother. This was a completely new situation for both of us. This in turn triggered something in my mother and she started to cry terribly. I instinctively comforted her, although at the same time I was still very angry with her for kicking my arse. Not only did I find her action outrageous, but she had also hurt me. But I also really loved my mother. She was my haven of peace in my life, my anchor, she understood me so well. She didn't think I was stupid, on the contrary, she thought I was very intelligent. She defended me against my father and my sisters with their insults and attacks. But that day, I had some-how unknowingly hit a sore spot with her, and we started talking about it after we had cried together. She made me realise that she was beginning to feel superfluous, unnecessary. Everyone seemed to no longer need her at all and were devoting themselves to their own interests; no one in the family except for me had any time for her anymore. Yet she had given us over 20 years of her life! She wasn't wrong and I had been disappointed with the others for some time that they had let our mother down like that. After what she had said, I decided to stay with her that day because she seemed so hurt. I reassured her that I still needed and loved her.

During this time, a new phase of arguments and discussions began be-tween my parents. They seemed to talk about things in the evenings that really upset them both. But we children weren't allowed to find out what it was all about. My mother didn't seem to be able to stand up to my father and was sad during the day. One day, after they had argued the night before, she cried so much that I asked

134

her to talk to me and tell me what had happened. But she wouldn't or couldn't do that. I said, "Mom, you have to talk to someone, it can't go on like this." So, she decided to call her sister-in-law Traude Holl. The two of them spoke in German and I didn't understand anything, except when the name "Hans" was mentioned. But my mother was clearly quite upset. She decided to drive to her sisters-in-law to continue the conversation. It took us about half an hour by car to get to where Aunt Traude and Uncle Gustav had their donut shop, a Tim Hortons. On the way there, my mother suddenly had a strong crying fit while driving. Her arms cramped up and she couldn't steer the car properly, so it started drifting into the next lane on the highway. We were honked at, but my mother didn't react properly. I shouted at her: "Mom, pull over and stop!" At that moment, she realised the situation and managed to pull the car over to the hard shoulder and stop, without having caused an accident. We stood there for a while. She cried and cried and in between she kept saying: "I'm sorry." But I didn't know what exactly she was sorry for. It was all terrible. After she calmed down, we continued to drive, but slowly. When we finally arrived at my aunt's house, I was lucky enough to be able to pick out lots of mini donuts. The two of them wanted to have an undisturbed conversation, and so I sat there alone and devoured loads of donuts. After visiting my aunt, my mother did something that probably helped her feel a bit better. She drove to "Holt Renfrew", a very exclusive clothing store in Toronto, parked right in front of it in a no-parking zone and said to me: "If a policeman comes, tell him your mommy went to the toilet." I just nodded and stayed in the car. I didn't want to ask her any more questions that day. After a while, she came back to the car with a smile on her face and a fancy shopping bag in her hand. She proudly told me that she had chosen a horrendously expensive silk blouse and added: "I paid for it with my credit card, so that your father could see the date and the price on the bill." She was delighted with her success. More importantly, she had calmed down for the time being and so we drove home, after a long day. From that time on, my mother was different. I still didn't know what it was about, but she seemed to have finally distanced herself emotionally from my father and was inwardly content with whatever she had decided for herself.

Shortly after this incident, my mother had another emotional low and it was just me at home with her again. She wondered and asked me what was to become of our European roots. She was annoyed that she had always wanted to teach us German, her language, but Carin and I had completely rejected it. She was under the impression that we weren't at all interested in her country of origin or her church. The situation was trickier this time. I couldn't fool her. In fact, I really wasn't very interested in the Germany we had learnt about up to that point. We had been allowed to give up our forced German lessons after half a year of complaining. Our parents couldn't get us back to Europe voluntarily, except perhaps on an interesting city tour, like the one to Paris that we did. There were certainly beautiful mountains in Europe, like the ones we had seen in Austria, and an endless amount of culture. But we didn't like the people in many ways, especially in Germany. They were often too unfriendly and unapproachable. We sometimes found them cold and, as children and teenagers, we usually had the feeling of being a nuisance. So why would we want to go there? My mother assured me that Germany, her home country, could also be wonderful and that children and young people were welcome in some places. She challenged me to broaden my knowledge and my horizons and asked if I would like to go to a nice boarding school in Germany for a year, to see for myself. I was to experience "her" home country for a year and get to know young people of my age. However, I was so happy with my life in Oakville that I didn't want to change anything. The present could hardly be better for me, and I had already planned a future there. So why go back to the "old" Europe? She made an almost desperate impression on me when it came to this topic. But I couldn't and wouldn't accommodate her.

At one of the many birthday parties, I was allowed to celebrate with my friends, I discovered my interest in a boy called Tom. He had often smiled at me nicely at school and belonged to the larger circle of our clique. I don't know whether it was because I was friendly or because I was already starting to develop breasts, but he was interested enough in me to ask me to dance. I really liked him and so we kissed that evening. It was nice, and I was a little bit smitten.

In June 1977, my father was elected as the new President of the Canadian German Chamber of Industry and Commerce. This was an honorary position that he had to fulfil in addition to his position as President of Robert Bosch (Canada). My parents were very proud of this appointment and my mother seemed to take a liking to her husband again. I knew nothing about all this beforehand. At home, we had subscribed to the Globe and Mail as our daily newspaper, which arrived early in the morning. My father and I had the same morning routine for a long time, even on weekends. We got up at the same time, got ready and usually went downstairs for breakfast at the same time. He fetched the newspaper, and it became routine for him to put the comics down for me to look at first, and then the regional section. There was hardly any talking. He was engrossed in his newspaper and I laughed at my comics and then continued reading. Sometimes we shared our "news" with each other. On this morning, my father put the business section in front of me and kept the comics to himself. I was a little irritated, but my father was always good for a surprise. So, I thought this was his way of telling me that I was now old enough to read the business section. Maybe he was right and so I accepted this new challenge without hesitation. As I looked at the business section of the newspaper for the first time in my life, what did I see? My own father! He had made it into the newspaper through his appointment as President of the German Canadian Chamber of Industry and Commerce, even with a photo! My own father was smiling at me from the newspaper. I was really impressed and had to tell him so. And he was visibly pleased with himself, and I think also pleased to for once be getting some recognition from his youngest daughter. He really deserved it.

Teenager

My thirteenth birthday was just around the corner, and I could hardly wait to finally be a teenager! I was so excited! Sue was already 20 and an adult anyway and Carin also made quite a mature impression on me, and I wanted to emulate my sisters. Compared to them, I still felt quite childlike, also with my still somewhat boyish figure. There were only two things in which I didn't want to be like them. They both had problems with their skin, they had acne. As we shared a bathroom, I regularly experienced the dramas they went through in the morning when they discovered a new pimple on their faces. The emotional outbursts ranged from sheer horror ("Oh, my God!"), to sadness (at the distorted beauty), to anger ("Today of all days"), to disgust ("My face is disfigured"). At times I could hardly believe how painful these disfigurements must have been on the face and soul. However, I was somewhat spiteful when one of them had been unfair to me again and then the next morning - as if it had been planted there by the hand of God himself - a huge pimple disfigured the face of the mean sister. I was able to rejoice at the compensatory justice. Albeit, I was rather worried about how my sisters would react towards me, once it was my turn as a freshly pubescent teenager to have a scary minute of truth in the morning. I didn't want to experience their nastiness towards me, and I also did not want to get the pimple plague myself, so I asked God to spare me from acne, in earnest prayers. My sisters with their mischievous ways kept telling me: "You'll soon have acne and a pimple face too." They could be quite scary, but I had connected with God in this case and felt as protected as possible from what might come my way.

The other thing I didn't want was to have a curvy figure like my sister Sue. Before today's times, when women make their curves possible with silicone, it was extremely rare, but sometimes there were women who were something of a natural biological phenomenon, without silicone. My sister Sue was such a phenomenon. For years, I had watched her bust grow from year to year and I was terrified that the same would happen to me. I observed a similar development in Carin, but it wasn't quite as pronounced. And so, I quietly hoped that my bosom growth would be limited, that it would be even smaller than Carin's. But Sue had a narrow waist in addition to her incredibly pronounced bust, which emphasised her bust even more. So, I was also hoping for a less pronounced waist. My sister's curvy figure was crowned by wide hips. My father liked to sing a lyric from a song about my sister Sue's hips: "She's got a pair of hips, just like a battleship". And referring to her overall figure, he said: "She'd actually need a firearms licence for that", which only he and our mother could laugh about. Sue was always annoyed by this, and I was terrified at the thought that one day I might look like her. I wanted to keep my boyish figure but was prepared to accept slight feminine curves.

When I woke up on my 13th birthday, I couldn't have been happier. I was finally a teenager, and I thanked God for everything I had because I realised how well I was doing. I was healthy and happy, I had a wonderful mother who even seemed to like my father again, I could put up with my sisters and father to some extent, I was happy with my school and had great friends, and I did sports that I enjoyed. We lived in a fantastic house and even had our own swimming pool. I didn't have to wish for anything - except to be spared the pimple plague and the busty miracle - because my life was paradise. I didn't have to dream or wish for a better home, because I was already living in paradise.

My mother had agreed that after much pleading and begging, I could finally go to see the movie "Star Wars" with my friends, to celebrate the day. At the time, the movie was groundbreaking, and you simply had to see it. Those of us who were allowed to go were therefore pretty much in tune with the times. But as the movie wasn't showing in the small cinema in Oakville, we had to go to Mississauga to see it, a half hour drive by car. It would have been too far on our bikes, so we had to be driven by car. My mother drove us, Kirsten, Janet, Matt, Scott and I, there and one of the fathers was supposed to pick us up. The movie ran from 19:00 to 21:00 and it was agreed that we would be allowed to wander around the shopping mall for half an hour afterwards and wait at the exit at 21:30 for the car to take us home. Normally, I had to be home by 9.00 pm, but as it was my birthday and I was out with reliable friends and would be taken straight home, my parents made an exception, and I was allowed to stay out until 10.00 pm. Great! We were all very happy about this. We all thought the movie was fantastic and afterwards we waited from 21:30 for our pick-up, which never came. At 10.00 pm we called the pick-up father, who was at his sports club, and reminded him to pick us up. So, we waited again, but he didn't turn up. In the meantime, we had called all the parents and explained what had happened. All the parents understood the situation, because it was conceivable that a parent might forget to pick up the children. My mother, however, told me that my father was already angry that I wasn't home yet. I on the other hand, was disappointed, because the other parents weren't angry. They knew that we couldn't help the situation and were relieved that nothing had happened to us. We continued to wait until 11.00 pm for our pick-up, but it still didn't come. So, we called the other parents again and, to our relief, Scott's mother agreed to pick us up. By the time she arrived and drove everyone home, I was the last one home at about 24:00. It was midnight! I entered the house, where it was completely silent. Then I went upstairs to tell my mother that I was finally home. I was relieved to finally be home, because sitting around outside a shopping centre for hours is not fun. And so, I thought my parents would also be relieved to know I was home and safe. But instead of receiving a sympathetic, warm-hearted or even relieved welcome, I realised that my father was furious. He just shouted at me that it was midnight and how could I think of coming home so late? I was probably imagining, he continued, that now that I was a teenager I could do whatever I wanted. I was completely taken aback by his accusations, especially by the vehemence with which he verbally attacked me. I hadn't done anything wrong! I repeated what we had already talked about on the phone. I explained several times what had happened, but he didn't listen to what I said. He didn't seem to be interested in what I was telling him. He belonged to a different generation. He was what you would call the 'old school' of upbringing: in his view, children had to follow and nothing else. They had nothing to say. And accordingly, he vented his rage at what he considered to be misbehaviour. He lashed out and hit me. He hit me so hard in the face that I fell to the floor. By now he was hysterical and shouting at me, but I couldn't understand him because he was shouting in German. I couldn't grasp what was happening. I was stunned! Then, when I was already lying on the floor, he wanted to follow up and hit me again. My mother rushed in to stop him and took the blow for me. Oh no, not that! I was horrified. After this second blow, there was a short but very violent argument between my parents, the likes of which I had never experienced before. My mother grabbed me and took me out of the danger zone and into my room. On the way there, she continued to shout at my father. But as she was shouting at him in German, I didn't understand what words she was throwing at him or what she was saying to him specifically, but I could guess. Her tone and body language were clear enough. She was beside herself with rage and about to burst! My mother stayed with me in my room that night. My fantastic day ended in disaster. What had previously been a temporary emotional distancing of my mother towards my father, which was just getting closer again, with this action, became a rift in their relationship.

The following days were horrible. My father stormed out of the house in the morning with the words: "You're grounded for the whole summer". Excuse me, I thought to myself. I hadn't done anything, and I was supposed to spend the next eight weeks in the house? My mother informed herself about the whole story from the other parents and knew, as she had already suspected, that I had not lied. She was so angry with my father about the whole thing that she didn't want to talk to him. She stayed in my room for a few more nights and then slept in the guest room for a few nights. That had never happened before. The incident was unacceptable to her, and she wasn't prepared to pretend that nothing had happened. As for my part, I hated my father for what he had done. For one thing, he hadn't believed me and for another, he had hit both me and my mother – even though her, accidentally. It still happened. From that point on, I couldn't stand him anymore and wished my parents would get divorced. In any case, I wanted to live with my mother in a different house to my father, with or without my sisters.

It was a blessing that Carin and I were registered for a two-week summer camp that month, at Camp Mini-Yo-We. As it was already paid for, I was also allowed to go, despite my house arrest. I was happy to be able to get away, but I was worried about my mother. She was more upset about my father than I had ever experienced before, and I wouldn't be with her for two weeks, to support her. She had been unhappy for months before that and now this incident. Everything in our blessed home seemed to be going wrong. I brought up the subject of boarding school in Germany again with my mother. Given my feelings towards my father, I might have been prepared to travel all the way to China to avoid him at this point. I no longer wanted to live under the same roof as him.

Camp Mini-Yo-We was a Christian recreational camp located about 200 kilometres north of Toronto on Lake Mary. In addition to Bible lessons, our daily routine included lessons in various disciplines such as canoeing, swimming, photography, nature study, including building a campfire. We slept in permanent tents and there were also "tipis". Although the location and the opportunities were wonderful, I only enjoyed it to a limited extent. I was worried about my mother, and I missed her very much, so I called her as often as possible from a pay phone. Unfortunately, she kept crying during our phone calls, and so did I. So, we decided that she would visit me at the weekend, although this was not appreciated. Carin was quite upset about our plan as she thought I was too old to need a motherly visit. But given the last few months and our mother's emotional state, I needed her to come for a visit, and my mother needed it too. It was nice to see her and it was good for both of.

Back at home, only a few days passed, before Carin and I went back to sailing school again for a month in August 1977. I was allowed to go there as well, despite being grounded, as this fell under the heading of "lessons". Overall, it was the same as the previous year and brilliant again. We got our second sailing licence. I also won the prize for the most loyal sunbather of the year, the "Sunbather of the Year Award", for the second time.

In the meantime, my mother and I had gathered information about boarding schools in Germany, from the German embassy. In view of the tensions between my father and me, it seemed like a good idea to go ahead with the plan for me to go to a German boarding school for a year. The summer had just ended, and Carin and I were in sailing fever. I was most interested in a boarding school near Lake Constance, in the southern part of Germany, where you could also go sailing. But they also offered horseback riding there and lots of other things. The boarding school seemed like paradise, and I was immediately impressed. The boarding school we chose was Salem Castle on Lake Constance. As beautiful as the castle was, the price to attend the boarding school there as a student from abroad was also high. In fact, I had chosen by far the most expensive boarding school in Germany. But neither my mother nor I really cared. When we presented our results to my father, he wasn't particularly thrilled when he realised the price. But my mother made him understand that she wanted me to go to Germany for a year and that she

141

would take care of the price herself, if necessary. However, she also made it clear to him that he owed me something big, after this action on my birthday. He nodded his head, which could have been interpreted as remorse. So, the matter was settled, and I would go to Salem. However, I still wanted to spend eighth grade in junior high school and agreed to skip the first year of high school, 9th grade at O.T. and spend the year in Germany. My father seemed to have nothing more to say at all, at this time and so he could only nod in agreement. At least that was a done deal and now we just had to get along for the year until then. The tensions between my parents were still enormous and so we were pleased that my father had to go back to Germany for a few weeks on business at the end of August! He could have stayed there for all I cared.

In September, I started grade eight at E. J. James. I was happy to see my friends again and was also looking forward to seeing Tom. Unfortunately, he had become interested in another girl over the summer and that seemed to be the end for us before anything had even begun. My father was back from Germany and gave the impression that he might have thought about his behaviour and his family while he was away. He was quite affected when he realised that neither my mother nor I were particularly thrilled that he was back, and he tried to be nicer to us from then on.

Beautiful blue eyes

Our father had just returned from his trip overseas and within the same month, our mother had to be hospitalised, in Toronto. She was told that cancer had been discovered behind her eye and that because of this, the eye would have to be removed, to get rid of it. What terrible news! We were all shocked. It was terrible. The answer to her increasingly poor vision was not age-related farsightedness, but a tumour. After the eye would be removed, she was to receive a glass eye. But it wouldn't be that bad, she was told. Other people also live with a glass eye, such as Sammy Davis-Junior, who was, despite this a very successful entertainer. I was completely shocked by this news and was very worried about my mother. I also couldn't imagine how she would cope with having to wear a glass eye in the future. Unfortunately, my mother had become somewhat overweight over the years, which she felt wasn't beneficial for her appearance, but she still had bright, beautiful blue eyes that gave her so much expressiveness. Of all things, this was now to be taken away from her. We didn't have time to get used to this development, because we were told that she had to go to hospital in Toronto as quickly as possible, as the operation couldn't wait. And gone she was. From then on, there was a dreadful uncertainty in our house, a sad emptiness filled the rooms. The fact that the operation couldn't be carried out in Oakville was particularly upsetting, as I had to rely on getting a ride to visit my mother. I would have loved to have been with her all day every day, but since that wasn't possible, I felt completely powerless in the face of the situation.

Due to my mother's serious illness, my father's position changed from being the enemy at home to being a fellow sufferer, as we were both very worried about her and suffered emotionally with her. Although I hadn't wanted him to return from Europe, I was glad that he was back home, because it meant that one of my parents was still there for us, at least in the evenings, during this difficult time. I could hardly bear the thought of my mother lying alone in a hospital in a big, anonymous city, having to cope with the pain and disfigurement of her appearance on her own. The same thoughts also seemed to weigh heavily on my father. In this situation, my father and I were suddenly united in solidarity. He promised to take me to the city again and again to see my mother.

We weren't allowed to visit my mother until the day after the operation. So, we drove to see her together, even though we hardly spoke to each other on the way. I didn't feel the need to talk to him about anything beyond the reason for our journey together. The memories of his tantrum in the summer were still too fresh in my mind. I was also worried about my mother's condition and the outcome of the operation. The tension was almost unbearable. But then my father told me that he had a present for her. Oh, I thought, how nice. I'm sure she'll be delighted. My father was excited about the surprise, almost like a teenager before a date and I didn't know him like that at all. He was looking forward to finally seeing her, but he didn't know what to expect either. We shared a mood that was a mixture of joy, fear and worry. But he had prepared himself and showed me what the surprise was all about. He pulled a small blue box out of his coat pocket whilst driving and gave me to look and as I opened it, saw a ring inside. I knew very little about jewellery, but when I saw this sparkling ring with its large and beautifully cut sapphire in the middle, surrounded by smaller diamonds, I had an inkling that this was an exceptionally gorgeous and valuable gift. It was only then that I began to realise that my father loved my mother very much in his own way, that she was very precious to him and that her illness affected him deeply. He asked me if I thought my mother would like the ring and I told him that she would absolutely like it! It was in her favourite colours, blue, white and gold, and apart from that, I thought that any woman would be speechless to receive such a gift. My parents had known each other all their lives. And even though they'd had differences over the past year, he seemed to want to do everything he could to make her feel better. It had only been two months since I loathed him deeply, but now I felt so much sympathy for him because he seemed so fragile and almost in need of protection. He of all people, my tall and sometimes oversized father, seemed as powerless and helpless in this situation as I was. I began to realise that it was possibly not me, but the knowledge of her health condition that had made him into what he had become towards me over the last two months. Unfortunately, I must have become a lightning rod for his helplessness, and when I realised this, I even began to feel sorry for him.

My father told me that my mother had always wanted such a ring. In Germany, the custom of the engagement ring didn't exist, but they had lived in countries where it was customary to buy your fiancée a precious ring with gem-stones. My mother was always asked if she didn't have an engagement ring. And so sometimes she did wish for such a ring. But my father said that they had started out penniless, then spent a lot of money on travelling and now built a big house. They had invested money in this, and his financial resources had their limits too, he said. After this bad year, he wanted to give her this ring for her birthday in November, but now he thought she desperately needed cheering up after her operation, so he brought the ring with him to the hospital that day. I was very happy for my mother that she would now be getting her "engagement ring" and shared the anticipation with my father, as I knew my mother would be delighted.

When we first saw her, we were both a little startled but instinctively tried not to let it show. She had a huge bandage over her eye and beyond and made a very terrible impression overall. She looked physically and mentally exhausted. But she was very happy that we had come. She held her hands out to us. I had always had the feeling that I was her favourite child, her little sunshine, and so I beamed at her as much as I could. As she was so unwell, so weak and the situation was painful, we were both even more pleased that my father had the ring with him. This lovely surprise was exactly what she seemed to need right now. When he gave her the ring, she was so happy that she cried with joy! But that wasn't good, be-cause crying caused her pain and brought her from her joyful high over the gift back to the gloomy present in one swoop. The mood changed so quickly that nei-ther my father nor I could react fast enough. Reminded that one of her eyes had

144

been removed, she was suddenly beside herself with rage. She shouted how ugly she was now and that she was impossible to look at and that she no longer needed or wanted the ring. She ordered my father to take the ring back, but he refused. The evening was suddenly horrible and all three of us had to cry. After we had calmed her down, also with the help of a doctor, and reassured her that we still loved and needed her, we had to leave because visiting hours were over. My moth didn't want to keep the ring, and my father didn't want to take it back. No one wanted the ring, so I took it and put it in my pant pocket, and we drove home. My father was devastated, and I didn't feel much better after seeing my mother in that state. He didn't say a word the whole trip back, and neither did I. When we got home, I put my mother's ring in her bedside table in the hope that she would at some point get over her anger and be happy to find it there.

After about ten days, my mother came home from hospital. But she was mentally and physically very unwell. She was very weak and still sad. She didn't want to be alone in her condition. She kept crying at the beginning, which caused her pain. So, I just stayed away from school as often as I could and stayed at home with her most of the time. I was 13 years old and tried my best to look after her, keep her occupied and cheer her up. Looking back, I don't know why there was no one else around to look after her. Didn't she have any friends? Or didn't they have time? Did my mother perhaps not want anyone else around her, other than her family? I don't know. What about her own mother, was she too old to visit her daughter or look after her? Why didn't she fly over from Germany? It seemed to me that no one was coming around to see her. And that made me sad. Could it be that she didn't have any real friends? If that was the case, was it probably because she had moved too often? Questions upon questions that I didn't know the answers to kept me busy.

My mother and I had to kill time somehow while her recovery was progressing very slowly. So, we kept playing cards. The problem was that she found it difficult to see with just one eye. But she had to learn. She hadn't yet mastered focussing on small things like letters and numbers with one eye. When I offered her the chance to look with just one eye so that we had the same starting position when playing, she was able to laugh again. So, we painstakingly felt our way from situation to situation. Day by day. But I was convinced that the two of us would somehow manage the whole thing.

My mother was soon to get her glass eye, which she was very excited about beforehand. But when it was inserted, she didn't like it at all. She kept saying that the eye was strange to her and that she didn't want to look like that. She was so upset about how horrible the glass eye was that she suffered a huge setback in the whole healing process. The hope she had of looking somewhat normal with a glass eye was taken away from her by this first replacement eye. We had a second eye made for her and fortunately she liked it better. But now she still had to learn to cope with this glass object. This would also prove to be an arduous process. I remember how she once wanted to sew something. She was a very good and practised seamstress. She was just trying to pull the thread through the needle, but she couldn't do it. She tried several times, but she didn't succeed even after several attempts. I was sitting next to her and was almost holding my breath with every new attempt she made. After several failures, she was angry and discouraged because she couldn't pull the thread through the eye of the needle. She now felt completely useless and was raging with anger and frustration, crying and screaming at the same time. As usual, we were both alone at home and all I could do was hold her and comfort her. I couldn't really understand how she was feeling physically or emotionally, but it was obvious that she was suffering terribly. She told me it was persistent pain in her head that was almost driving her crazy and that she was also suffering from the side effects of the painkillers. She was more aggressive than usual and had also put on some weight, which made her even angrier. What made my moth even sadder was that she felt like she looked like a monster, as she told me. But I reassured her that she didn't look like a monster and that I didn't care what she looked like. I was just glad she was alive. The time I spent with her took its toll on me. I did my best to be there for her and suffered with her in her helplessness.

Life went on and so my mother decided to try her best to take part in life again. She needed a change and wanted to accompany my father on a business trip. She was in a bad way at the time, but they both thought that a trip and a change of scenery might do her some good. She should regain her self-confidence and get her mind off things. In November 1977, they travelled to Edmonton, Alberta.

In his role as President of the German Canadian Chamber of Industry and Commerce, my father was to officially attend the opening of the branch office there. The Alberta Premier and the Ambassador of the Federal Republic of Germany from Ottawa attended the ceremony. Other personalities from business and politics were also present, including the then head of the airline Lufthansa in Canada. There was also a German-born Alberta minister named Horst Schmid. Back at home, my father told me that Mr. Schmid had asked him to introduce him for his speech, as Horst T. Schmid. My father replied that this was no problem at all but asked why with a "T". Mr. Schmid replied: "Sometimes, when I pronounce my name "Horst Schmid", people think I said, "Horse shit". To avoid this misunderstanding, he therefore always introduces himself as Horst T. Schmid. We all laughed out loud at this story and I thought it was so funny that I kept asking my father to tell it to me, for years afterwards. The trip had been a success for my father, but unfortunately not for my mother. She came back and was devastated. She told me that she had never felt so unwell in her life. She felt so ugly with her glass eye and so fat with her extra kilos that she was embarrassed. She said she never wanted to travel again under these circumstances.

For me, life went on at school. I wasn't always there and when I was at school, I wasn't particularly focussed. The subject matters only went into my head to a limited extent. The teachers complained to me because I didn't do my homework. They were not satisfied with the explanation that my mother was ill. I was completely exhausted and felt misunderstood. What I did notice during this time, however, was that a very nice boy showed interest an in me. His interest didn't fit in very well with what was going on at home, but he was very nice to me, and I couldn't and wouldn't ignore him. It felt good that someone asked me how I was doing and was genuinely interested in me. But I always wanted to go straight home after school to be with my mother, so I didn't have time to talk to him for a long time in the schoolyard. And so began a time, in which we would walk home together after school and talk for a while. These walks together became the highlight of my day. However, because the walk was too short and we wanted to talk for longer, Brent and I started talking on the phone for long periods in the evenings. We got along very well and just enjoyed talking to each other.

In the fall of 1977, my father was watching the international news with particular interest and waited for a certain report. I had never seen him watch television so anxiously as he did at the time. There wasn't much reporting about the rest of the world back then. But one evening it was reported that in Germany, the President of the Association of German Employers had been kidnapped by the German terrorist group 'Rote Armee Fraktion', Red Army Fraction, or RAF for short, to free some of its members from prison. My father had followed this development on the news for weeks and told us that he had met this man on his last trip

147

to Germany, that he appreciated and liked him, and he also told me: "This man is a family man." All he ever said about the terrorists was: "Those bastards", words that I didn't recognise from him either. My father was visibly moved by the whole story. When the murder of Hanns-Martin Schleyer by the RAF was reported, my father was shaken. He had been sitting on the floor, to be as close as possible to the television, and after the report he began to cry bitterly. That was also new to me. This whole story with the terrorists in Germany had really affected him and it worried me. Now I had gained another negative impression of Germany, namely that there were terrorists there. This whole concept, which my father tried to explain to me, didn't go through my head at all. I couldn't understand the principle of kidnapping, blackmail and murder for political purposes. Suddenly Germany seemed dangerous and somehow crazy on top of everything else that I had thought about the country. I had lived for years in a functioning democracy in a country where people were nice to each other and the highest form of political protest was when the postmen went on strike. There were always some Québécois, the inhabitants of the province of Quebec, who wanted to become independent from the rest of Canada, but these discussions were resolved through referendums without violence. I only knew peace and had no interest in moving somewhere where there were such dangerous nutcases. My interest in my year in Germany was diminished.

Christmas 1977

In December, my mother had to go back to hospital in Toronto. As I understood it, this hospitalisation was "only" for a few weeks. She had problems with the medication and was also getting weaker and weaker. Basically, it was about finding the right medication for her. She was supposed to be back home for Christmas, but that wasn't possible after all. And now, we were supposed to spend Christmas Eve, the feast of feasts, without our mother for the first time. We couldn't do it without her, so we decided to take Christmas to her and celebrate with her in hospital. We packed some presents, candles and Christmas cookies and drove to her on 24 December. When we got there, much to our surprise, we realised that she was doing amazingly well! It seemed like a Christmas miracle. And for all of us, the best present ever. We sang German Christmas carols with her, which she had sung with us all those years before, sitting at the piano and playing. We children didn't usually know more than one verse of each song, but our mother sang the

148

remaining verses to us. She seemed so invigorated and cheerful to me that I was sure she had survived the worst and would be home again in a few days. What a huge relief after weeks of uncertainty. We all kissed her goodbye, and I told her as always that I loved her. As we drove away that evening, I was sure that everything would be fine. This thought relieved me because I was exhausted inside and desperately needed some good news. I couldn't have endured much more of the hard times.

My intermediate report in grade eight was poor, even though I still had a C average. My music teacher, of all people, with whom my mother got on so well, had written me a bad but accurate assessment: that I was constantly absent and lacked concentration. In contrast to all my previous reports, this time it didn't matter at home what kind of report I had brought home. For the first time, my father didn't get upset because he knew why my school performance was worse than usual.

We spent the next day, 25 December, with my mother's brothers and their families. So at least we had our traditional extended family celebration, which did us all a lot of good. The next day, my uncles were going to visit their sister in hospital, so she had visitors again. We were therefore able to celebrate Christmas Day with Ed's family, where we were invited to for the first time. Stella, Ed's mother, knew that our mother was in hospital and so she wanted to invite us girls to celebrate with her. She was a warm-hearted woman and suffered with us girls when our mother was so unwell. She was always worried about us and asked how we and our mother were doing. She also knew that Sue, at just 21 years old, had a lot of extra responsibility, often driving her sisters around and being responsible for buying the groceries. And all this on top of her studies! We girls were all quite overwhelmed in our own way and were happy to receive invitations from relatives and friends. It gave us support and was a great help during this difficult time.

We all took a break for two days, during which we did nothing. That was good for all of us because our mother had been unwell all year and we were all affected. However, my father had to go to the office during the day and went to see her after work. On 29 December, I finally wanted to visit my mother again. My father was at work and wanted to go back to the hospital on his own afterwards. I was so annoyed that I wasn't supposed to go that I threw a tantrum at home at lunchtime. My sisters were also at home that day and had witnessed my tantrum. They didn't know how to help me and told me to go to bed and take a nap because I seemed exhausted, mentally drained. I was, but I was also angry and frustrated that I couldn't see my mother! No one seemed to understand me. Although I didn't like listening to my sisters, I did this time because I realised how little strength I had left in me.

That evening, our father came home looking terrible. I told him to lie down first and although he had never listened to anything I told him, he did. Carin, meanwhile, was out at rehearsals again. I told Sue to get Carin and bring her home, which amazingly she did. My father and I were home alone when the phone rang. Normally I would have gone, but at that moment I just couldn't. It rang and rang until my father finally answered the phone. I was already on my way upstairs to ask him who was calling when my father started screaming. He was screaming loudly and in pain, shouting, "No, no, no!" At that moment, I knew that my mother had died. I stopped in the middle of the stairs. At first, I didn't know what to do, but then I went to him. He was sitting on his bed and was a pile of misery. He could hardly breathe. He was crying and screaming and gasping for air at the same time. He was completely beside himself. When he saw me, he tried to say something, but nothing came out at first. Then he kept saying "Your mother, your mother..." but that was as far as he got. I took my father in my arms and said: "I know."

When I was taking my afternoon nap that day, I dreamt that my mother had died or was in heaven. In my dream, she spoke to me and told me that she had to go now. But she also told me that she wouldn't be far away and that I could talk to her any time. I had never dreamt anything like this before. When I woke up in the afternoon, I was afraid that she was really going to die. Now it had already happened.

Shortly after the call from the hospital, Sue and Carin came home. I went downstairs, looked at them for a long time and then said, "Mom has died." We all hugged each other and cried together. At some point we went to our father's room and the four of us cried. Then my father packed us all into the car and drove us back to the hospital in Toronto, even though it was already rather late. He felt that we should say goodbye to our deceased mother, and so we did. In retrospect, I think it was the right decision for our father to take us there, not only to say goodbye, but also to see our mother's lifeless body. If I hadn't seen with my own eyes how my mother's dead body lay completely motionless and observed for myself that she had stopped breathing, I might always have doubted that she had died and not just disappeared without a trace. If I hadn't felt her cold, lifeless hand with my own hands, I wouldn't have had the memory for years of what it was like when she stopped responding to my squeezing her hand.

When I realised that my mother was dead, I ran out of the room. I had gone into some room, and I don't know how long I was there before a pastor came to me. It must have been at least 10 pm. He came up to me with the good intention of comforting me. He told me that my father had told him that we were Protestant. To my "So what?" he replied that that was good, because as Christians we believed in eternal life, life after death. If that was the case, he continued, then I would know that my mother was now in heaven, with God. I should know that her time here on earth was over and that God had decided to take her to Himself. He said that as a devout Christian, I should find comfort in the fact that my mother was still alive in heaven. In theory, he was right. But I told him that I didn't really give a damn where my mother was floating around, if she wasn't here on earth with me. But he said that it had been God's will to bring her to himself. At this, this whole story about God, church and religion ended abruptly for me. I told him that I wanted nothing to do with a God who takes away the mothers of children or teenagers. I asked the pastor to leave me alone and he left.

That night seemed never-ending. Back at home, none of us could sleep. I went to Carin's room, and we went to Sue's room together. The three of us sisters fell asleep in Sue's bed sometime in the early hours of the morning.

Days of confusion followed. But first we had to talk about how it was possible, that our mother could have died so suddenly. I couldn't grasp it because she had gone to hospital to have her medication adjusted and when I saw her a few days before she died, she was making a good impression. Only then did my father come out with the whole story. Our mother had cancer. She and my father didn't want to spoil Christmas for us and as the doctors said she had two or three months to live, it would suffice to tell us the truth later. But then, unfortunately, she unexpectedly died earlier. Of course, I was shocked and angry. I had been robbed of the possibility to say goodbye to my mother! And Carin and I - because Sue already knew - had no idea that our mother wasn't suffering from the consequences of the eye operation in the last few months but was battling terminal cancer! What words fit my feelings; anger, horror, frustration, mistrust, simply everything. I felt lied to and betrayed, even though my father insisted that concealing the truth had been a joint decision of our parents.

151

In our otherwise rather strict and very orderly house, there were suddenly no more rules except that everyone had to be in bed by 11.00 pm. That didn't deviate from my usual daily routine anyway. I usually went to bed shortly before 11.00 pm and got up again shortly before 8.00 am. As each of us started our day independently and each of us had breakfast on their own as we were accustomed to doing, what we missed most, was having dinner together with our mother. It was only then that the big emptiness set in, which we all couldn't really cope with.

At first, I called all my friends to tell them that my mother had died. When I rang Suzanne, she wasn't there, and I spoke to her mother. I must have sounded lost because she told me to come over, which I did. Although it was dark, I walked alone through the nature reserve behind our house, which we were generally forbidden to do, but I didn't care that night if someone attacked me or not. Suzanne's mother, who I knew to be a very disciplined, reserved Northern German who was always correct and showed little emotion, opened the front door and took me in her arms. She didn't just offer me her condolences; she seemed to feel with me, and it was only at that moment that I began to realise that something terrible had happened.

Carin and I didn't really have a role at home these days. Sue and our father had to prepare the funeral, which wasn't easy because of the public holidays around New Year's Eve. My father expected us all to wear black clothes to express our grief to the outside world, in keeping with tradition. However, black was not a fashionable colour back then, and when the three of us girls went shopping for our mourning clothes, the task turned out to be more difficult than we could have imagined. When we asked for black skirts, blouses or sweaters, a saleswoman looked at us uncomprehending and commented that black really wasn't a colour for girls and women as young and as we were. Sue then flipped her lid and said: "Black is exactly the colour we need because we want to wear mourning clothes as our mother has died." The horrified look on this poor saleswoman's face again gave me the feeling that something bad had happened.

The funeral parlour, "Ward Funeral Home", was quite large and quite elegant. My father had prepared everything there with Sue. They had chosen a very beautiful coffin and decorated it with a huge bouquet of 100 red roses from my father. We daughters each had a bouquet of 50 yellow roses in front of the coffin. There were also flowers and wreaths from my father's friends, relatives, acquaintances and business partners.

152

We attended a service in the Protestant church. We probably looked like watered poodles. Now we suddenly needed the help of the pastor and his church to bury our mother according to her faith. It was a strange feeling for me to know that the pastor's presence at the funeral would play a role that deeply moved my father and would have meant a lot to my mother. However, as my parents' church was still closed to me, I felt like an observer at his religious ritual.

In this funeral parlour, I felt like an observer anyway, rather than a participant in anything. People came up to me and expressed their condolences. I thanked them, but didn't fully realise what was happening around me. Suddenly my class teacher, Mrs. Harcourt, stood in front of me and I thought to myself: "What is she doing here?". I really liked her; she was a charming person and had a strong personality. She and her husband both drove Corvettes, which we students thought was cool. Everyone in the class liked her and she liked us too. On this day, however, she didn't have her engaging smile and positive charisma as usual. She was dressed in dark colours and looked very sad. She came up to me with a huge bunch of flowers in her hand and said: "These are from your classmates." That caught me off guard and I was speechless. I couldn't believe that they were thinking of me and expressing their sympathy for my sad event in this way. Then she hugged me and expressed her very personal condolence. I was not prepared for this heartfelt expression of empathy and began to cry bitterly. She continued to hold me in her arms, and I cried and cried and cried.

Many of Carin's friends came to the funeral parlour, including some from the church, of which she was not allowed to be a member. My father didn't like this at all and would have liked to throw them all out. We were all emotionally upset, but Carin and I made him realise that these people from the "sect", as he always said, had been our friends for years and it was good for us to have them with us at this time. It was then agreed that they would sit in a side room during the funeral service so that my father wouldn't have to see them and so that relatives and friends of the family could sit in the main room. The German ambassador also came to my mother's funeral. In the end, there were so many people that they could barely fit into the funeral parlour and had to queue outside the door in the freezing cold for a long time before they could get in.

In the days that followed, we received many calls from friends, relatives and neighbours. Every family I had ever babysat for also called. Most of the calls were for Carin and me, but the callers often also wanted to express their condolences to our father. We would hand him the phone with the words "Mr. So-and-so" or "Mrs. So-and-so". He always looked at us with that "who-is-this look" and so we briefly explained to him who it was. He had received so much sympathy from people he didn't even know, but who all knew who he was. Some of these people had been friends with us children and our family for almost four years. It had completely passed my father by that we children had become part of the community and that these people were also interested in our family. For the first time in our lives, Carin and I had become an integrated part of a neighbourhood and a community, and this was very strongly expressed during those days.

We were very touched by the empathy of the neighbourhood and our friends and their families. Everyone seemed to sympathise and wanted to help us in some way. Once, when I thanked them on the phone for their sympathy and said that we didn't need anything, Sue said jokingly in the background: "We need someone to make us dinner." I repeated what she had said, quicker than she could tell me she wasn't being serious, but that got us an invitation to dinner. I thought this was rather good! If it hadn't slipped out, so to speak, we probably wouldn't have gotten one. The change of environment and the care we felt on the evening when another woman cooked for us, did us all a lot of good. And so, I always dared to answer the question: "Is there anything we can do for you?": "Yes, we need someone to make us dinner." This led to out being repeatedly invited to dinner by our neighbours and friends. My father was quite stunned by how many neighbouring families I knew and by the fact that they knew me. He hadn't realised how much I had settled into the neighbourhood and how deeply rooted I was. He also seemed surprised that some people liked me, simply because of my good nature or my character. It almost seemed as if he could hardly believe that anyone liked me at all. But that was the case.

We also received messages of condolence from my father's employer, Robert Bosch GmbH in Stuttgart. In a letter to our family, the company wrote that they would donate 50,000 Canadian dollars to the Canadian Cancer Research Foundation in honour of our mother. We were speechless! The amount of 50,000 Can-$ was very high at the time. Anyone with an annual salary of that amount at the time was already considered to be earning very well, so I was hugely impressed by the size of the donation. I was not aware of the fact that my mother was also highly respected and not just my father. She certainly hadn't realised it either. It was just a shame that she hadn't been aware of it beforehand. At least my mother's death, apart from being meaningless for me and our family, had resulted in a positive contribution to a good cause through this money for research purposes.

Note: as I translate this to English in 2024, the value is five-fold.

On the third of January, we took our mother's ashes to the cemetery in an urn. It was indescribably cold on that January day. The weather could not have been more fitting. The cold wind blew in from Lake Ontario and made everything even frostier. It was grey, cold and windy. Apart from my father and sisters, Ed was with us at the cemetery, as he was already part of the family at that time. My mother's brothers, Gustav and Martin, were also there. My father didn't want anyone else there.

A few days after the urn burial, my father asked the three of us sisters for a talk. He wanted to discuss with us what the financial situation would be like for us, if he were to die now. We were still in mourning and didn't want to deal with the idea that he might also die, and we would be left without parents. But he insisted on discussing the matter here and now. We sat at the dining room table, where we had never sat to talk before. My father had documents on the table. He explained to us that half of the house belonged to us due to our mother's death, but that there was still a mortgage on the house. There was also the balance in a savings account, which he would divide by three and pay out to each of us at the age of 18. So, we were told that we had inherited. He went on to say that there was no life insurance on our mother. Our parents had always made their financial decisions together. My father had categorically refused to take out life insurance on his wife because he had always told her that he didn't want to make money from her death. I found that very touching and decent. But apparently, he hadn't considered that our mother, by being a housewife and mother, also did work in the household and in raising children and that this work would have to be continued. Perhaps they both simply didn't consider that she might die at the age of 47 instead of in old age.

I was surprised by this conversation in more ways than one, because we had hardly ever talked about money or property in our family. The idea had never occurred to me that half of the house we lived in could belong to my mother. And even if it had, it would never have occurred to me that her share would now go to us daughters. I certainly assumed that everything belonged to my father, as he was the one who earned the money. At my age, I wasn't concerned with legal issues and questions of ownership. Our father went on to explain to us that if he died, the second half of the house would also go to us, making the three of us the owners.

He also explained that he had taken out various life insurance policies on his life. Originally, he had wanted our mother and us children to be taken care of if something happened to him as the head of the family. Now she was no longer there, and he said that we could manage with the money that would come our way, but that we would have to move into a smaller house, to reduce the running costs. He was sure that all three of us would be provided for and could finish our schools and then universities in peace and take care of ourselves later. What he explained to us sounded reasonable and I would not have to worry about our financial situation, should our father also die. It was a reassuring feeling.

Our family constellation had changed. Six months earlier, I had wished my parents would separate. I had hoped that my mother would leave my father. Now there was a separation; she had left him. However, my wish had been to live with my mother and not with my father. But now she had died, and I was living with him! Instead of having him as far away from my life as possible, she had disappeared from my life as far away as possible. I had wanted a divorce, not a death. There were now four of us in the family for good.

My father now sat in the living room evening after evening with a look of emptiness on his face and spoke next to nothing. He was an abandoned man. His expressionlessness went so far that I was worried about how he would cope with the loss of his lifelong partner. He had changed abruptly with the death of his wife. There was nothing left of the restless, tigerish man who had been too strict with me for my liking and had the occasional outburst of anger. He seemed weak and sometimes even fragile. This new man, who was still a stranger to me in this form, was suffering. I felt very sorry for him in his suffering. Just as he was grieving, he received the news that his father's health was very poor. The news of our mother's death had taken its toll on our grandfather Paul Bauder, who was already in poor health, and weakened him further. So, our father decided without further ado to fly to Germany, as he really wanted to see his father again, should he also die. My father also wanted to visit his parents-in-law to tell them about their daughter's funeral and show them photos of it. They had explicitly requested a visit from him so that they could grieve together, as they couldn't take the strain of an overseas flight because they were also devastated by our mother's death. He wanted to fly to see them anyway, at a later point in time, but now there was a sense of urgency, and he had to leave immediately.

After his return from this trip, he spoke even less than before. But he told me that he had said goodbye to his father, which had been very, very difficult for him. I was still very sad about my mother and this pain was difficult for me to bear. But my father was also in mourning and now had to assume that his father wouldn't live much longer either. What an additional blow! Just a few months ago, we were united by our shared concern for my mother, but now we were even more united by our shared grief. My father lost his wife after 22 years of marriage. Not only that, but they had also known each other all their lives. They had built a very nice life out of nothing, had three wonderful daughters, and had lived in several different countries. They had built an exceptionally interesting and successful life together. There was a lot that bound these two people together. I now clearly felt that my father had lost his other half. And I had lost my anchor, my haven of peace. Now my father continued to sit there evening after evening, speaking almost nothing and sometimes staring silently ahead of him. As he seemed so empty, I even began to wonder whether he might end his own life.

My sisters didn't suffer at all like my father, and I did, at least I couldn't recognise any deep pain in them, even if there might have been some. They seemed to be getting on with their lives and their interests, which they were already pursuing. Sue had to go to university, had her boyfriend and his family, who certainly gave her support. Carin had all her hobbies, at least outwardly she was a strong head person and less emotionally driven. She seemed to have accepted our mother's death as a fact and somehow gotten over it. However, I have to say that the two of them were never particularly close. It was completely different for me, and the absence of my mother left a huge vacuum. I felt empty and abandoned. I had no support, protection or help. Although my father, but also my sisters, had mellowed because of my mother's death and no longer annoyed me, I didn't know how long this state would last. They all seemed to be too preoccupied with themselves to want to annoy me like they used to. But I still remembered their attacks and nastiness from the past and I didn't know if or when they would start again. Who would protect me then? But now they hardly seemed to notice me.

A month after our mother's funeral, my father's father died at the beginning of February. My father was now devastated. Within a few weeks, the two people he loved the most had died, first his wife and now his father. Nothing could have been more inappropriate for my father at this time. Having just returned from

Germany, he flew to his father's funeral and stayed there for another week. We three girls stayed at home alone again and Sue was again in charge of us. Poor Sue!

On the flight back from Germany to Canada, my father met a woman on the plane. It was February, usually the coldest month in Canada. This woman said she was on her first trip to Canada, to get to know the country and its people. Her plane ticket was so cheap that she simply had to buy it. The fact that anyone could even think of flying into the frozen Canadian winter as a tourist amused my father. He explained to her why her ticket was so cheap, namely because there was very little to do in February and advised her to come back to Canada in the summer. He found this story hilarious and told it to us on his return. Otherwise, however, he had little to laugh about and looked terribly worn out. He seemed exhausted and still had to process the impressions of his father's funeral. He said that his siblings had been very nice to him. They sympathised with him because his wife had just died. For this reason, he was the first of the seven siblings to say what items he wanted in memory of his parents. He wanted the family Bible that his father had always read from. He also wanted his mother's silver cutlery and a cobalt vase that had been a gift from my parents. Finally, he wanted a crystal vase and a crystal plate with a dedication that his father had been proud of. His siblings agreed to everything and gave him priority. What bothered my father, however, was how his siblings otherwise discussed the estate. He told me that it really disgusted him at times. His father had barely died, and his siblings were discussing the estate fiercely, sometimes "like vultures", as my father put it. I asked him if he had inherited anything else from his father apart from the items I mentioned? He replied yes, money. The amount seemed a lot to me, especially since his father was 80 years old, and the total amount was divided by seven children. I asked my father if he had the money with him on the flight? He laughed and said that firstly, his father's house or villa had to be sold, and the entire estate settled. Secondly, he said he would then leave the money in Germany. I asked him why he needed money in Germany, as we were living in Canada. He replied: "You never know." And he added that it was always better to spread your money around or not have it all in one country. He said that this was the case for people who had lived through times of war. His father had done the same and had money in Switzerland as a reserve. I found all this interesting because it was something I had never thought about before.

It was the end of February, and our father had only been home for a few days. After a week at the office, he decided to take a week's holiday to recover from the stress of the two deaths. He spontaneously booked a trip to Acapulco, Mexico. He had last been on holiday there with his wife a year before her death and they had enjoyed it very much. From Mexico, he wrote a postcard to his parents-in-law, as he did from almost every trip, in his usual manner. It read: "Now I have managed to go on holiday for a week after all, but without the children. I had a very good rest; the weather is marvellous." While swimming on holiday, our father saw a woman in a Triumph bathing suit and approached her with the words: "Triumph crowns the figure", the company's former advertising slogan. This is how these two German tourists began an acquaintance in faraway Mexico.

In the meantime, the three of us girls were home alone again. After all, we also had to go to school and university. However, during this time Ed, who also came round to look after us when Sue had to stay at university, acted as a sort of big brother. At first, I was a bit taken aback by this, but then I thought it was good to have someone at least halfway grown up in the house. He proved to be a good provider and took us to McDonald's, like he used to. He was really worried about us and helped where he could. He also grieved, after all he had known our mother for five years and the two of them had gotten along well. Ed developed a kind of protective instinct, especially towards me. He was a bit like a big brother and sometimes caring like a mother. In honour of his efforts during this time, I gave him a Mother's Day card as my new surrogate parent for Mother's Day!

My boyfriend Brent was also a great support for me during this time. We spoke on the phone almost every evening as usual. When he told his mother that our father was away again, now for the third time, and we three girls were on our own, she invited me to come to her house anytime for dinner or whatever. She was so sweet and said that, with or without Brent, she would always be there for me. As I was also allowed to come for dinner, I did that once. When my father was back from his holiday, Brent understood that I wanted to stay with my father in the evenings and so we spoke on the phone again almost every evening, for quite a long time. He was incredibly understanding of me and my situation, even though he had never experienced such a loss himself. He always managed to cheer me up and make me feel liked and needed. I couldn't have had a better friend. His mother was also very nice and always asked me how I was doing. It was strange. Just that summer, I had been punished by my own father for not being home at 10 pm as agreed. Now there was no one there to check up on me and the matter was no longer so important. Brent's mother had thought it to be exceptional that the three of us were at home without an extra adult while our father was away. But when she

159

found out that he'd gone on holiday without us, she thought it was strange, that he left us alone too much and expected too much. That's what I thought as well. After all, he could have waited until the next school holidays and taken us to Mexico, because a holiday would have done us good too! But we didn't get one.

My friends were also a great support during this time, especially Janet, Kirsten and Shelli. I was allowed to call them all at any time and simply express that I sometimes felt bad, or sad. They were always there for me. They also came over more often and invited me to their homes. I felt good and well understood by these friends, also by Suzanne and Jacquie. The six of us girls had done and experienced many things together in the four years we had known each other. We had all taken it in turns to have sleepovers, sometimes all together. We had gone through this pre-puberty phase together, discussed our first bras, talked about boys and had our first parties. When Kirsten's younger sister became difficult, together, we took more care of her and included her in our clique. Sometimes we studied together for school, we did a lot of sport together, and in the summer months we often went swimming either at Kirsten's or my place. We knew all the family members, the siblings and the parents and, as with Shelli's home, not only the dog "Ruffy", but also the entire "zoo" that her brother had in his room. In short, we had been through all the developments, challenges and crises that girls between the ages of 10 and 13 can have together. I couldn't have had better friends.

Confirmation classes

My father now had the task of making sure that Carin and I went to confirmation class, as this had been one of the last wishes of our mother. We were less than thrilled about going to Toronto for classes every Saturday from March to May. Sue wasn't thrilled either, as she had to drive us there most of the time. But it wasn't our fault that we were required to attend these classes, nor was it our fault that Sue had finally taken over most of our mother's responsibilities, including grocery shopping and driving us to our appointments. Confirmation classes could hardly have come at a more inopportune time. Carin had been denied her wish to join another church the previous year. Accordingly, she showed little interest in the Protestant church. But there was no way round it for us. We didn't hide our disinterest, on the contrary. We told the pastor why we were there, and he said that it would not be easy for him to teach us under these circumstances. Much to our

160

pastor's astonishment, Carin was well versed in the bible. Her expertise combined with her inner rejection of the situation soon led to a kind of exchange of blows between the two of them. Whenever Pastor Knaack explained something to us according to the Protestant faith, Carin would quote some passage from the Bible that said something different on the subject. It was unbelievable how much she challenged him, and I simply agreed with her without knowing the facts, no matter what it was about. As far as I was concerned, I knew that God had taken my mother from me and so I wanted nothing more to do with him. For this reason, I stood by my sister in solidarity when she tried to take poor Pastor Knaack down as part of his role as a representative of the Protestant church. After all, this concerned the very church, which she had rejected. My knowledge of the Bible was nowhere near as good as my sister's, but I usually agreed with her arguments just to be against this church. This was my way of expressing my rejection of such a mean God who takes away children's mothers. Perhaps the confirmation classes were misused by both of us to rebel, which is what young people our age sometimes did. Surely, the lessons were also used as a type of lightning rod for our bottled-up anger and disappointments. Pastor Knaack had a really difficult task ahead of him to teach us and change our minds within three months.

After several attempts to teach us something, Pastor Knaack said to us one day that we were like a pair of pliers. No matter what he said, one of us would squeeze on one side and the other on the other, like a pair of pliers. He said that there was no point in continuing with us as we obviously didn't want to participate. He would call our father and let him know. We were overjoyed at this news and Carin, and I could not have been happier about our victory. From our point of view, the confirmation classes had been successfully cancelled! However, we hadn't expected a stern talk from our father about this for him unpleasant development. We thought we would simply tell him that Pastor Knaack was somehow no longer interested in teaching us. But our father hadn't accepted our version quite so blindly. I can't remember what he said to us in response to Father Knaack's complaint. He may have reminded us that it had been our mother's last wish, for us to take part in these lessons. However, it had the effect that we remorsefully called Pastor Knaack to apologise for our misconduct and for having been difficult confirmands. We even asked him to give us lessons again.

Toronto 1978, Carin, Pastor Knaack, Claudia, Confirmation.

We were only allowed to come back to class under the condition that we no longer argued with him. From then on, we didn't. By the end of May, everything was over for the three of us, and Carin and I were confirmed in the first week of June at St George's Lutheran Church in Toronto. After some initial difficulties, Pastor Knaack was convinced of my good inner core and gave me the confirmation motto: "Blessed are the pure in heart, for they shall see God" (Matthew 5:8).

At the age of 13, Brent and I were madly in love with each other. I was convinced that in him, I had found my partner for life. He cheered me up after that sad winter and made me laugh and I even loved him for that alone. At the time, he seemed to understand me better than anyone else that I knew. There was no question that we wanted to stay together. He was charming and funny, considerate and very athletic. He loved playing ice hockey, so his mother and I sometimes came with him to his games. From spring onwards, he played baseball instead of ice hockey and it became my favourite pastime to watch him play baseball after school. I watched him practice at school and sometimes accompanied him to his games, away games. While watching, we girls would sometimes sit or lie on the edge of the pitch and watch the boys, sometimes lying on our stomachs. The boys often had something to giggle about, but what it about remained a secret amongst them, that we girls weren't supposed to find out. At some point, I got on Brent's nerves so much, wanting to know what was so funny, that he had to tell me the secret. He said the boys had found a new definition for the word "impossible". The definition was "for Claudia to lye flat on the ground" It had not escaped the boys' attention that I had not only been mourning over the winter, but also growing, particularly noticeably, my chest. I hadn't really noticed it myself. But when he told me about the definition of "impossible", I also had to laugh. It still makes laugh today! What did however get my attention, was that I had been spared the acne plague thus far. My sisters always commented that with: "Wait and see, you'll get it too." Inwardly, I prepared myself for the plague to hit me, but it never did. I also was expecting that I would develop the same voluminous bust as my sisters, but that remained within limits, at least for the time being.

There was nothing that could have come between Brent and me at that time. We had been through such a difficult situation together, that some couples might not go through in a few years, and that at our age! Yet there was also a promise I had made to my mother, that I wanted to keep. After all, I had promised her that I would spend grade nine in Germany. Summer was approaching and Brent and I discussed whether it was still necessary to keep this promise. I concluded that I absolutely had to keep it. Somehow, I couldn't let go of the fact that she wanted me to give her home country another chance. At this point in my life, shortly before my 14th birthday, I was very clear about what I wanted in life: To spend that one year in Germany to at least try to get a slightly more positive impression of the country. And then, the issue of my parents' home country would also have been ticked off for me and I could prepare for my future in my home country, Canada. After a year, I would return to Oakville and attend grades 10 to 13 at O.T. and hopefully be back with Brent. That sounded good to me! After high school, I planned to go to university, following my sister Sue's lead, and enrol at the University of Toronto. I had no doubt that I could do it all and was looking forward to the wonderful years ahead of me. Only one more year would separate me from my future and that's how I explained it to Brent. He didn't want me to leave, but he was understanding. On the one hand, he understood that I wanted to keep my promise. On the other hand, I convinced him that if the two of us really wanted to stay together, we would manage this one year of separation. To me, the matter was decided. After grade eight, I would go to Germany.

I had planned to stay at home for the whole summer. I wanted and needed to rest, and I also wanted to spend time with my friends, who had been such a great support over the past half a year. But our father told us that we had to go to Germany for the summer to visit our grandparents. As our mother's parents were apparently endlessly sad about the death of their daughter, we girls were supposed to go and visit them so that they wouldn't be so alone in their grief. That seemed reasonable, although at the same time I felt it was a bit much to ask of us. However, knowing how much my mother had loved her parents, I agreed to spend my summer holidays with them.

But first, I really wanted to fly to my aunt Trudel and my uncle Alex in New Jersey. I had the feeling that I desperately wanted to be hugged by Trudel, as she was the person whom I loved most in the whole world, after my mother. Apart from that, it was always fun for me being with Trudel and Alex, where I had always felt safe and loved, even as a small child. My father agreed to my wish, and I flew to see them for a few days, at the end of June. Only Brent was not thrilled about any of this. First, he had reluctantly agreed to my 'compulsory year' in Germany. Then, he had to do without me for the summer, so that I could visit my grandparents and now I wanted to spend a week with my great-aunt and great-uncle in New Jersey. He was rather annoyed due to my family commitments, and rightly so. But what was I supposed to do? We weren't a normal family where all the family members lived in the same area. As interesting as the international dimension made us for some, it also had a downside: one must travel to see each other and that is time-consuming and expensive. The time Brent and I still had together became less and less and there was nothing that he could do about it.

So, I flew to my beloved great-aunt and her funny husband. It was the first time I was flying alone, and I was quite nervous about it. But the flight from Toronto to New York was quite short and therefore over quickly. Nevertheless, I was travelling from Canada to the USA and was quite scared to cross the border alone, without my parents. Every entry into another country made me feel uncomfortable; the stern looks from the border police when they looked at the passports, the many questions they asked people like us, who had many stops registered in their passports, the armed police officers walking around. Once you had your suitcase and finally wanted to go out of the building into freedom, you still had to go through customs, again subjected to stern looks, this time from the customs officers, and again from the armed policemen. I hated all of it and felt uncomfortable every time, as if I could be grateful if they didn't do anything to me. Nevertheless, I had to cope with the situation on my own.

When I finally arrived, it was a very happy reunion for the three of us. As always, the days with Trudel and Alex were fun and enjoyable. We were still a close-knit team, just like from the beginning. I always found Alex's driving the funniest: when turning the car to the left or the right, he looked left and Trudel looked right, and before he drove off, he asked his wife: "Everything clear at your side?" If she answered "Yes", he drove off without even checking whether what Trudel had said was correct. The two of them were unique! And this turning ma-noeuvre was like out of a movie. At some point during the visit, Trudel came up to me and slipped me $20 with the words: "Don't tell Alex about this." What was funny, however, was that Alex came up to me shortly afterwards, also slipping me $20 and said: "But don't tell Trudel about it." It was hilarious and I kept quiet.

We drove to the seaside as usual and walked along the boardwalk. Since I could trust them, I told them that I was in love for the first time and that I had a very nice boyfriend. They were very happy for me. We also talked about how much I liked horses and riding and how I intended to have my own ranch with horses one day. During those days, Alex, who was deeply affected by my mother's death, told me that of all relatives, he had loved and cherished my mother the most. Alex told me that he wanted to bequeath his favourite grandfather clock, one of several that he had made with his own hands, to Magda. It was the very grandfa-ther clock that used to keep Carin, and I awake as small children when we spent the night at their house. Now, that my mother was no longer alive, I was to inherit it. At least, I was very happy about this news. It was lovely to know that one day I would have his favourite grandfather clock with me and with that, also a little bit of this funny little man.

He was not his usual funny self, at the time. He couldn't hide his sadness about my mother's death, and he also told me that he was very worried about us children, but also about Hans. He said that my parents needed each other and that he didn't know how Hans would cope without Magda. She had always been his support, the strong woman behind the successful man. He was serious about his worries, just like the ones he had about me. He thought I was far too young to manage without my mother. I told him that I would go to a boarding school in Germany for a year and that would take care of me. He didn't like that idea at all. He said that we should and had to stay together as a family, and then we might be able to manage without Magda. But not otherwise, he said. Strong words, I thought, and I could not evaluate, if that was correct.

The fact that I even wanted to go to Europe completely upset my dear Uncle Alex. He talked to me for days about how I shouldn't go there, under any circumstances. He said: "Don't go to Europe. Everything is so cramped there, people have so little space, which makes them so unfriendly and aggressive." I replied: "But Alex, it's only for a year!" He literally begged me not to go. Like Brent, he didn't think I had to keep my promise after my mother had died. I couldn't understand why he appealed to me so passionately not to go, but I sensed that he was very serious about it. My great-uncle had never asked me to do anything or told me what to do. I knew that he loved me and only wanted the best for me. But he started to scare me with his pleas for me not to go to Europe. He only stopped when Trudel said to him: "Alex, stop it, you're scaring her." He had indeed succeeded in doing so. I decided to reconsider my intention to stay there for a year. I now had two good reasons not to go and was looking forward to returning to Oakville. After all, I had already missed everything and everyone there terribly after this short absence. I wouldn't be able to stay away for a whole year now.

Back at home, I wanted to take some time to think about the necessity of my year in Germany. But events were already coming thick and fast. Shortly after my return from New Jersey, the 8th grade prom took place. It was a farewell to "being a kid" and to junior high, before life at high school would begin. My friends and I were all terribly excited about the evening ahead. The dress code told us to be "formal", in evening wear. The girls were talking about nothing but what colour their dress would be and where they would buy it. The evening was coming up and I hadn't really thought about how to go about the dress issue. So, the first thing I did was ask my father how much money I could spend on an evening dress. Without even having to think about the subject, he replied, "Nothing. Your sister Carin had the same graduation party two years ago and I paid $50 for her dress, which she only wore once". So, he thought I should wear it now. What? I could have fallen over on the spot. How could my dad ask me to wear a dress that my own sister had worn to the same party at the same school two years earlier! He said I would survive and besides, he had just paid for me to fly to New York and that was an expense as well. I felt I had no choice and tried the dress on. Carin was about three centimetres shorter than me and half a dress size smaller. So, I could wear her dress, but it was a little too short and a little too tight, which I didn't think looked good. Sue understood that I was a bit embarrassed and tried to talk to our father to change his mind. It was the first time she stood up for me and I was very grateful

166

for her support. Unfortunately, my father remained stubborn in this matter, and I had to wear this dress to graduation. The shoes I wore were borrowed from Sue. I had to put my $40 from Alex and Trudel into a savings account and was not allowed to spend it on a new dress. I was very annoyed with my father!

My attempts to make the doubts about my overseas plans heard, that had arisen in the meantime, failed. Everyone was preoccupied with themselves and their worlds. Carin had decided to start the summer in Germany with a 10-day trip to Switzerland to go hiking in Valais with a group of young people from the Protestant church. Our grandmother had chosen and organised this recreation for her, so Carin flew off to Europe, before Sue and I did. It was made clear to me that I would be going over for the summer.

My father was working, and Sue was busy. So, I was worried that no one from my family would come to my graduation. Eventually Sue came and I was so grateful to her for not letting me go there alone. Looking at her, I was proud of her. She was a very attractive young woman, and I hoped to look as good as her one day. And she was developing into a good surrogate mother. She had even helped with the preparations for the evening. Mr. Mugford had told her that too few parents had come forward to help prepare the event. So, without further ado, she decided to help. She was more exemplary in her new role as a substitute mother than some real moms! Sue and I had finally stopped being hostile towards each other. Our mother would have been very happy if she could have lived to see this. But as sad as it was, it was that hardship, that had finally brought us closer.

After the official part of the event, my sister went home but allowed me to attend our farewell ball. It turned out to be a wonderful evening in which Brent and I danced almost inseparably. What I found sad was the song "Sealed with a kiss", which is about a couple breaking up for the summer and it being a cold, lonely summer. The lyrics fit our situation perfectly, as it would be a cold and lonely year for us if I couldn't convince my father that I wanted to return to Oakville after the summer instead of staying in Germany.

The next day I started packing my bags. I only had a few days left before I was due to go with Sue, to our grandparents, for the summer vacation. As the flight was already booked and I would be away before my 14th birthday, I was at least able to invite all my friends to a pool party as a farewell. Everyone was there: Janet, Jacquie, Shelli, Suzanne, Kirsten, Brent, Matt, Manuel, Kirk, Scott, Chris and Chris. It was a lovely farewell, and I was sure that nothing would break up these friendships. I had the best friends in the world. With a love letter from Brent in my pocket, I left for Germany together with Sue the day after the party.

Oakville, July 1978, pool party.

Happy Birthday

It was my 14th birthday, 10 July 1978, and the phone rang at our grandparents' house. Grandma called for me to answer it and receive my birthday greetings. It was my father, and I thought he wanted to wish me a happy birthday. He asked how we were doing and without any further introduction he continued: "I'm going to sell the house in Oakville and will be working in Germany again soon." This news was like a slap in the face for me and so, in shock, I couldn't say anything at first. I was speechless. He went on to say that he had spoken to a neighbour who worked as an estate agent, and she had promised him a good price for the house. He asked what I thought about all of this, and I replied, "Daddy, it's my birthday." He replied, "Oh that's right, I knew there was a reason I wanted to call today. Well then, happy birthday!" he said in such a joyful voice, which would have been appropriate for a normal birthday, but it was completely out of place considering the new developments that he had just informed me of. He wished me a happy birthday by telling me that he wanted to sell my home. Was that a joke? I didn't realise what was going on but told him he couldn't sell the house; it was our home. You can't just sell something like that, I thought to myself. Besides, I had only agreed to come to Germany for a year at most, and I wanted to go back home and go to high school next year. There had never been any talk of staying in Germany for longer or possibly forever. Was I never going to be able to go back home? He replied that this was no longer possible because the matter had been decided, and everything had already been organised. Now I was almost breathless! Everything decided? But we hadn't discussed anything. How could any decisions have been made? Apart from that, could he even sell our half of the house? I reminded him that we children owned half of the house, and he certainly couldn't sell it, if we were against it. But he said that he could and went on to tell me, without any transition, that Carin and I would both have to go to boarding school. What? That was probably already a done deal. I was speechless again. I couldn't say anything, again. He had probably interpreted that as an affirmative acknowledgement and went on to change the conversation. Finally, he said: "By the way, tell Susi to choose a boarding school for the two of you." I head was spinning, I felt dizzy, I could hardly grasp what he was saying. We had lost our mother six months ago. Now, my father told me within a few minutes, that we would soon have to give up our house. We were going to lose our home and what's more, our homeland? Our home, the country we loved, Canada? We were to leave it forever. What about the friends we had made over the last few years, who had stood by us in times of need and supported us so much? Should we just leave them behind and possibly not even be able to say goodbye to them? What about our schools? We loved our schools and intended to continue attending them. Should Carin never be allowed to go back to her school and should I not be allowed there in a year's time either? And Sue, was she not going to go back to her university and finish her studies? What was going on here?

My father would move back to Germany, and <u>he</u> had decided that the three of us should give up everything so that <u>he</u> could work here? How? Was there no work for him in Canada? Wasn't there a company there that would be happy to employ him? And what about our plans? Did our plans no longer exist? Was there no future for Sue with Ed? Hadn't we three daughters already planned our future? Apparently, all of this was suddenly irrelevant.

The news that there would suddenly be no present and no future for us three sisters in Canada, my father had told me to tell my sister Sue. What was I

169

supposed to do? I was supposed to tell her. Why me? I understood that even less. This was about his plans, so he could tell her himself that her plans for her future, were null and void. But he said he didn't have time for that now and he had to go. My eldest sister was supposed to look for a boarding school in Germany for us. How did he imagine that would work? It was the summer holidays, and the schools were all closed. Where was she supposed to go to get information? Besides, we were here in the countryside in a small town. We weren't in a big city like Stuttgart, where it might have been easier to find information.

At least I managed to tell my father that Carin would never agree to move to Germany and go to boarding school here. He said it was all final and that he might even have a buyer for the house already. He went on to say that he had written Carin a letter for her birthday on 6 July, four days before mine. He had sent her this letter for her hiking recreation in Switzerland, informing her of the news. He had told Carin in her birthday letter that Canada was over. I couldn't believe what I was hearing. She was alone in the mountains with strangers. How could he be so heartless as to write her such life-changing news, and in a birthday letter and expect her to deal with it all on her own? How was she supposed to find comfort now? My poor sister, I thought to myself. None of the family will be with her when she hears the bad news. She must deal with this news all by herself and on her 16th birthday! What kind of person was my father? I was horrified. Had he planned to give us each a shock on our birthdays? It seemed to me that he had, and he had succeeded. There was no end to my bewilderment.

I had been in Oakville just a week before and had no idea of his plans. This new development couldn't possibly have happened within a week. Or could it? I wondered how he could have tinkered so quietly and secretly with his life, his job and his work without giving the three of us the slightest consideration. How was such a thing possible? Or had he thought of us after all? Had our needs been considered or did he not care about them at all? This flood of bad news overwhelmed me - completely.

Nevertheless, I asked my father why Sue should look for a boarding school for us, as I was planning to go to Salem, just as my mother and I had decided. He said that one year for one child would be fine, but paying for the remaining school years for two children at the most expensive boarding school in Germany would be too much. He said that although he earned well, he was an employee, albeit a manager, and not a self-employed entrepreneur. His financial resources are limited, he said. Now the situation had changed, and his employer wanted him back in Germany. He had been in Canada for seven years, although he hadn't planned to stay that long, only three to five years. Right, I said, then why did we build such a great house four years ago? He didn't answer my question directly. He went on to say that his employer, Bosch, had only let him stay in Canada for so long because his wife had fallen ill. One shock followed the next. What kind of things was I hearing? My father knew in advance that he would have to leave Canada and that we would have to move with him. Why had we never discussed this? How did his employer know that my mother was ill when I didn't even know?! Had they been waiting together for her to die? That's what it sounded like to me. How long had they known about it while I was unaware? Were my father and his employer so close to each other that our family matters were discussed there, rather than at home, within our own four walls? It didn't just look like that was the case, it probably was. And I felt betrayed, more than ever. To be more precise, I felt lied to and cheated. My father and the Bosch company were sneaky and mean. Why weren't we children prepared for these developments? I hadn't been informed about my mother's terminal illness the previous year. And this year I wasn't informed about my father's career changes! Was I, were we children, just puppets in my father's life? Silly puppets, without emotional needs or our own thoughts?

Why didn't my father simply refuse a transfer and look for another employer in Canada if necessary? Did he want to go back to Germany, voluntarily? Didn't we have a fantastic life in Canada? What did he miss there? Why did we girls have to go to Germany at all, if he wanted to go there so badly? Were we at his mercy? Obviously, we had no say in any of this, and no influence. Now I felt strongly what I had already been thinking about, shortly after my mother's death: Who would protect me against my sisters or my father now that she was no longer there? I realised that no one could protect me against my father's power and decision-making ability. Questions upon questions raced through my mind. I had been betrayed. It was obvious to me that our mother was no longer there to represent our interests or needs, and that we were directly at the mercy of our father's determination. I was angry and had a renewed hatred for him, but a deeper hatred than ever before. The fact that I felt we had grown closer to each other in the last six months, now seemed like an illusion.

At least I had been able to say goodbye to my friends for the planned year abroad, but not Carin. She had only reluctantly agreed to come to Germany for the summer. For her, the country, our parents' homeland, was already a closed topic and she had firm plans for her future in Canada. I realised, that all the arguments which I had brought forward to my father were useless. Our father had already decided everything. I would spend the next five years and Carin the next three years at boarding school in Germany, and our opinions or thoughts about this had no relevance.

Sue hadn't known about the whole thing beforehand either and was shocked, at least she pretended to be. I wasn't sure if I could believe her. After our mother had died - surprisingly for Carin and me - it turned out that Sue knew in advance that our mother was in the final stages of her battle with cancer and that it was only a matter of a few days or weeks before she would die. But Carin and I didn't know! We hadn't been told. My father said he had not wanted to tell us how serious it was, until after Christmas or the holidays, but by that time she was suddenly dead. So, we couldn't say goodbye to her. The last time I visited her in hospital, I was under the impression that she was doing well again and would soon be coming home. I had no idea that she had been given morphine in preparation for our visit and that's why she was so cheerful and outwardly pain-free. I had been so angry that Sue and my father hadn't taken the time to tell me the truth, supposedly to spare me. Then the reality set in, and the shock was enormous, since I hadn't been prepared. I was angry with Sue, my sister, for not telling me the truth at the time. She said she was sorry and that it would never happen again, she promised. Now I looked at her six months later and asked her if she had known about the move in advance. She claimed not to have known anything and that she was just as surprised as I was, honestly. She convinced me of her sincerity, and I was sure that she had understood that sisters should stick together and tell each other the truth, always.

Due to the new developments, she was now also faced with the decision to move to Germany with us, or to possibly stay behind in Canada on her own. Unlike Carin and I, who were still minors, she was already of legal age and was therefore allowed to make her own decisions. As far as her current task of organising everything for us regarding a boarding school was concerned, she wasn't enthusiastic either and did not have the slightest idea how to go about it. In a phone call with our father, she asked him just how he imagined the practical realisation. Should Sue and the two of us be travelling from one place to another by train for the next few weeks? The train connections in a rural area like Heubach were poor. There were none. One first had to go by bus to the next small city with a train station. Sue was on the verge of refusing to do any of it. But, as he was dependent on her cooperation to make his plans happen, our father told her to buy a car, and she could take DM 10,000 from his account. What a mockery, I thought to myself, of course my father had money in his account in Heubach. He had said to me a few months earlier, that he would leave the money he had inherited from his father in Germany because "you never know...", but he probably knew at the time that he would be coming back to Germany and had therefore already left his money there. Did not only his employer, but possibly even his siblings, perhaps even his entire family, including my grandparents and of course my mother's siblings, know about this transfer in advance, even before we children were allowed to find out about it? Anything seemed possible to me now. The money for the car seemed like a bribe to get Sue to look after us. Did my father have legitimated concerns that she might abandon us? But she assured me that she would look after us out of concern for our wellbeing, otherwise what would happen to us? She was worried about her future and about ours. She had been given a sort of no choice, with a "swim-or-drown" option, had to decide not only for herself, but with the responsibility for us as well.

Now, Sue was trying to find a car on her own. But she had never bought a car by herself, even in English, but certainly not in German! She barely understood what they were the potential sellers were trying to sell her. In addition, there was the problem that Sue had only ever driven an automatic car and did not know how to drive a manual gear shift at all. But all the cars she looked at had manual gear shifting! That narrowed the available cars down to next to nothing. She was close to giving up the whole project, out of despair. But then an uncle and a cousin stepped in to help her. Suddenly there was support from our German family. Together they looked for a car for Sue and taught her to drive with gears in a very intensive crash course. The fact that the three of us were not comfortable with the fact that Sue would be driving with manual gears after just a few trial lessons remained our problem. She had to learn to drive, and Carin and I sat by and could only hope that everything would go well.

Sue had already studied at the University of Toronto for two years and now approached a university in Stuttgart to enquire about possible admission. She was told that a Canadian degree, or two years of it, would not be recognised and that she would have to start from scratch. Excuse me? We three sisters all found this announcement from the German university quite shocking and didn't understand why two years at one of Canada's oldest and possibly best universities should be worth nothing. When we told our father about this on the phone, even he was upset about the attitude of the German university. He said it was typical German; they were so convinced of themselves that they couldn't imagine that one could do or achieve anything anywhere else in the world, other than in Germany and that this was a combination of arrogance and ignorance.

At this point, Sue had already been together with Ed for five years. She was faced with the question of giving up Canada and Ed to move to Germany with us, or going back to Canada alone, without her family. She would no longer have a home there either, no parents and no sisters, the latter who often annoyed her, but were still family! But at least she could then continue her relationship with Ed and continue her studies, which were already halfway completed, and then graduate with a bachelor's degree in two years. Should she just throw away a relationship that had lasted five years? Should she also throw away two years of time and money invested in her studies? She was probably facing the most difficult decision of her life.

It was the middle of July and the almost impossible search for a boarding school began. We three sisters, aged 14, 16 and 21, travelled from one school to the next. We had only found them through hearsay or recommendations. The first time we set off in the morning, we had to drive up a steep hill, which was also a very winding road. The route was a real ordeal for Sue with her limited experience with manually shifting gears. She struggled. When we finally reached the top, we were in for a real surprise: a police checkpoint! Apparently, they were looking for terrorists, which also explained why some of the policemen were carrying machine guns. Right, there was something about Germany and terrorists... It certainly looked strange to us to see armed police officers standing in the country, in the middle of nowhere and surrounded by fields. The terrorists they were looking for were both men and women and some were around 20 years old, which is why Sue was scrutinised by them, very closely. What a welcome that was! It seemed like we were not spared of any challenges. In any case, it was not easy for Sue to explain why she had a German passport but spoke only broken German. She also had to explain that she owned this car, which was a Mercedes and quite expensive as well as exclusive at the time, particularly for a young woman of her age, as it was registered in her name, but that she had bought it with her father's money, who was unfortunately was not in Germany at all, but currently still living in Canada. At the time, this was a completely unusual story, as people did not come from families with an international background. It probably looked and sounded like illegal money, and a crazy made-up story. None of it made sense to them. The fact that Sue

174

had a registered car, an international driving licence and two teenagers sitting in the back of the car who couldn't even speak German, was enough to worry the dear police officers. However, after they had searched our car, they discussed the situation for quite some time - still standing in the field - and then, suddenly and much to our surprise, gave us permission to drive on. They had decided that nobody could have made this story up and that it must therefore be true. We were immensely relieved and just wanted to leave. Yet now, Sue now had to reverse the car out of the field, which she had not yet practised in a gear shift. It was an awkward situation. After some initial difficulties, she finally managed it and we drove on, we were all a somewhat annoyed, but very relieved to not have been detained.

Our first destination was a boarding school in the Black Forest, which I didn't like at all, but Carin did. I still had Salem Castle as my baseline in mind and this one seemed too off in its appearance and from what they had to offer. No, I wasn't going for that. Sue was undecided. Our second destination was a boarding school in Baden-Baden, which Carin and I thought was fine, but Sue didn't. She insisted on reminding us that it was not us, but ultimately her, who would make the decision, as she had the task of finding an appropriate boarding school for us. We had now visited two boarding schools, and we all knew that, at least in our first round of searching, there were only three boarding schools on our list. The search had come up with no other options. We were still a long way from achieving a positive result. Regarding the scenery, our trips were very lovely, down in the Black Forrest and the surrounding area, and we also made the odd cultural excursion, including to Hohenzollern Castle. That was a pleasant change, to see and do something nice, but we couldn't really get excited about it much. We were all still stunned or shocked about having to give up our home country.

The third school on our list was a boarding school in a suburb of Heidelberg, which was also Protestant. Our grandmother had made enquiries and learnt that a certain Silvia Sommerlath from Heidelberg had once gone to this school and gone on to become the Queen of Sweden. Great, we thought somewhat cynically, if that's not a reference! Our grandmother was very worried about us girls being motherless. For the life of her, she couldn't imagine how Carin and I would manage over the next few years. She wanted to find the best solution for us and was very pleased with the results of her enquiries about the right boarding school for us. She was most worried about who would cook for us. She didn't know anything about our ability to handle the can opener, but she certainly wouldn't have been thrilled about that either. If she only knew, how often and how much we liked to eat instant meals out of the can, or the freezer, she would certainly have been even more worried about our health. It was better to keep it our secret. In her opinion, it was of utmost importance that we were well looked after in the coming years, which was synonymous with having freshly prepared, hot lunches, and that we were protected, looked-after, sheltered. She wanted us to have the best foundation for our future and she was sure that if we attended this school, we would be well prepared for our future, by which she certainly meant like Silvia Sommerlath. However, the fact that there were only a limited number of future queens in Europe and that the likelihood of one of us being hit was zero was not considered. From her point of view, one could never be sufficiently prepared for the ranks of nobility, just in case. Apart from the unlikelihood of that happening, we rather rugged, and somewhat roughneck Canadian girls weren't interested in cultured and historic European nobility, as much as I was fond of Salem Castle, but particularly due to it being close to Lake Constance and the many sports options it offered. We were more interested in having fun, preferably outside and spending time at rugged Canadian cottages.

Carin and I didn't feel, or comprehend, that we absolutely had to be cooked for and looked after. Our needs were completely different; we just wanted to go home again, where we could take care of ourselves. This nightmare we were now going through could have ended abruptly at any time and we would have been happy to return to familiar, beloved surroundings. We were sure we could cope there. We had already learned to cook a little at school. If necessary, we could also get our food from a tin or call the Chinese takeaway service. We didn't see any reason to go to a boarding school just because of the hot food in the afternoon. Aside from that, our father could have simply organised a housekeeper, cook and maid, just like my friend Kirsten's father did! What was the problem here? It seemed to work well there. Why didn't we just get a housekeeper? Had our father possibly not considered all the options? Or had he decided to deport us, to get rid of us, so to speak? That's exactly how I felt. So many questions remained open. We had no answers, and every thought was painful to us.

This boarding school near Heidelberg was an all-girls school and Protestant. When Carin found out, she was furious. She had no intention whatsoever of being locked up in a "convent" to be "moulded". She had just turned 16, old enough to get her driving licence in Canada and take her first steps towards adulthood. She didn't need any more supervision now! She only had three years of school ahead of her before starting university, where she wanted to study law. In

Oakville, she was not only in the school orchestra, but also in the Oakville town orchestra. She was successful at all levels and very quick to go her own way. What on earth was she supposed to do in a "convent" now? A school without boys was unthinkable for her. The third boarding school was already out of the question for her.

As I had just left my first love behind in Canada, I had no need to get to know any more boys. I was still sad and shocked about the whole situation. Therefore, I did not care about the co-ed or segregated aspect of the school we were looking for. That was pretty much my last concern. The school had a very good reputation, and the boarding school was considered the best girls' boarding school in Germany at the time. We might not have gone there if I had been as vehemently opposed to the idea of a "girls' school" as my sister was. But I was till shocked to the bones from the phone call with my father on my 14th birthday and simply couldn't believe what was happening to us. I did not have the strength that my sister could still muster up to fight vehemently against this school. The real issue for me was that the rug had been pulled out from under our feet. My thoughts were not on the upcoming school year, but on the years to come. What other options did I have to return home to Canada? What would become of my relationship with Brent? How would I qualify for the University of Toronto? No, the school choice was not really my biggest concern at the time.

After the first schools were rejected, time was pressing for us to decide. Our father had told us that if we couldn't find a boarding school, we would have to live with our grandparents, who were now 77 and 78 years old, and go to school in Heubach. As much as I loved my grandparents, I already suspected that this proposal would not be feasible. Our worlds were simply too far apart. With every visit to our grandparents and to Heubach, Carin and I endeavoured to kill time every time we went there. The town was too boring for us, even though it had a large swimming pool, its own small airport and beautiful mountains all around. But we weren't part of the community there, we didn't have any school friends, we were always seen as the "girls from Canada", we were outsiders. Everyone just looked at us. In addition, we had experienced incredible freedoms and opportunities at home, which didn't at all match the ideas and possibilities of a very loving, but strictly puritan Protestant retired couple. They tried to send us to bed at 9 o'clock in the evening during the summer holidays, which led to an exchange of words between Carin and Grandma every evening. She had values and parenting ideas that were certainly good, but which we felt were completely outdated. As like almost everything else we found or experienced there, whether it regarded upbringing or technical devices. We were used to a house with central heating and air conditioning, with a perfectly constant annual temperature! We were not fond of individual stoves, some of which used wood or even coal. We had a side-by-side freezer and fridge combination in our kitchen, not a toy-like mini-fridge or a windowsill used as a fridge extension. It would have been too much to ask of us to take a permanent moral and technical leap back 50 years!

We lived more in the "here and now", were loud and active and not at all "ladylike", as our grandma imagined. She once called our father and complained that we were walking around in 'sports shoes' day in, day out, which was not done where she lived. She asked my father what that was all about, it wasn't appropriate for young ladies to wear trainers outside of physical education lessons. And she asked for his permission to take us to the Salamander shoe shop and buy "proper" shoes for us. He agreed to her request, and we had to go shoe shopping with our grandmother. With our grandmother! That was pretty much the most unpleasant thing that could have happened to us, getting fashion advice from our grandma. No matter how hard we tried, we couldn't get her to understand that our sneakers were not just fashionable where we came from, but also an expression of an active lifestyle. When we told her that even our mother didn't mind us wearing them, she replied: "That was only because she was so ill, otherwise she would have taken more care of you." Well, this comment went way too far for both of us. How could she say that our mother did not look after us? She was insulting our mother who, despite her constant and ultimately serious illnesses, had looked after us wonderfully in her own way over the last few years. She didn't try to impose her ideas of fashion on us, unless we went out in the evening event or had a celebration. Then we had to wear dresses. But during the day and at school, we were allowed to wear whatever was in fashion. We were allowed to pursue our interests to the fullest and develop according to our ideas and abilities instead of being tamed, as we felt that our grandma wanted us to be. Our mother had supported everything we wanted to do. She organised and paid for music lessons, sports lessons, events, everything. Even when she was hospitalised in Oakville and Carin visited her after school and told her she wanted to go to Toronto for a concert. That was no problem for our mother; she made a few phone calls from her hospital bed and the concert was organised for two people; this having been in a time before automatic debits from bank accounts! In those days, such things could only be organised through connections or with a good name. Our mother had both and could do that.

178

The situation with our grandma had become unbearable for us at times. We could feel her sympathy and concern for us. But we thought we didn't need what she was willing and able to offer us. If we had moved there, apart from the fact that our grandparents had a washing machine and a television, it would have been almost like travelling 50 years back in time. We had no interest in that. Why should we go backwards when we were well on our way forwards? There wasn't even a working hairdryer in the house. Our grandmother, who had long hair like the three of us did, didn't mind not having a hairdryer, unlike us. She had her own way of drying her hair and wanted to show us how to do it. Sue was the first to learn how to dry her hair, without using a hairdryer: Grandma opened a window, placed a chair with the backrest against the wall in front of the open window and said to Sue: "Please, sit there." We waited anxiously for the "hairdryer", which was supposed to work without electricity. Grandma fetched a pillow, placed it on the windowsill and told Sue to lean her shoulders and the back of her head against the pillow, let her long hair hang out of the window and let it dry in the direct sunlight. We were speechless at first, because our grandma was being completely serious about it. But then the three of us were overwhelmed by an incredible fit of laughter. We sisters just couldn't believe how Sue let her long hair hang out of the window and just waited for it to dry! This situation was just too funny for us! We laughed and laughed until we were in tears. Sue, who always had to translate things into English for us, pointed to the chair and then to the cushion lying on the windowsill and said to Carin and me: "This is a German blow dryer". At that, we really could not stop laughing any more! Our poor grandma couldn't understand why we were laughing, and we couldn't really explain it to her. Although we had laughed at the method as technically outdated, we did realise that this method worked. Of course, the prerequisite was that the sun was shining, and you had to sit in the sun long enough. And from that point of view, it wasn't funny, but a very old-fashioned way of drying your hair. This woman was born around 1900, had learned to get by without electricity and had survived two wars. She had a solution for pretty much everything, and most of them worked. But the three of us were too young at the time to accept the practical aspects of her experiences and knowledge. We simply thought that this hairdryer without electricity was hilarious and that all other similarly practical "appliances" were cumbersome.

I might have lasted a year with my grandma. After all, with her we would at least have had some continuity in all this confusion. But our worlds were too far apart. As far as Carin and our grandma were concerned, the differences were too great. As if we had been waiting for proof of this, one day our grandma told us that she wanted to teach us something important for our future. Carin and I sat in the back room, interested, as Hedwig proudly pulled out a basket of torn socks, darning thread and sewing needles. She explained to us how important it was to look after ones' clothes and to be able to repair them yourself, because you must be able to cope on your own, especially in difficult times. There it was: the time travel. None of her words could arouse our interest in this learning skill. Coming from North America, we were used to buying sturdy jeans with all the other clothes and wearing them until they were worn through and then throwing them away. Nothing about sock stuffing was interesting to us. We were interested in horseback riding, gymnastics, sailing, music and boys, but not in torn socks. Knowing that in future we would either come to terms with Hedwig in Heubach possibly darning socks, or find some other solution, we travelled to Heidelberg. In view of this choice, we had already decided in favour of Heidelberg in advance, unless we could have found another boarding school that still had two spots available for girls of our age.

From North America to Europe II

On this day and with our last chance to find somewhere to stay, the three of us introduced ourselves to the head of the boarding school, Benita von Egen. Firstly, her physical presence was unmistakable, as she was a very tall and slim woman, like our Aunt Trudel. Her style of dressing was decidedly classic, even aristocratic, and on this day, she was wearing a dark green suit in which she looked as if she had just come from her country estate. But this was not entirely far from the reality, as the main house of the boarding school was called the 'castle', the Schloss, and the grounds were a large park. She also had a strong personal presence and exuded a self-confidence, which I had only ever experienced to this extent with my grandfather, Paul Bauder. As with my grandfather, I was initially somewhat intimidated by the strength of her charisma. But when she sat with us at her antique round coffee table and started talking, she became less frightening to me. She first told us that she had spoken to our father at length and, that she knew what this was all about. That surprised us at first. She went on to explain that she had really understood him and our family situation well because, like us, she had also lived in South America. Now we were even more surprised. We were dealing with a "woman of the world", which made things easier for us because we didn't have to explain that we came from another country and were now supposed to live in Germany. She herself had already experienced what it was like to move from one country - yes, even from one continent - to another. She understood that our backgrounds were different from those of people who have lived in one country all their lives. She sympathised with our situation from a professional and practical point of view and had basically already won us over. She had already told our father, that she was willing to take us. From the boarding school's point of view, however, it was not just a rule, but her own explicit wish to get to first get to know us personally, as she explained to us, before a final commitment. She wanted to know from us, whether we even wanted to join her at the boarding school. The fact that she wanted to know whether we had been "forced" to go to this boarding school or had come voluntarily made her very likeable to me. After all, boarding school children are also a business and getting two at once is double the turnover. But she was interested in what we wanted. She was the first person whom we encountered this summer, who was interested in hearing what we wanted. That was a change. What we really wanted was to keep our home and return to it in our lives in Canada. But that wasn't possible. So, we had to accept that we had to stay in Germany and go to this boarding school, as it was the only one, we hadn't turned down. The choice was ours; this place one or grandmas' house. Hence, we were indirectly forced into it, because we didn't let the head of the boarding school know that.

Be we went there, Sue told Carin that she should keep her mouth shut during the visit, so as not to jeopardise our chance at getting accepted. Sue had gradually had enough of having to look after us. She wanted us to be accommodated for, so that she could take care of her own life. After all, the rug had been pulled out from under her feet and she still had important decisions to make, in a very short space of time. As this was the only alternative to "Hedwig" for Carin, she followed the instructions and held back with her provocative questions. As I hardly spoke any German, Sue taught me to say a complete sentence in German in the car on the way. Mrs. von Egen told us that she had never had a situation where three sisters introduced themselves to her alone, without their parents, two of whom might be coming to her boarding school. She admired our courage and our strength. Above all, she admired Sue, who was supposed to make a success of this task at such a young age. In contrast to the other boarding school heads, we had met so far, Mrs. von Egen had recognised what a difficult situation we were in and what a burden Sue had been given. I was impressed by Mrs. von Egen and her ability to recognise the situation, as well as her knowledge of people.

When Mrs. von Egen told us that another girl from Canada would be attending the boarding school, Carin and I immediately sympathised with the boarding school, despite all our other reservations. Shortly before the end of the conversation, I asked my question, the one sentence I had memorised: "What do the girls do in their free time?" The answer came a little hesitantly, but it was: "In their free time, the girls go for walks and some play music." I didn't have to look at Carin at that moment to know that she was fuming. Going for a walk? What kind of free-time activity is that? That was something for old people! She couldn't seriously think that dynamic young people would voluntarily do something so boring. We could never imagine taking up walking as a hobby, or leisure activity. We were used to gymnastics, horse-back riding, swimming in our own swimming pool, riding around freely on our racing bikes, sailing, meeting up with friends, going to the cinema, dancing and meeting up with boys. Everything else except but going for a walk! I could literally feel Carin's tension growing as she realised that although there were things to do in and around Heidelberg, the school or boarding school had almost nothing to offer that we were interested in. We whispered to each other that it couldn't possibly be as boring here as it sounded. That couldn't be possible, could it? Sue sensed our concerns and literally pushed us out of the conversation before we could discuss the subject further.

Time was of the essence, because although the Canadian summer holidays lasted until the first week of September, the summer holidays here were already over in August. By now it was already the end of July. So, on top of everything else, we had to give up a month of summer holiday. Although we hadn't officially accepted yet, Mrs. von Egen gave us a list of things we would need to acquire, for our life at the boarding school. This list included the number of towels, cloth napkins, bed linen and blankets we should bring. We also needed a reading lamp for our desk and other school supplies. Whilst we were still discussing the options and trying to influence the decision, Sue specifically started shopping for these items with us. She realised that a decision had been made. That decision was Heidelberg. We called Mrs. von Egen and informed her of our decision. I for one was convinced that we would be in the best care with her. The boarding school costs, including school fees, were around DM 10,300 per child per year.

Heidelberg 1978

Our decision was made for the Elisabeth-von-Thadden-Gymnasium, secondary and boarding school in Heidelberg-Wieblingen, in the Klostergasse. Unfortunately, the address is „Klostergasse", meaning abbey or convent alleyway or lane, increased Carin's rejection, as she wanted to have nothing to do with a convent, as anything remotely close to that. But I didn't mind, after all, the location and surroundings were beautiful.

The entire property, the old Wieblingen Castle with its park, had then in 1978 been privately owned for roughly 200 years, as I soon learnt, the park grounds dating back to 1727. The school itself had started teaching in 1927 and had therefore been in existence for 51 years with interruptions. It was founded by Elisabeth   von   Thadden   and   was   originally   called   "Evangelisches

Landerziehungsheim für Mädchen Schloss Wieblingen", meaning Protestant country boarding school for girls. This meant that Carin and I had both ended up at a boarding school in Germany, a girls' school and a Protestant school, and one with a long tradition! The differences to our lives, which we had involuntarily and definitively had to give up a month earlier, could hardly have been greater. Carin had not returned to Canada at the end of the summer and her only option was to inform her friends of this development, was by letter. I wouldn't be coming back to Oakville after my "year in Germany" either. That was it. We had built up a social network of friends and acquaintances, communities of interest and school activities. We were both still there in our hearts, as well as Canadian at heart, because we had spent over seven years in a country of almost unlimited possibilities, friendly people, fantastic nature and the hope for a bright future. We had learnt to sing the Canadian national anthem "O Canada" at school. We were completely unfamiliar with the German anthem. We were also used to having a photo of Queen Elizabeth hanging at the front of every classroom. The Canadian flag was everywhere, the sight of which we took for granted. And now we were here.

Wieblingen Castle, Elisabeth-von-Thadden School.

There was no flag flying anywhere in our new home. We didn't hear the national anthem at school either. The Queen was nowhere to be seen and, as we realised, no one else was in her place either. How monotonous and unpassionate I found it all to be! You weren't encouraged to be proud to belong to this country. No one sang the national anthem anywhere, and surely not wholeheartedly with your classmates in the morning. Why was this the case? Was it because this country had nothing to be proud of in the present? Or was it, only the past that you couldn't be proud of? For me, it didn't matter what the problem was. There was no joy in being here. How could we identify with our new home when there were no outward signs that we were part of something good? What were we a part of now? It felt like a big nothing to me – aside from residing on lovely grounds.

For Carin, living in a boarding school was completely against her nature. She had been something of a lodger or housemate in our family for years. She came and went as all her interests and appointments scheduled, which were a lot. My parents had never really had Carin under control. She was far too wilful and independent and preoccupied with herself and her world. Our parents had not brought her up in the usual way. She did and didn't do as she pleased. She was certainly at home at night and had no interest in drugs or alcohol, which some girls did at her age. It wasn't about her rebelling within the family. No, she was an independent person within the family. She didn't care about norms or rules in the slightest – yet at the same time, was not rebellious. But it wasn't necessary to give her many rules either. She was always a straight-A student without ever seriously having done any homework, she was excellent at playing the flute and at times even considered making a career out of it. She did gymnastics both in the school team and in the club, and she was a devout Christian! I didn't turn out too badly either as a grade B student who had a passion for horseback riding and wanted to develop this, and was otherwise nice and polite all round, but I didn't excel like she did, in anything. Therefore, for me, the ways of boarding school life, in a regulated and scheduled manner, wasn't necessarily against my nature, because I was never as independent or freedom-loving as she was, I was a bit more conventional and conformist. At the time, I was just happy to know that we could stay somewhere, no matter where, because we no longer had a home.

It wasn't the first time in my life that we were without a home. We moved from Germany to Canada in 1971 without having a permanent residence at first. I was only six years old at the time and didn't feel any great loss from the change of country, although I was sad to have to part from my friends. After all, I had already moved to my fourth country and hadn't been anywhere long enough to consciously feel part of something bigger than my family. Now we had moved from Canada to Germany in 1978 without having a permanent residence, yet. Surely, I could assume that my father would sort out the residence thing somehow and at some point, as had been the case in the past. This time, however, the situation was fundamentally different for me. I can say that this was the first time I had consciously lost my "perceived homeland, and that was a terrible feeling! Lost is lost. Perhaps the circumstances under which you lose your homeland are of secondary importance. It was a loss of belonging to a place. And the whole thing happened six months after losing my mother. It was too much, too soon. My father had always commented on how attached the two of us were to each other by saying: "They forgot to cut the umbilical cord between you two." Metaphorically speaking, that was true. I didn't just miss her because the umbilical cord had been cut for good. She wasn't there to support me during this time of upheaval. She had always been there for every other move. She was my anchor, my stability, the reassurance that if we were together, all would be good. She carried us, as a family.

My corner of the room in the "Little House"

186

Mrs. von Egen had assigned me to the group in the "Häusle", which meant the little house, outside the walls of the castle and the park. Hildegard Schmid was to be my family mother, as it was assumed that she would cope best with my wounded soul. And that was the case. Mrs. Schmid, then in her late 30s, had something calm and warm about her and I immediately felt comfortable with her. The room on the first floor on the left became my new home, but I shared it with two other girls, Stephanie, called "Steffi" and Verena, called "Veri". Both came from towns not very far away and, unlike me, had not suffered one or more hard blows of fate. They were both at the boarding school by choice, and of their own willingness, and had been there since grade five! I could hardly believe it. Both were very nice, even-tempered, friendly and calm. From that point of view, they would have been good advertising as happy and content, even convinced boarding schoolgirls. They were very much interested in their new roommate, and I felt very welcome in their room. Our room was painted in a soft pink colour. Otherwise, everything else in the house was painted a sober and functional white and grey.

Even though I had two nice roommates, I would have preferred my sister and I to have a room together, but that was generally not desired by the boarding school. Siblings were always separated to encourage contact with other children and you were supposed to be in a room with people of the same age, as one could assume a similar level of development. The girls could and should also help each other with their homework. The explanations were plausible. Nevertheless, I would still like to have at least my sister close to me. She was all I had left from my previous life! Everything else had been taken away from me, and I was not coping well with that.

But Carin lived in the "barn", inside the walls. She also had two roommates. As the name suggests, the building used to be used for supplies such as hay or grain but had since been converted into living quarters. We liked to say that pigs had probably lived in there in the past, alluding to the lack of luxury and the unsurpassable sobriety in which they now lived. A typical "family", as the residents of a particular house at the boarding school were called, consisted of about 15 girls and a family mother. Carin was placed with a family mother in her late 40s, who we were told, like Carin, was also very much interested in music and played an instrument.

What was completely new to both of us, was that there was usually only had one bathroom in our "families". It wasn't like at home, where we were used to having two large bathrooms for five people and an additional guest toilet. In addi-

187

tion to the one bathroom here at boarding school, there were usually only two toilets for all 15 people, instead of the three for five that we had. The number of sinks was half the number of girls, so you had to share a sink with another girl. At least that was familiar to me. The 15 girls also had to share the three or so showers per "family". And what was difficult for us, was that there were not individual cubicles separated from each other, but the shower heads were lined up next to each other, so that the three girls showered in a row next to each other, without partitions and no privacy. My sister and I found this to be a particular imposition. Showering naked next to strangers really surpassed our notions of shame at the time. What was pretty much the most intimate thing to do at our age, namely, to strip naked and wash in the shower, should we now do in front of others? We both would have preferred to leave for that reason alone. But now we had no choice but to stay. There were also times when we had to queue to brush our teeth, go to the toilet or take a shower! What a shock that was to us! Having to queue for necessities! This was supposed to be Germany's best girls' boarding school. Best in what? Not in bathroom facilities. Carin and I really struggled at first with this institution, which seemed more like a military institution, along with the associated changes. For us, this seemed unhygienic and downright undignified. Fortunately, the girls in Germany didn't wash as often as the girls in Canada, otherwise we would have had to queue even more to be allowed to shower! As they didn't wash as often, we found that some of them smelled a bit like sweat, which took some getting used to for us. Something like that didn't exist in the culture we came from, at least not in our environment. We were quite shocked to realise that not only did they wash less, but almost none of them shaved under their arms and their legs at all! For us, being conditioned at the onset of puberty, to engage in grooming and shaving, the lack of it was a bit disgusting. In Canada, girls usually started shaving as soon as they had hair growth, so around junior high, seventh or eighth grade. As a girl in Canada, shaving under the arms and on the legs was part of personal hygiene. Here in Germany, we sometimes felt like we were surrounded by half-Neanderthals, at least as far as development in this direction was concerned. What some of these half-Neanderthals also did, or allowed themselves to do, was to not wear bras. Our concept of body culture also meant that girls our age wore a bra as soon as their breasts started to grow and fit into the first cup size, or at the very latest from the second cup onward. But here, people seemed to take a more "natural" approach to their breasts, simply letting them bounce freely. Girls who, in our opinion, should have been wearing a bra long ago, simply didn't wear one. So much naturalness

188

was not easy for us to digest. And then there was greasy hair. Of course, you didn't wash it every time you showered, but maybe once or twice a week. Oh dear, what a change! In one respect, however, Carin had it even more difficult than me. There was a girl in her house who was anorexic, and she even shared a room with her. We had never seen anyone so painfully thin before in our lives. We didn't even know that such a thing existed! Back home, people we knew were healthy. But this girl had more bones sticking just beneath her skin, than we even knew existed. That was not healthy. At least I didn't have to see with this sight in my room or in the shower, but Carin did. We couldn't really be asked to understand the fact that anorexia was a disease, could we? Wasn't that a bit much to ask?

House rules

From day one, we had to familiarise ourselves with the contents of the house rules, which consisted of 21 points. That was about 19 more rules than we had at home! There, everyone was supposed to be present at dinner, if possible, so that we could eat one meal a day together as a family, which was not a problem for me. Everyone was supposed to be in bed by 11.00 pm, but I usually fell asleep at 10.45 pm, so that wasn't a problem for me either. Carin still read in bed at home and often didn't switch off the lights until midnight. At home, everyone was responsible for themselves in the morning, and so I usually got up at 7.45am, to be at school an hour later. But that was now a thing of the past. We were no longer independent in our decisions and actions but had to adhere to strict rules, which were simply to be obeyed, mindlessly. This was clearly a huge step backwards in our development!

The first point of order was that the start and end of the day were fixed. Everyone had to get up at 6.30 a.m., breakfast started for everyone in the dining room at 7.00 a.m. and ended at 7.30 a.m. at the latest. The fourth point stated that we should all arrive at the table punctually and in an orderly fashion, which is why the door to the dining room was demonstratively closed punctually at 7.00 a.m. and after that, it was no longer possible to enter unnoticed. Then, as point five of the rules said, there was a minute of silence before the start of each meal, which we held standing behind our chairs. This was to give everyone the opportunity to pray silently at the table. Only then, when everyone had finished, were we allowed to sit down. Anyone who was late had to wait outside the door until one of the house mothers checked a few minutes later to see if anyone was standing outside and then asked them why they were late. Only when the answer was acceptable was the girl allowed to come in and go to her seat, walking past all the other girls who were already seated and eating. It was extremely embarrassing to be late because everyone stared at you. But one had to come to the meals, because point six of the rules stated that meals were compulsory.

Point eight of the regulations stated that entering the kitchen was only permitted with authorisation. This meant that when bowls, dishes, plates or drink containers were empty, someone from the table was allowed to go to the kitchen window with the empty container to ask if there were any second helpings. We were not allowed to take anything from the table with us, we were not allowed to keep any perishable food in the room and alcohol was strictly forbidden.

We used the remaining 20 minutes after breakfast until the start of the first class at 7.50am to get our school things out of our rooms and make our way to school. School went until 13:00, five days a week. We were fortunate at our new school that they no longer held classes on Saturdays. Between the six classes of 45 minutes each, we had four short breaks of 5 minutes each and one long break of 20 minutes. During the long break, there was a snack available outside, on the terrace in front of the dining hall for the "interns", as the girls who lived in the boarding school were referred to. This snack consisted of a drink and a sweet pastry, or a bread roll, fresh from the bakery, which was new for us and which I thought was amazingly good!

After school, we would quickly rush take our school things to our rooms and sometimes be happily surprised to see that we had mail, to then hurry and be on time for lunch at 13:15. What we found very strange was the principle of the hot lunch. How could anyone insist on having a hot meal in the middle of the day and possibly even bring all the family members to one table? That was completely out of touch with reality as we knew it and, in our opinion, unnecessary. Because of this hot lunch, schools in Germany had to finish at 13:00? All mothers endeavoured to put a hot meal on the table for the children and, if possible, for the husband too. But why? Why should everyone sit together during the day when they could sit together at the end of a full day? It was incomprehensible to us then and it still is to me today. We had survived the seven years without a warm lunch quite well and in the best of health, and we had our warm meal with the family in the evening. We also found this to be much cozier for the family, to get together in the evening, because then everyone could talk about what they had experienced after a full day. We had lived healthily by taking our "lunch box" to school with us, with sandwiches, vegetable strips, fruit and things to snack on, and we liked it that way. However, we didn't like our new daily routine at all! We also found that a hot lunch in the middle of the day only made us tired and we couldn't work afterwards. Sport was out of the question in the afternoon. What was the point of all of it?

After lunch, we had another 15 minutes to go to our rooms to start our mid-day quiet time, nap time, or siesta, at 2.00 pm, as stipulated in point two of the rules. For the girls from grades five to ten, this meant that everyone had to lie on their beds and be quiet or take a nap. What? Where had we ended up here, in a kindergarten for teenagers? The older girls, from grade 11 onwards, only had to keep their rooms quiet. They were allowed to sit quietly at their desks instead of having to lie on their beds. This afternoon quiet time lasted 45 minutes and was based on the grounds that some of the younger girls, who were only 10 years old, still needed to take a nap. This nap point seemed to me the craziest of all the order points. Carin and I had seven years of an all-day school system behind us, and we had been very happy and content, surviving with no nap time. School in Canada started just before 9:00 am and ended seven hours later, just before 4:00 pm. We were not familiar with the principle of midday rest and felt it was not only a complete waste of time, but also not natural for people our age. Who sleeps in the middle of the day, apart from small children and older people? We were used to being out and about all day, at school learning and doing sports. And that was good.

Twice a week, on Tuesdays and Thursdays, we had to get changed after our siesta, from 14:45 to 15:00 and make our way to afternoon sports, the so-called boarding school sports, which took place in the school gym. As stated in regulation thirteen, participation in these sports lessons was compulsory for all boarders. Sports lasted until 15:45, and we had 15 minutes to go back to our rooms and change, get our school things together and be at homework supervision on time at 16:00. Here, all the "interns" from grades five to 10 sat together in different rooms (per grade) and were supervised by a teacher, or supervisory person, whose duty it was to make sure that every single person completed the tasks entered in the "homework books", of their respective classes. We were not allowed to speak, except to quietly explain something to a classmate, until everyone had finished all their homework. We then had another 15 minutes to make our way to dinner, which started at 18:15 and finished at 18:45. The so-called dinner was a "Brotzeit", meaning bread time, which was and still is the norm in Germany. Instead of having a cozy, warm evening meal, as we were used to, we now had to resign ourselves to eating a piece of bread with sausage or cheese and usually cucumber. Not only did we find this extremely boring, but I also usually still felt hungry in the evening.

After dinner, all 90 of us "interns" quietly and devoutly walked to the chapel on the estate and adhered to rule three, which stated that we were to remain silent on the chapel path and in the chapel. During the service, Mrs. von Egen usually held a sort of sermon, but these were also sometimes held by family mothers and sometimes by the girls themselves. Songs were sung from the hymn book and prayers were said. Admittedly, I liked the singing right from the start. After 10 to 15 minutes, the evening service was over, and everyone tried to walk back along the chapel path in silence. After the service, we had about half an hour of free time to meet up with other girls in the courtyard or walk in the park. I tried to use this time to finally see and talk to my sister in peace. Other than at this time, the strict scheduling of the day did not leave us the opportunity to do this, unless we did our errands in the village together, which we sometimes did. At 8.00 pm, everyone had to be in their "families", or the "little ones" even in their own rooms. The "little ones" went to bed soon after that. We in grade 9 had to switch off the lights at 9:30. For Carin in grade 11, "lights out" was at 10 p.m. These were all strict rules and huge changes for us. It was not what I had imagined boarding school would be like! It felt like a penitentiary, albeit in a lovely surrounding.

Now, my sister had to have her entire daily routine dictated to her and she was already struggling with this fact alone. We both felt incapacitated instead of challenged in a positive way. From the very beginning, Carin suffered from no longer being able to live the free life she was used to. Her family mother was a woman who was very strict about punctuality and keeping to the rules. It was a clash of two worlds, like with our grandmother. Had we made the wrong choice after all? Would we perhaps have been better off with a good-natured grandma instead of in an institution run like a military camp? In any case, I began to feel that we had made the wrong decision and felt like I was being punished for it on top of what I had suffered over the past year.

I didn't like all these rules either, but at least I didn't suffer as much from that, as my sister did. I missed my home and my mother. I was sometimes sick with grief over everything that I had lost. In this respect, I was relatively well looked after in my strictly structured environment. I might otherwise have spent a large part of my day alone in my room with my grief. Even that would not have been possible here, because as regulation point fourteen said, entering the boarding school rooms during school mornings was only allowed by arrangement with the family mother. In practical terms, this meant that it was forbidden to go to your room during school hours. Nobody could go to our house anyway, the one that I live in, outside of the walls, as it was locked at the start of the school day and only unlocked again at the end of it. The "permanent programme" meant that I was always on the move or off to somewhere and at least during the day, could not take time to think about and process what had happened to my family.

On Mondays, Wednesdays and Fridays, instead of boarding school sports, we had the so-called "village walk". We were allowed to go shopping in Wieblingen for things we needed, such as stamps, stationery or drugstore items. As I was usually frustrated, like many others, I would rush straight to the bakery and buy sweets or sweet pastries and then sit in the park on my own and eat them. We all received a monthly allowance. In grade nine it was 15 DM and in grade 11, where Carin was, it was 19 DM. That had to be enough, even for our stamps.

I was lucky enough to be in grade nine, because according to the house rules, point eighteen, radios, cassette recorders and record players were only permitted from grade nine onwards. When I asked, they confirmed that I wouldn't have been allowed to have a radio in my room if I had still been in grade eight. That was unbelievable to me! At home, I already had my own radio in my room at the age of seven. It seemed to me as if we were supposed to be cut off from the outside world.

There were no girls from the boarding school in my class. Steffi and Veri were in parallel classes where they learned Latin. They had chosen a language stream in which they took Latin grade five, English from grade seven and French from grade nine. This path was out of the question for me, as I wouldn't have been able to catch up on the four years of Latin. Instead, I ended up in the maths and science stream. Here the pupils had English as of grade five and French as of grade seven. I saw this as a clear advantage for me in terms of a knowledge advantage, as I had learnt French from grade six and had English as the language at school.

I wasn't particularly looking forward to the first day of school. As my German language skills were poor, I was reminded of 1971, when I first went to school in Canada and understood very little English. That feeling of being a foreigner was there again. Only this time, strictly speaking, I wasn't a foreigner because I did have the German nationality. But what does a passport mean if you feel like a foreigner and can't express what you want to say? After the first lesson, a girl from my class greeted me warmly with the words "Hello, I'm Feli, welcome to our class" and she introduced me to other girls, including Baerbel and Katharina. I was so grateful that she had approached me and that I wasn't just looked at by everyone and left alone. It wasn't long before a second girl introduced herself to me with an equally friendly "Hello, I'm Gabi. Welcome to our class." So, on the very first day I experienced two nice greetings and thought to myself that my new classmates might not be so bad. It was these two girls, Feli and Gabi, who became my friends.

In August 1978, I received a postcard from my father in Oakville depicting part of the harbour, where my sister and I had spent a month each of the previous two summers, taking sailing lessons. In the centre of the picture was a Canadian flag waving proudly in the wind. Looking at this postcard, I didn't know whether to cry or rejoice. "My hometown!" I thought, feeling warmth and security in my heart. "My home, where I will never live again!" I continued to think and felt sadness. He wrote: "How are things in Heidelberg and how are you? Oakville is - almost- as usual and says hello. Did Sue visit you at the weekend? I hope all is well and that you survive." How could he of all people, the man who had taken our home away from us, ask me if everything was all right? Of course nothing was fine! Was he even thinking about what he was writing? Maybe he was trying his best to deal with our situation and just wanted to send me a greeting. But I couldn't find anything positive in what he wrote. He was in my or our home country and he seemed to be doing well. I was in his home country and not just me, but Carin too. We weren't happy at all. In fact, I somewhat hated him.

On one of our first "boarding school home weekends", i.e. every second weekend when all the "interns" had to stay at the boarding school, we all went on an excursion together. The purpose of a mutual trip was to give the new girls in particular the chance to get a bit familiar with the landscaping or scenery around Heidelberg. It was also intended to give them the opportunity to get to know each other. I found this excursion quite fun. We travelled up the Neckar by train, then we walked a bit, and at the end we boarded a boat on the Neckar to go back to Heidelberg, which was all good fun. Sitting in the train and looking at the scenery, we discovered how beautiful the area around Heidelberg was. During our walk we also experienced in what was for us how surprisingly good physical shape Mrs. von Egen was in. Although she was as always, dressed properly in a skirt and matching blazer suit, one could have been led to assume that she was not particularly physically active, or sporty, but to my surprise she had no trouble in rushing us along at a rather athletic pace. Even when a large fallen tree had blocked our path, it didn't stop her. With the words: "We'll have to go over it", she pulled up her calf-length skirt a little, swung one leg over this huge tree trunk, sat there briefly as if on horseback, then quickly pulled up the second leg over, and she was on the other side. This was followed by "come on girls". Mrs von Egen was such a classy lady and generally didn't let anything get in her way, which I found exemplary and inspiring. I admired this woman.

Due to this, it was even more surprising for me that my sister was summoned in for a conversation with Mrs. von Egen after just a few weeks. There she was told that she should please adapt to the more civilised and orderly boarding school life, instead of behaving a bit wild at times. My sister didn't like this request at all, and she expressed her displeasure with the boarding school - which she perceived as a re-education institution - and her headmistress by telling Mrs. von Egen, among others, that she was a "stupid cow!". She didn't care that it wasn't appropriate to speak to adults like in this manner, nor did she care that she had used this inappropriate insult, which was bad enough, to address the head of the boarding school informally, which was unacceptable. Carin had vented her justified frustration, but in the wrong place. Mrs. von Egen wasn't to blame for our situation. On the other hand, my sister was not able to manage the balancing act between her actual Canadian, wildly independent "self" and the well-behaved, well-adjusted "higher daughter" manner desired at this school in Germany. Worlds collided.

When Carin told her friend Susanne, who also lived in the barn, about the incident with Mrs. von Egen, Carin had become a heroine in the eyes of her "fellow inmates" because she had dared to stand up to the headmistress and to the system. I, on the other hand, was a little embarrassed by the incident, because I realised that you weren't allowed to talk to a headmistress like that. Apart from that, this boarding school at least offered us an accommodation, a roof over our heads, which we didn't have otherwise. I was grateful for that and felt that I was in good hands. And fitting in wasn't so much of a problem for me. But my sister had always been fearless and sometimes disrespectful towards authority figures. Apart from that, she had felt attacked in her personal development and therefore fought back. The real fault, if you like, lay in the cultural differences. We hadn't grown up in this country and we could no longer be suppressed and moulded into conformist and adapted young ladies or "Fräuleins", as we were already far too free in spirit for that. As a punishment for the things she had said, Carin - as well as other "bad" girls - had to sit at Mrs. von Egen's table in the dining room for three months, directly under the strict eyes of the "sovereign", whilst the other girls were allowed to enjoy a new table arrangement every month.

We were allowed to go home every other weekend. Unfortunately, however, we had no home to go to. Our father was still in Canada, finishing his work there. So, not having a home here, we went to Heubach for the first few weekends and stayed with our grandparents. But after just a few visits, Carin could no longer bear to stay there and preferred staying in Heidelberg. However, this was not appreciated by the boarding school, as the family mothers were also supposed to have these weekends off. The rule was that only the girls from abroad were allowed to stay at the boarding school on the 'away' weekends, because they had no home in Germany that they could go to. Logical deduction led us to understand that hence this rule also applied to us, did it not? We were also from abroad and we didn't have a home. But it wasn't seen that way. People spoke of our grandparents almost as if they were our parents. We were regarded as German children and not as foreign children. But we felt like foreign children! It seemed as if we couldn't please anyone. We were expected to go to our grandparents. But we defended our position and made it clear to everyone that our grandparents were not our parents, and that their house was not our home. Our arguments on this matter were reluctantly accepted and a compromise was reached. We were to visit our grandparents every other 'away' weekend, so only once a month instead of twice, and we accepted that, out of necessity, having no other choice. However, I was happy to be able to go to Heubach once a month, as I didn't want to live at the boarding school permanently. Apart from that, I felt somewhat at home with my grandparents, it was after all the family home of our mother, and I also realised how much it meant to my grandmother to have her grandchildren with her. It was good for me to be in her home, which always functioned immaculately, and to experience this continuity, which I had already been experiencing from her, since I was a small child. I also enjoyed the peace and quiet there, which meant unbearable boredom for Carin. However, given the circumstances, we thought it was a good compromise and hoped that our father would soon come to Germany and buy a new house so that we would have a home again. Our longing for this was enormous.

In the fall, I received a postcard from Vancouver from my father in which he wrote, among other things: "I may be travelling to Germany next week. Maybe we can look at houses in the Stuttgart area". "YES!", I thought to myself. There it was at last! That was exactly what I wanted to hear. For Carin and me, the wait for clarity had already become too long. For us, the helplessness of our situation was unbearable. Sometimes I woke up at night and thought, "Where am I?" When I realised that I wasn't experiencing my interesting "Germany year" at Lake Constance but had ended up in Heidelberg with a one-way ticket, I became more than just sad. I felt desperate, lonely and abandoned and couldn't fall asleep at first. Sometimes, however, I would cry myself to sleep again. I was often quite upset during the day after such nights and couldn't talk about what was bothering me. We were at the mercy of our father's decisions, his work and his employer. This time, it really got me down. Emotionally, I was really battered by it. Maybe my father wouldn't come to Germany next week and maybe we wouldn't look at houses. The fact was that this man was making decisions or pursuing goals regardless of what we wanted or needed. Were we being sacrificed for my father's career advancement? We were 'parked' at boarding school and didn't seem to have any influence on what our father would surprise or shock us with next. Did he perhaps already have a new woman at his side? Was a new woman possibly behind the fact that we had to go to boarding school? Had we been sacrificed for our father's new personal happiness? Questions upon questions kept me up at night.

Shortly after this sign of my father's life, the house in Oakville was sold. There it was the final blow. There was no going back now. Sue had to go back to university, but she also had to help clear out the house. This included our mother's things; books, a decent collection of clothes, art and real jewellery, a shelf full of handbags, shoes and furs, all things none of us had touched before. This difficult task was now hers alone. It would have broken my heart to take these things into my hands for the last time and have to say goodbye to them. Poor Sue, she was now quite lost without a home and didn't even know where to move to. It was her good fortune that her boyfriend Ed's father owned an apartment building in Mississauga, on Hurontario Street, not far from our first home in Canada. Ed's parents were very worried about Sue because they had known her for six years, ever since she had been with Ed. Sue had returned to Canada alone because of Ed and for her studies. His parents, Stanley and Stella, now wanted to help look after her, as Sue and Ed certainly wanted to spend their futures together. Stanley told my father that Sue could and should move into his apartment building. This seemed like a good solution to both fathers, as Sue would be in a more protected environment. Stanley wanted to help us deal with the whole situation as best he could. He offered my father that Sue could live there rent-free, as she was already part of the family. My father really appreciated Stanley and Stella's dismay and concern, and agreed to

Sue moving there, but he insisted on paying rent as well. When I asked him later why this was so important to him, he said to me that he never wanted to be accused later of not having paid for his daughter. He said it would be different if Sue and Ed were already engaged or living there together. But my father felt it was important to have separate bills until that time. Sue and Ed were conservative and had very clear ideas. They didn't want to get married until after their studies and didn't want to move in together before then.

Our substitute sister

Whilst we were having our difficulties adjusting in Germany and felt out of place and all too often misunderstood, there was to be unexpected support for us. The Canadian "fellow detainee" Heidi was to become like a light in the darkness that we had been groping around in during this difficult time. I would never have imagined in the first days at the boarding school, when we had our awaited first encounter with her, that things would turn out so positively.

She came from Montreal and had English as her first language and French as her second. As her father was from Bavaria, Heidi also had to learn German, which is why she was at boarding school. I found her language skills very impressive, as she switched from one language to the other without any problems, even though she was only in her second year in Germany. However, when we finally had the first opportunity of making her acquaintance, she was very busy talking to her many friends about her summer holidays. She obviously knew many of the girls and they all seemed to want to talk to her. So, she didn't have time to deal with us at first. She simply left us standing there, put us off until later and moved on. I had interpreted her actual joy at seeing her friends again as a lack of interest in us and was very disappointed. I also thought she was arrogant and didn't want to have anything to do with her, out of sheer disappointment, but my sister didn't let herself be shaken off as quickly as I did and continued to seek contact with her. She succeeded and the two of them became friends. Carin assured me that Heidi was not arrogant, but very nice and very funny. All right, I thought to myself, maybe we were not dealing with the most arrogant Canadian girl of all of Canada here in Heidelberg after all, so I'll give her another chance. In addition, we wanted and needed some information from her, if nothing else. What we really wanted to know from Heidi was, whether all these rules we were living by were real or just on paper. We were dying to hear how one comes to an agreement with the family mother, or if there were any other ways to get more freedom. She answered our questions with a simple "no" and explained that it really was that strict here and that there were no other options. We could hardly believe that it would be hopeless to change the quality of lives here and were reluctant to acknowledge this information but had no choice. It was upsetting.

Heidi had told us that she had agreed to her parents' request to come to Europe for a year or two to learn German. This part of the story sounded familiar. However, as Heidi was a passionate skier, she was thinking of a sports boarding school in the Swiss Alps for her stay in Europe. But poor Heidi ended up far away from the Swiss mountains, in Heidelberg! We made the joke out of this logistical misplacement that her parents probably thought "Heidel-Berg" was something like a Swiss mountain. I told her that my father had probably mistaken Lake Constance for the Neckar River, which flowed right past Wieblingen. We joked that I could go sailing on the Neckar and she could go skiing in the nearby Odenwald, the nearby low mountain range! Ha! That gave us something to laugh about! The dark humour, the situation comedy, helped us to get over the disappointments of not being where we wanted to be. As we learnt over time, Heidi's father was a well-known self-employed sportswear designer. He had his own brand in Canada, and it was he who had originally developed the Moon Boots! He came up with the idea when he saw the moon landing on television. We found that interesting and impressive.

It was good for our wounded souls to be able to speak English with Heidi. If I had still had my faith in God back then, I would have thanked him for the encounter, the support, the understanding and the friendship that had just begun and would continue throughout the school year. No one else around us could understand what a culture shock we were going through. We were athletic and modern, self-confident teenagers, with our own styles, opinions and expectations. Now they tried to dress us like German "higher daughters", to mould us, to tame us. The three of us were amused to realise that most of them were little "princesses", but hairy as monkeys! When we told Heidi about our astonishment, she laughed terribly: "That's right, I thought the same thing a year ago!" she said. But she said that you would get used to some things over time and that many things would seem completely normal. But we couldn't imagine that! So, within a very short space of time, the three of us had a few jokes of our own about living in this situation comedy. Sometimes we only had to say a keyword and we were already laughing! We felt

199

like we were observing a different culture but living in the middle of it. It all felt like travelling back in time for us. We kept saying that the "Germans" did this and the "Germans" did that. But for Carin and me, there was no going back to our present, out of this journey through time. It wasn't long before Heidi realised that she was a lot better off than we were; she still had her parents and her home country. She sympathised with us and at the same time was very grateful for what she had at home. How envious I was! How I wished we were like her: she didn't have the one-way ticket, but a flight back to her former life. Within a short space of time, she became more than just a friend to us, she had become a substitute sister.

Heidi taught us the essentials to survive "here". She told us that there was an English-language radio station called AFN, the American Forces Network. We were very excited about this news. Because hearing English spoken was balm for our souls. As there was a large US army base in Heidelberg, this radio station served the armed forces. Neither Heidi, Carin nor I had ever had anything to do with the armed forces before, so the parts of the programme that dealt with the military were completely foreign to us. Our families had nothing to do with the military either. But we were far away from home and for us, German was a language that still had to be learnt. Even if some American dialects hurt Canadian ears, they spoke the language on this radio station that we were used to hearing and that sounded so familiar to our ears. So, we started listening to this American military radio station in our rooms, which admittedly added to the feeling of being in a military camp.

My room mates usually didn't mind, because they viewed the station, along with me, as a good opportunity to learn English better. My sister's room mates, however, found it rather annoying to have to listen to this station. It is also understandable that the German girls wanted to listen to a German station to keep up to date and to listen to "their" music. It was a difficult situation for both sides. We wanted to listen to English, the others German. Could we only listen to the radio in our language if it was accepted or tolerated by our room mates? That seemed to be the bitter reality, and we had to come to terms with it. But wasn't it also important that we also felt comfortable? For us it was, but our family mothers and the head of the boarding school seemed to be interested with total conformity and not with our sense of well-being.

The boarding school prided itself on being internationally orientated and looking after girls from different countries. My sister's "family" also included a girl from Venezuela, my country of birth. She also had German roots. But what did the school do for those of us from foreign countries, offer to us or accommodated us with, so that we felt comfortable so far away from our home countries? I can't think of anything. And I can't remember receiving any support from the boarding school in terms of integration. We were expected to comply with the house rules immediately: to function, to adapt, to be inconspicuous. It seemed to me that we were supposed to shed our own identity, our "I" of our previous lives to become one of "them" as quickly as possible. We, however, felt infinitely overwhelmed and annoyed by the expectations of the boarding school to conform as quickly as possible. It was hard enough having to learn the language! But had we ever agreed to a re-education? We were happy with the way we were. Why should we change? After all, we had been raised to be independent and self-confident girls, obviously ahead of the times of what was expected of girls here. On top of that, after everything we had been through in the last few months, wasn't it asking too much of us to also give up our identity and individuality? We became increasingly frustrated, as there seemed to be no other way out, other than to reject what was expected of us internally and at the same time pretend to conform, at least a little, on the outside.

Our Sunday programme included nothing other than going for a walk along the Neckar or visiting another "fellow prisoner". Some girls visited each other in their rooms in the afternoon and drank tea together. We new arrivals were completely dumbfounded by this limited choice of Sunday activities. Going for a walk and a "tea-drinking culture"? Wasn't that something for adults or even old women? Strolling and sipping sounded like a senior citizens' programme to me. Wasn't it against the nature of young people to sit together in a room and drink tea on a day off from school? In my eyes it was. Where was this going to lead and what would we have to do next? Like darning socks or knitting? We were used to riding our road bikes across Oakville to visit friends. At lunchtime, when it was warm, we often liked to meet up for a swim, sometimes at one person's house, sometimes at another. Or we would cycle to downtown Oakville to my favourite ice cream parlour "Baskin Robbins". Or we did sports together or went horseback riding. We were always outside in the summer months and out and about in the winter months. We would visit each other at home or go ice skating or watch an ice hockey game. We were somehow always on the move. Heidi told us that she often even went skiing at home on the weekends in winter. But here, there was nothing going on. Here, it was all about drinking tea and possibly having a nice chat. Perhaps that was what "higher daughters" in Germany did in their free time. But that didn't seem at all desirable to us as a leisure activity and completely uninteresting as a lifestyle. For us, it was at least another boarding school shock, if not a culture shock.

Out of boredom and desperation, Carin and I usually met up in her room on Sunday afternoons. From 2 p.m. to 6 p.m., the "American Top 40 Countdown", the chart hits of the week from the USA, was on AFN, hosted by Casey Casum at the time, who we listened to with great attention. We let him tell us what we were missing at home or almost home and what the latest musical developments were. He also made us laugh, which, apart from Heidi, pretty much nobody else had managed to do. Carin and I disappeared into our own world for those four hours, almost every week. Sometimes I cried, sometimes she cried, sometimes we both just felt abandoned and miserable. The pain of knowing we were far from home was temporarily acknowledged during this time. All the listeners were "from over there" and now stationed here. Almost always, when greetings and requests for a special song were read, written by members of the armed forces to loved ones left behind back home, we felt that we too were experiencing this pain of separation and that it was entirely justified. We experienced sympathy for our situation from the radio, something we didn't experience in everyday life. The "Top 40" was ended by Casey Casum with the sentence: "Keep your feet on the ground but keep reaching for the stars". This became our guiding principle. The boarding school was the ground on which we found ourselves, as if set in concrete. The freedom outside of this institution was like the first stars we were reaching for. Ultimately, the big star we were really striving for, even if only in our minds, was the return to our home country.

As there were many Americans living in and around Heidelberg, Carin and I also enjoyed going to Heidelberg on the Saturday afternoons when we had our "city walks", meaning that we were free to stroll around or shop downtown, without having supervision, in the hope of meeting some native English speakers. We didn't necessarily seek contact with members of the military because, as we realised after just a few conversations with young soldiers, their worlds were very far removed from ours. But one could hear a lot of English being spoken in the old streets of the historic centre of Heidberg, by the American forces stationed there, as well as by the many tourists from all over the world. There was a concentration of

Americans in the pubs, but my age group was strictly forbidden from visiting them. Instead, we went to McDonalds, where there were also lots of Americans. So, Carin and I always went to McDonalds on our stroll through the city, just to hear English, because English sounded like home and was very good for our us. McDonalds became a balm for the soul. Sometimes we were approached there because we were speaking English to each other, sometimes by young German men and sometimes by young American men. The young German men were looking for contact with American girls, presumably to improve their English. But the American soldiers were also looking for contact. This seemed to be a sought-after commodity in Germany: Girls from North America, who spoke English. So those who approached us asked us if we were American. American girls? Who, us? No, we always replied, because we weren't. According to my passport, I was German, but in my heart, I remained a proud Canadian. Although Canada and the USA are neighbours and look very similar from a European perspective, and use the same language, we were just neighbours. This is comparable to Germany and Austria or, to Switzerland. Our two countries in North America have similarities, but also differences, which from our point of view were significant. The countries were not a single entity, but were once separated by war, and of course Canada had developed better than the USA, from my point of view. And it was a part of the Commonwealth, making it more international. To avoid any further misunderstandings about our origins, we got ourselves as many Canadian flags as we could in sticker and fabric form and stuck and sewed them everywhere in plain sight. We didn't want anyone to miss where we were coming from. And no one missed it either!

When I told my classmate and new friend Gabi that my sister and I spent most weekends at boarding school, she was quite surprised. She had assumed that we would be travelling to visit relatives. She had also assumed that we at least had an interesting leisure programme on the boarding school weekends. But when I told her that we did virtually "nothing" on the weekends, she spontaneously invited me to spend a weekend with her in her family. I was very happy about this invitation, as it seemed to be the first step towards a normal life for me. But it wasn't quite as easy as we had imagined. Now I got to learn more about the rules and procedures of our "institute". First, I had to get my father's verbal consent to spend the weekend with Gabi, which I got with a phone call. My father didn't know my girlfriend or her family, so the first thing he asked was what the father of the family did for a living. When I replied that he was a "doctor", so my father said without further hesitation that I was allowed to go there. I was lucky that Gabi's father had a profession that could be clarified in one phone call and was also highly recognised internationally. The first hurdle was cleared.

Next, the boarding school, which was responsible for the safety of all the girls, had to make up its own mind about the family that an "intern" wanted to visit, whether for an afternoon or a weekend. It wasn't enough that our 'external' friends were at the same public school as us. My house mother had to inform the head of the boarding school of my wish. The head of the boarding school informed the head of the school, Mrs. von Rad, who in turn asked my class teacher, Mrs. Königsbüscher, about the friend. If the friend had been a pupil who attracted negative attention, the plan would have been ended right there. But Gabi didn't attract any negative attention and so the process continued. Gabi had two brothers who were also not known "negatively", which would otherwise have harmed the process. The brothers didn't go to our school, but it was part of the process to enquire about siblings. The school also informed the boarding school whether at least one of the parents was personally known to the school. The head of the school knew Gabi's mother, so the process was almost over. Mrs. Schmid told me that both the girl and the family had been approved, in principle. That was nice to hear, but I thought the whole procedure was rather exaggerated. Our head of boarding school explained to me that she had a special duty to look after the girls' welfare, especially in the case of girls whose parents lived abroad. She was personally responsible for us and couldn't just let us go anywhere we wanted to go. After this explanation, I was somewhat more capable of understanding the procedure. It was also explained to me that if a family had already been checked and accepted as being suitable, they didn't have to be checked again every time we wanted to visit them. Well, at least that was a good thing! I tried to explain all this to Gabi without upsetting her. She was very understanding and immediately agreed to come to the 'little house' where I was living, after school to meet my house mother, and see the boarding school "from the inside". Luckily for me, Gabi was a very nice and sympathetic person and probably answered the questions she was asked to Ms. Schmid's satisfaction. It was certainly a good thing that Gabi was the class representative, which helped her cause. Next, a visit from Ms. Schmid was supposed to be made with my potential host family. However, I resisted this step. I was so happy that one of my classmates had invited me to her house that I didn't want to express my gratitude by thoroughly investigating the family and their home. The whole thing seemed excessive to me, and I was a little embarrassed by the thoroughness of the checks. After all, I wasn't a millionaire's daughter who was in danger of being kidnapped! Even if I was, the danger wouldn't come from a classmate, would it? Much to my surprise, my house mother realised that I was getting increasingly annoyed about the whole thing. So, we agreed that she would at least drive me there when I went to stay with them and then that way, come to the door and greet the parents, so that she would be able to say to Ms. Von Egen that she had been there. Well, good thinking, I thought. This was the first time I had rebelled, albeit gently, against a rule, but I had won in the end. After all, I didn't want to be completely incapacitated.

After the long preparation procedure, I was finally allowed to visit Gabi's family in Schwetzingen, about a half hour drive away, for the long-awaited weekend. I was warmly welcomed there and was so happy, not only about the warm welcome, but also about being able to take part in normal family life! What a relief that was! Gabi's little brother was very cute, but still a bit small. He was interested in the visit "from abroad", which got on our nerves at some point. Despite his beautiful eyes, he did what little brothers usually do: He was a nuisance. Gabi's older brother came across to me as a bit of a "busybody", as I was used to from my sister Sue. It seemed to be the role of the first-born to act like the boss. I found it a bit strange that he wanted to join a new political party that was concerned about environmental issues, the "Greens". Ha, I thought, what's that supposed to be? What does the environment have to do with politics? Gabi's brothers were what I was familiar with from my friends in Canada: Just normal annoying siblings. But I loved this piece of normality and would have loved to move in straight away, because I thought this family was wonderful. Gabi's mother had probably realised how much I missed being mothered and took great care of me and my emotional needs. But the weekend soon came to an end and on Sunday evening, she drove me back to boarding school. On the way back, I pointed out to her that she was driving in the middle of the country road, as if there was no oncoming traffic. Yes, there would be, she explained to me. But she would deliberately drive in the middle of the road so that oncoming cars would have to swerve as far to the right as possible to avoid a collision. Only at the last second would she herself drive further over to the right so that the other car would have room. That way, she said, she would always have enough space and wouldn't be pushed to the side of the road. The whole thing made me a little nervous, but I realised that it worked. I silently thought to myself: "My mother would have come up with such a crazy idea as well", and I already felt safe with her.

Extra help classes

On Monday morning, the school routine was back. The relaxation from the weekend was blown away. I immediately realised again that the school and the boarding school had the task of teaching me German as quickly as possible. For this reason, I initially had an hour of tutoring in German every day, during homework supervision, which always became my "torture hour". The ambitious tutor had set out to teach me the grammar of the German language and she tried to explain to me that there was not just one article "the" as in English, but several articles "der, die und das". I was still able to accept this fact, although I found it rather superfluous as a rule. A simple "the" was enough in my opinion. Why complicate a language unnecessarily? She also told me about gerunds, accusatives, datives etc. until I didn't understand anything at all. After about a month of "torturous lessons", the tutor gave up. She hadn't been able to teach me anything. I was as happy about my victory of getting rid of this woman as I was about our supposed victory a few months earlier, when we had managed to get our pastor to stop teaching us confirmation classes.

I was very relieved that this tutoring thing had come to an end. You can't learn a language like that, I thought to myself. But Mrs. von Egen proudly told me that she had found the right person to teach me German. I would have lessons with Frau Dr. Rech, starting the very next day. I was speechless, because I had thought I had gotten rid of the plague, but now it was to continue the next day with a different person. Mrs. von Egen also told me that she had a very high opinion of Dr. Rech and that I would certainly learn something from her. My daily routine was changed, however, as I had already lost a month's time and now had some catching up to do, not only in learning German, but also including in the other subjects. So, I had to give up my midday rest, which I was happy to do, and meet with Dr. Rech every day directly after lunch, from 13:00 to 14:00. "Every day?" I asked. Yes, "Benita", as we interns called our headmistress behind closed doors, replied confidently, I was to have one hour of German lessons five times a week. Five times?! Yes, and that until I was at grade nine level. Great! I imagined another woman in a green suit, possibly a friend of "Benita". Perhaps her friend had a whip with her, with which she would somehow whip the German language into me. My enthusiasm was correspondingly low.

But what awaited me the very next day, exceeded all my expectations. A small-figured person came along, a rather old woman who could barely walk, with a hunched back. She had white hair, her hands were shaking and, as I was soon to discover, her teeth were rattling. I was speechless when I saw this woman coming towards me, because she was coming straight towards me! I suddenly realised how serious the situation was. If there was no one else who could be trusted to teach me German apart from this person, I must have been considered as a rather hopeless case.

Dr. Rech briefly introduced herself to me and explained that she was fluent in written and spoken German, English, French and Russian, just as it used to be for the education of a woman from the upper classes of society, to which she unmistakably belonged to, due to her self-confident appearance and fine manners. She also knew Greek and Latin. After this introduction, she said resolutely that she would now teach me German. Then she took a booklet out of her little purse, which had a picture of a kitten on the front of it and said it was a second grade reading book. The lesson began with the words: "We are now going to do a dictation". She read aloud, her teeth chattering, her hands shaking and so did the booklet. I had the task of writing down what she had read to me, which I tried to do. However, I also tried to explain to her that I couldn't write German, but that didn't change her approach. After the dictation was over, she corrected my sheet and underlined every word that was misspelled, which were quite a few. My homework was to write each misspelled word 25 times. As there were around 50 misspelled words, I thought that she couldn't possibly be serious about me writing each word 25 times. But she replied curtly: "Every word". To make sure I understood her, she said it emphatically in English: "25 times, each word"! I realised then that she was serious and that there was no way around this mountain of a task. And so began a time when I had to write 1000 or more words a day in a small notebook. My family mother, Mrs. Schmid, had witnessed my ordeal, due to her having to proof-read my work for weeks, and she felt sorry for me. However, we both realised that this method worked, unlike the last one. Within a few weeks, Dr. Rech and I had finished the second grade reading book and had arrived at the third grade reading book.

Unfortunately, in the meantime, I had understood far too little in the other subjects at school, so I also needed extra tuition in the other subjects, to cope with the day-to-day lessons. I got maths tutoring, even though maths had always been my best subject, but I couldn't understand the lessons in German, which was very frustrating for me. Then I got physics tuition for the same reason.

Much to my astonishment, I was even bad at French lessons. But not because I didn't understand the French part, but because I didn't understand the German part! I was completely frustrated when I realised that I understood the French texts but couldn't translate them into German. So even in one of my favourite subjects, French, I was bad. Why couldn't the school allow me to translate into English? After all, the point was for me to prove that I understood the French texts, which I did. Wasn't it unfair to penalise me for learning to translate French into English? I was increasingly becoming infuriated and despaired. I had up to three tutoring sessions a day, mostly from students who had the ambition to help me with my subject. But I couldn't prove any success in any subject apart from German. The more I learnt, the more I seemed to spiral downwards. Because of all the extra tuition, I was no longer able to do my regular homework. Mrs. Schmid recognised my desperation. She tried to stand up for me to the heads of the school and boarding school. However, they argued against her objection by saying that other girls like Heidi and Carin were managing the expected workload and therefore there was no reason to reduce the pressure on me. But maybe I didn't have the intelligence or stamina of other girls and that could have been taken into consideration. Or maybe I had the intelligence but was too emotionally burdened and therefore couldn't learn any more or any faster? Perhaps a child psychologist should have been called in instead of assuming that I was too lazy to learn. However, nothing was changed in the procedure. Mrs. Schmid had at least managed to ensure that I only had to write each misspelled word 10 times when it came to German tutoring. At least that was a relief, but I still wasn't happy with the overall situation. She knew that I was doing everything I could to learn German. But I still had to study for my other subjects. We reduced the frequency of my German lessons to three times a week. I couldn't understand why nothing seemed to be going into my brain. But I knew that it wasn't going to get any better if I continued to have loads of lessons force-fed to me.

Even my previously brilliant sister Carin had several hours of private tuition a week in German, maths and chemistry. At school itself, the worst lesson for her was history, because she didn't understand either European or German history. I felt the same way about history lessons. I had Canadian history in grade seven and American history in grade eight. But I didn't know much about Europe, or to be more precise, almost nothing. That school year, Carin had to read "The Sorrows of Young Werther" by Goethe. Even though for her and me "Werther's" were a brand of sweets, she read the book from cover to cover and from then on was proud to be able to say that she had at least read Goethe once, even if she hadn't understood any of it at the time!

Neither Carin nor I particularly liked the food at boarding school. It seemed like we were constantly eating potatoes with sauces, strange vegetables and indefinable meat dishes. At home, we ate a lot of pasta and rice dishes. There was none of that to be seen here. I didn't know what was healthier. I only knew that the spices were completely different to what I was used to, or more precisely, that they were non-existent. Everything seemed more natural, which was possibly even the higher art of cooking. But I found it bland and unappetising. So much naturalness was too much of a good thing for me. The meat was a colour between grey and light brown, which I had never seen before. Heidi laughed when I asked her what it was. She said that at some point she had stopped asking or thinking about the food and would just eat it. From that day on, this meat, which we couldn't categorise into any known meat group, was given a name: "mystery meat". From then on, everything that was unfamiliar to us was "mystery meat" and there was also a variant: "mystery vegetables". Carin, Heidi and I had something to laugh about again along the lines of: What's on the menu today? "Mystery food?". We were very happy to have her there and she was also happy to have us. We understood each other in joy, sorrow and mystery food. Heidi became a great support for both of us. She often picked us up when we were emotionally down, which was often the case.

At some point in the fall, our father finally came to visit us in Heidelberg. He was in Germany for a few weeks, and we were supposed to see each other three weekends in a row, although two of them were in Heubach. Much to my own surprise, I was happy to see him again. He also seemed happy to see us. However, he was speechless when he saw us for the first time. I had put on about 5 kilos and Carin about 10! Our father thought we looked like steamed dumplings (a pastry made from a yeast dough that becomes round like a ball when baked in the oven). Despite our weight gain, we had called him to complain about the food and so he had assumed that we had lost weight. My father couldn't understand how we could gain so much weight in such a short time, if we didn't even like the food! We couldn't explain it either. But our father wanted to do something good for us and took us to a really good restaurant on the weekend we spent together in Heidelberg, to which he had already been with our mother. It was in one of the best hotels in Heidelberg, the Hotel Ritter. When he told us how he had been there with his wife, he sounded very romantic and in love. How could this man, who could talk so romantically about trips with his wife, be so inconsiderate when it came to their children? He was a mystery to me.

We had ordered steaks as we hadn't eaten any since we had been in Germany, but at home we must have had steaks once a week. Our father watched us eat and when we had finished, he said we had eaten like we were starving. He had never seen anyone eat a steak as quickly as we did. He also said that we now had table manners 'like pigs'. He was horrified and asked if we had been taught to eat like that at our expensive boarding school? We said "yes" of course, where else would we have learnt such manners? At home, we had learnt to sit up straight at the table and keep our elbows as close to our bodies as possible while eating. If we neglected this way of holding our arms several times in a row, it was quite possible that our parents would fetch a book and shove it under our arms. We then had to continue eating with the book tucked under our arm. Apart from that, our mother had a big book called "Knigge" (etiquette), which describes the correct way to behave in any situation. And it was from this book that she drilled us, especially when it came to table manners. But on this day, it looked like the book had also been buried.

At that time, Carin was certainly not on good terms with our father either. In response to his comments, she made it clear to him that we looked and ate the way we did because he wanted us to live in a boarding school. Carin did five to 10 hours of gymnastics a week at home in addition to the 4 hours of school sports. We went swimming every day in the summer. Our boarding school didn't have a swimming pool and there wasn't one in the town. She made it clear to him that we were completely lacking in exercise and that he shouldn't complain about the state that he found us in. After all, it was the result of his actions! The situation threatened to escalate in the middle of the "Ritter". Our father thought about it and said, in a rather friendly tone, that he could understand the manners thing. He had grown up with six siblings, so you had to eat as quickly as possible to get enough. He thought it would probably be the same at our boarding school, where eight of us sat at one table. It was a successful de-escalation. I was amazed at how quickly he had changed his mind and then reacted directly. Our father seemed to have realised that day that something had fundamentally changed between him and us. We were suffering the consequences of his decisions about our lives, and he realised that we were no longer letting him order us around in our state of suffering, as we used to. In our eyes and hearts, he had lost the position of the admired father, that of a successful businessman who had also demanded a lot from us, but had also given a lot in return, above all a better quality of life. For us, selling our house behind our backs was a sale of our stability, our home. It was also a breach of trust. He could no longer expect us to respect him. Those days were over because of the betrayal. We didn't really care whether he was "forced" to move by his employer or whether he himself had expressed a desire to be allowed to return to his home country. Everything had taken place without our having been actively involved in the considerations and without having been presented with alternatives.

We felt that our father had been treating us like young, stupid children whose opinions and feelings didn't count. Perhaps we were still small and stupid when we made the move from Germany to Canada, eight years earlier. But we weren't anymore, and he had underestimated this fact. In the meantime, we had developed feelings of belonging in Canada that he should have better recognised. We had opinions that he should have listened to. And we had plans for our lives that he should have considered. But now it was done. In our eyes, the damage had been done and could no longer be undone. We made him feel that from then on. We had a legitimate claim that our now ruined lives should at least be arranged according to our wishes and ideas, moving forward. So, we kept asking when we would finally have our own home again. However, he said that his employer had not yet decided where exactly he should work next, in Stuttgart or just under an hour's drive to the west in Karlsruhe. We were not particularly impressed by this information. In plain language, he told us that he had given up everything in Canada without knowing what his new job would be and where he would even be working! Why had he acted so quickly? Why couldn't our father and his employer have just left us in our familiar surroundings for another year so that we as a family could first learn to deal with the changed situation? We couldn't understand it. None of it at all. Had it really happened that a bunch of grown men, my father and his superiors, men who ran companies, who had to deal with difficult situations daily, were blind to the simplest things in life – the needs of children who had just lost their mother? We didn't understand any of this and could only shake our heads at this version of the story. It seemed impossible to us to be the truth. Or had our father perhaps gone mad? Had he been unable to cope with the loss of his wife and no longer knew what he was doing? Had he not found an employer in Canada who could offer him a job with 28 days holiday, a good basic annual salary and a secure pension? Possibly not that easy. But couldn't he just leave Bosch anyway, if Bosch no longer wanted him in Canada? After all, he had a financial cushion from his father's inheritance, which was equivalent to a full year's net income.

Now we didn't know where the journey was going. The base in Canada had been taken down, so to speak, and we were pressing for a solution to this situation. So, we started by looking at condominiums in Herrenberg, which is I found to be a rather quaint small city with a beautiful historical town centre, about a half hour south of Stuttgart, but which seemed somewhat far away from everything else, Stuttgart, Karlsruhe and Heidelberg. The train connection for us was not good. We also looked at a convenient place in Karlsruhe-Durlach, which is a mid-sized borough of Karlsruhe, also with a historical town centre, obviously going back hundreds of years. It was very impressive, and one could tell that the 'well-to.do' of Karlsruhe lived here. I did like it, and the condominium that we looked was higher up and had a lovely to the distance, overlooking Karlsruhe. As luxurious as it was, the condo only had two large bedrooms, instead of three. That meant that Carin and I would have had to share a room. There was no way that that was going to happen, regrettably so, because otherwise, I did like the area. But condominiums? Why were we looking at condos? We wanted to move back into a house! And there were plenty of lovely houses here, large and small. We had never lived in a condo for as long as I had lived. Our father told us that a large condominium in Germany cost as much as a medium-sized house in Canada, depending on the location. Excuse me, I thought? As a kind of subordinate fact, we had just learnt that there would be no more house to live in either. Why on earth would anyone voluntarily move to a country where a good salary could only afford a condominium? That was absurd! Where was the quality of life in that? I increasingly understood why our mother had valued her life and our life in Canada so much and wanted us all to stay and have a future there. But our father also argued to us that he didn't want to have a house anymore, as there were only three of us left. Oh yes, that's right, we had "lost" two family members in one year, one through death and the other through relocation. Our father asked who was going to look after the house? Our mother was no longer there, nor was our older sister. We were still schoolgirls and too young to run a household. Maybe he was right. But you could hire domestic help if you were on a director's salary, couldn't you? Once again, we had been confronted with a pre-decided information and were not at all impressed. At that moment, my father seemed to me to be quite lost and overwhelmed at of our reactions. I also thought he was rather stupid. Hadn't he thought about the possibility of a household help? Would it have been so absurd to bring help into the house? Even his father had a housekeeper and cook, who was there every day. I didn't like the fact that my life was in his hands. I was under the impression that we were facing chaos. What about our mother's thoughts or ideas? Did they no longer count? She had realised that we children needed stability and continuity after so many moves! Should we now need less stability and continuity to cope better with the loss of our mother? I don't think so. None of this made any sense to me.

After his first visit to us in Heidelberg, my father seemed to have brought reinforcement with him on his next visit. He came with a woman we didn't know. Again, no prior information about someone accompanying him. Although we were not getting along, we did need to spend time with each other, but he chose to bring a stranger to our meeting. She was quite small, a bit chubby and quite young. My father introduced her as 'Amelie' and that was it. There was no more explanation. And so, he seemed to have just introduced his girlfriend to us, briefly and concisely, and of course again without any preparation. Despite this approach, which again I didn't think was right, I realised that she was a likeable type of woman, and she had a good laugh. When we visited Heidelberg Castle with her, I asked my father what this woman was all about. He said he liked her and hoped we did too. We thought so, but how were we supposed to understand the whole thing? Did he now have a steady girlfriend? Or was he even planning to marry this woman? Had he just introduced us to our future stepmother? My trust in my father was pretty much at zero at this point. Something about this story didn't quite add up and I started to look for what it was. When I asked him why he had chosen this woman, he said she was young, and that he hoped we would get on well with her. Amelie was in her late 20s and therefore 20 years younger than our father. I didn't like that at all, and it almost seemed like a provocation to the memory of our mother, who was only two years younger than him, a worldly, elegant and well-read, experienced in life, marriage and raising three daughters. This seemingly random choice of a woman gave me the impression that any female could now take my mother's place as long as she was young and could laugh. Were these my father's new expectations of a life partner? Wasn't the task at the side of a successful man more comprehensive than just smiling, being female and young? As she was far too young for my father in my opinion and too young to be accepted as a stepmother, I asked her what she thought was so great about my father. Nothing really came as a reply, after some teenage-like giggles. The fact was, that my father seemed to have blossomed in the arms of this woman and appear a lot younger. This oddly, did make me happy for him. Still, I thought, this situation can't go well. Amelie then said she thought he was great and that they both laughed so much together. She then awkwardly said that they also had a lot of fun when she visited him in Canada in the summer. She said we had a great house. That left me speechless. Now I could assume that my father had spent the summer that we had to spend with my grandparents with this woman, in our house in Canada. Now I felt really betrayed. Was her visit to him the reason why we had to leave home so quickly? Did I now have to assume that this woman had made herself comfortable in the house that our mother had so lovingly decorated, filled and furnished? In our belongings? Did I even have to assume that this woman had slept in my mother's bed not long after she had died? I found the whole thing distasteful and was very upset. Our father was a widower, but our mother had only been in the ground for six months when Amelie had visited him in the summer. Was he in such a hurry to find a new wife? He did have the right to have a new partner. But did his claim to a new relationship justify the fact that I felt hurt by his behaviour? Maybe this woman just made him laugh and he needed that. But the whole thing didn't make me laugh.

All the stress and pressure from school was really getting to me. I constantly had stomach pains, but I didn't complain because I felt so bad overall that I didn't even know what was bothering me the most. It was October when Mrs. Schmid had to take me to the doctor because another teacher had noticed that I kept putting my hand on my stomach, holding it. When the doctor asked me what the problem was, and by that he meant how my stomach pains could have come about, I didn't know what to answer. Should I say that a year ago I lived in a family of five in another country, then my mother died and there were only four of us left? Or should I say that I no longer had a home because my father had sold it, and we didn't have a new one yet? Or should I tell him that I was forced to leave my home country and our family home forever and was parked here at boarding school with my one sister, perhaps so that my father could devote himself to his potentially new wife? Or should I tell him that we lost our eldest sister because she had decided to return to her home country, Canada, which was no longer to be our home country? Should I explain that we had shrunk from four family members to three? Or should I tell him that my father didn't know where he would be working next, as his employer hadn't told him yet? While I was thinking about what to say, Mrs.

Schmid replied to the doctor that I was under pressure to learn German fluently, by Christmas. After Christmas, in the second half of the school year, I was expected to be able to participate fully in the regular lessons of grade nine. The doctor explained to her and to me that I had gastritis and was possibly on the way to developing an ulcer. He also said that at 14 I was still a bit too young for something like that. He kindly warned me that I was under too much stress. I was given medicine for my stomach, but the stress didn't subside. I don't know why he didn't put me on sick leave at the time. Under the circumstances, the doctor understood that I was suffering from a lack of motivation. Whether there was another serious psychological or psychosomatic illness behind the stomach issues, was not considered at the time. They recommended a medication called "Aktivanad", which was supposed to energise me with caffeine and vitamins. But that was all he did for me. He also didn't come up with the idea of getting me psychological treatment or counselling. The stress was affecting me mentally and physically.

Flying home

When the fall break came, my sister was the one who put pressure on our father. We would have had to go to our grandparents' house during the holiday, as the boarding school would be closed during this time. But Carin categorically refused to go there. She told our father that he had already ruined her summer holidays. She would not allow him to continue to ruin her holidays and force her to spend them with her grandparents, again. Our father decided on the spur of the moment to let us fly to Canada for the holidays. Perhaps he was now feeling somewhat of a guilty conscience regarding us, which is why he gave in. We flew out on the very first day of the holidays. Henny, Sue's friend, who had flown to Canada with her seven years earlier, picked us up from the boarding school and drove us to the airport in Frankfurt, which was quite a trip for her to make. We were completely dependent on the help of others and grateful for it. When we arrived in Toronto, we both had mixed feelings. We came "home", but there was no longer a home. We arrived at the apartment building where Sue and, temporarily, our father lived. It was a strange feeling to be there, because it was now obvious that our house had been sold. The rented apartment contained some of the furniture from our house, which reminded us of our former life. But it was in the wrong place, which I found to be rather painful. This sight made it unmistakably clear that there was no other environment for our furniture. Our friends were all at school at the time, as there were no fall holidays in Canada, like in Germany. Due to having school, they all had little time to meet up with us, but at least we could talk to them on the phone. Sue was at university during the day, our dad was at work. So, Carin and I were on our own, again. The real problem now was that we were not in Oakville, where our friends lived, but in neighboring Mississauga, where we had no friends. The connection between the two places by public transport was still poor at the time. Neither of us had a driver's license, although Carin would now have been old enough to drive a car in Canada. We could only hope that friends or their parents would pick us up in Mississauga and drive us to Oakville to meet them there. And they did, but usually only in the evening, as everyone was busy during the day. One time we drove to Oakville and visited friends at the high school, O.T. This, I found to be particularly sobering. They all seemed to be bubbling with energy. They told me about the different subjects they took, the extensive sports program and all the after-school activities. They were unstoppable with their enthusiasm for high school life! This colorful bunch of positivity was the opposite of my black and white life that I was living in Heidelberg. I had never met anyone there with such enthusiasm for school, or anything else. Every meeting with our friends was nice, but also painful, because the next separation was only a few days away. Compared to what we experienced with the German school system and at our boarding school, it was almost unbearable. Of course, I also saw Brent. We talked about the situation that we would not be able to continue our relationship at the end of the school year because I could no longer come back. We both felt betrayed but were powerless to do anything about it. How would we ever find out whether we belonged together after all? The time came when we had to say goodbye. Our friends had helped us cope with the grief of our mother's death in the winter. Now they helped us again, this time over the grief of losing our home. Our friends from the RLDS church, who we were not supposed to have anything to do with anymore, were also there for us. After many visits, many hugs and a lot of bitter crying, our vacation was over, and we had to fly back to Germany.

In November it got colder in Germany as well, just like we were used to in Canada, although not quite as cold. We knew winters that lasted four months, long, hard winters with lots of snow and cold winds coming from Lake Ontario. But we had grown up with it and had no problem with it. Now, in Heidberg, it rained the whole month. No snow. I waited for the rain to finally turn to snow, but it didn't happen. Advent had already begun, but the snow still hadn't arrived. We weren't used to so much rain and it was depressing for both of us. Carin also waited in vain for the rain to turn to snow. Then one day I said to her in a comforting and joking way: "That's snow, transparent German snow!" We were laughing so much that we could hardly calm down: Transparent snow! Another difficult situation had been temporarily saved by our humor, like the summer when we laughed our heads off at the German hairdryer. But would we really spend Advent and possibly Christmas with transparent snow? That seemed like another imposition to me. Would we have to give up everything we loved and were used to? In a phone call with my dad, I complained that there wasn't even snow in "this stupid country"! And I also told him that it was too much to expect us to spend Christmas without snow. Our father had taken so much criticism from us that he could hardly react to it anymore. We were just complaining about everything. He thought for a moment and then said: "It may be that there is no snow in this "stupid country", but it borders on a great country where there is endless snow, Switzerland." He continued: "If you need a white Christmas, then you shall have one, we are going to Switzerland to go skiing over the Christmas vacation." Crazy, I thought, to be going to Switzerland to go skiing! That finally sounded like some good news, very good news, in fact. Finally, there was a ray of hope in what had been such a dark six months for us – other than our very sad and tear-filled visit to Canada, to part from our friends. Carin and I couldn't ski, but Switzerland sounded very nice. Dad also said that we would spend Christmas together as a family and that Sue would fly over from Toronto to be with us. After all, he didn't want her to be alone without us at Christmas. Another piece of good news.

Shortly before Christmas, our father and Sue picked us up in Heidelberg and we spent a few days in Heubach. In between, we drove to Stuttgart to buy ski clothes and equipment for all of us in a bit of a rush, and then the four of us drove to Switzerland to go skiing. After years of being at home over Christmas, we were now going on a skiing vacation, and I was very happy about that. On the way there, a little while after the Swiss border, we were impressed by the landscape. It was very exciting for us to see how the mountains were building up before our eyes, more and more and higher and higher. It was also a relief and a liberation to have left Germany, even if we had only driven to the neighboring country.

Our destination was Leukerbad in the canton of Valais. After a half-day drive, we finally arrived there. We had rented a beautiful, large holiday apartment, for two weeks in a residential complex called "Utoring". On the first evening we took a walk through the town, which was beautiful and idyllic. My father said he deliberately chose Leukerbad, because it was a beautiful place, a somewhat larger Swiss mountain village. It was a very well-kept spa town, and we were all enchanted by the chalets and everything that came with them. Our father had made a good choice.

The next day we went up the mountain to ski. We were very lucky that our father had chosen an apartment building just a few meters from the station of the cable car. So at least we didn't have to walk far in our new ski boots and with our skis balanced on our shoulders. We sisters took turns laughing about how clumsily we moved in our ski clothes and equipment. It was a skill that had to be acquired. It was entertaining though and that was a good thing, because we finally had a lot to laugh about. One funny situation followed another. Once we got to the top of the mountain, we first had to strap our skis to our feet, which wasn't as easy as it looked. Sue was the most amused, literally doubled over with laughter at the sight of her sisters and their dexterity exercises. I had never seen her laugh like this before!

Once strapped to the skis, we were supposed to ski. Our father, who had already skied a lot in his youth, was still a master of this sport. He simply went ahead and, when we reached the bottom of the "baby hill", signaled with a wave of his arm, that we should come down too. Sue went first and after just a few meters seemed to be slowly but surely getting the hang of her skis. However, she was smart enough to ski in the beginners' snowplow style. Carin followed her example and skied slowly but surely down the hill. Then it was my turn. I also tried to ski slowly down the hill in a snowplow, brake and carry on. That went reasonably well until I lost control of my skis halfway down. They just kept going and I couldn't brake or turn! I got faster and faster and headed straight for a big red "Pistenbully", a snow plough. It looked like I was going on purpose, but it wasn't. Luckily for me, the snowcat driver also noticed that I had no control over my skis. He was able to lower the front of the shovel a little in time and I crashed straight into a shovel filled with snow. Fortunately, I didn't hurt myself. My sisters, who were very concerned about my well-being, did what they did best: They laughed at me! It must have been a very strange idea, because Carin said that it was even better than the garbage can incident in Bremen. From that point on, I had various nicknames and at every opportunity my sisters pointed to a "Pistenbully" and said something like: "That's not a brake!" or: "Don't drive into it!" Although I was once again the one being laughed at, it wasn't as bad as it used to be. The main thing was that we could all laugh again.

In the mornings, we had breakfast together, and at lunch we ate pasta up in the hut on the mountain. However, we all found that so horrendously expensive that we preferred to go back to our apartment and make pasta from a can. We also found that rather funny. None of us could cook.

Christmas, the celebration that had always been such a big event in our house, came. Our father simply said he was fed up with Christmas and that was the end of the matter. We didn't even celebrate but went skiing instead. We noticed that the slopes were empty that day and so we decided that this was an additional reason to go skiing. The first anniversary of our mother's death was already approaching. We thought about how we could mark the day in a dignified way. But, like Christmas, it was not given much attention. My father said, "What are we going to do? Sit at home and cry all day?" He was right, that didn't seem like a good plan, so we all went skiing that day as well. That was our way of dealing with the grief.

Leukerbad, Christmas 1978, Claudia, Carin, Sue.

While skiing we met two brothers from Sweden, Hans and Anders, who were better skiers than we were. They were on vacation with their parents, were about the same age as Carin and Sue, and lived in the same apartment building. These Swedes were very funny and could laugh a lot. We discovered that Swedes and Canadians have a similar sense of humor, like being out in nature, and were full of mischief. The older of the brothers and Sue were allowed to drink alcohol and did so when we went out together in the evenings. The three younger ones then guided the older ones safely home after going out and drinking.

There was also a single woman from Hamburg, with two teenagers our age, staying in our apartment building. Our father and this very tall, slim, dark-haired woman with the pleasant smile seemed to get on very well, right away. She had told us that she had fled East Germany, the GDR, with her children. This story was incredibly fascinating for all of us, because we had never heard anything like it before. It was the first time we had ever encountered the issue of the divided Germany. Before that, it was something of a foreign matter, very far away from us. I could hardly grasp that a person could be so desperate and convinced of wanting to live in freedom that she would risk both their own life and the lives of her children for it, but she did. I was deeply impressed by the story and especially by this brave woman. I also liked that she had children of her own, which made her a more suitable potential stepmother in my eyes. And she was also closer in age to our father than the first candidate. We and her children joked among ourselves that we might become related if the two got married. It was a nice thought. As things were, we sometimes went out to dinner with them and then sometimes out with the Swedes. We had a full program all around, which really was a lot of fun.

Then came New Year's Eve. Here too, we went skiing and, in the evening, we went out to dinner and celebrated with our friends and possible future relatives. It was the first time for me to take part in a New Year's Eve party outside of the house. That was great fun, too, as was the whole vacation. But I did wonder if we would have experienced all of this with our mother.

Less funny was that we had to show our father our parents' reports from the boarding school. The boarding school report was divided into three parts: 1. Health, 2. School and 3. Personal development at boarding school. Under "Health" it said "Good" for me. That wasn't quite right, unless gastritis or an almost ulcer was considered "good" there.

The "School" section said: "For Claudia, the adjustment to German school conditions and the higher performance requirements were not easy... In addition to her lacking mastery of the German language, she also lacks some basic knowledge in other subjects." Since I didn't master the language, I wondered how I would have understood the lessons in the other subjects. I also wondered how they would know whether I lacked knowledge if I couldn't express myself sufficiently due to a lack of language skills. They simply assumed that I lacked basic knowledge and that was the reason why I had difficulty following the lessons. We also wondered why the teachers assumed that the performance requirements in Germany were higher than those in Canada? We did not find them to be higher, but rather the entire lessons, as well as the style of teaching, to be boring and monotonous.

What Carin and I knew for sure was that we didn't like the school or the school system. We didn't think much of the way the lessons were taught, primarily through monologues from the teachers rather than involving the students and supplemented by practical exercises in class. We also found the music and art lessons, which focused primarily on theoretical education, incredibly one-sided and boring. How can you understand music and art when you almost only talk or read about them? The only thing missing from all this theoretical teaching was for us to be told about sports instead of letting us do them! But the two hours of sports we had per week were just boring, like the rest. The school or the German school system didn't catch our interest. It was as if we had experienced and participated in school in Canada in colour and now, we experienced it in black and white. The emphasis of the lessons was on learning in the sense of memorizing, rather than experiencing and comprehending. For us, that was a step backwards in our educational development. In addition, we were not used to absorbing huge amounts of material just to be able to repeat it when asked – basically from memory. Where was the learning effect?

At the mention of our observations and our comparisons of the two school systems, other students told us that we were lucky to be at Thadden School, because state schools were much worse. The notion of that was incomprehensible to me. How inadequate if only part of our abilities were addressed, mainly that of learning by heart. The German school system did not seem to place any value on the ability to think for oneself, to work in groups, to create things in class. No, this type of teaching that we had been presented with, in our experience, only developed part of a young person and hence did not appeal to us. A bunch of lone fighters were being trained here. They did not practice in groups or learn to play in a

221

team. They all went home at 1 p.m. to study in their own rooms at home. Each on their own. How could any feeling of community or belonging together arise among the students?

In the section "private lessons" it said that I had German three times a week, French two times, and math two times, seven hours in total. But it was usually more. Carin had five hours a week. My workload had only been reduced in December, in response to my complaining, and refusing to take any more lessons. What a relief for our father that all the lessons were paid for by his employer! This was standard practice at the company, where the "Bosch family" was always referred to when an employee's children had to change language or school system due to a transfer and therefore needed additional lessons to master the school material.

In the section "Personal development in boarding school" it said, among other things: "Claudia settled in quickly and has adapted well at the boarding school." I did not necessarily share this opinion. I had resigned myself to this dull, patronizing system rather than settling in well. Sometimes I was simply so emotionally exhausted that I went with the crowd. I had learned to live with the system, so to speak. After I was praised in my report with words like "open-minded, sociable, cheerful and orderly," I was harshly criticized: "We hope that Claudia can expand her contacts with people her own age in the future and not limit herself so much to her relationship with her sister and other older girls who also come from Canada," which from our point of view was the crowning glory of my boarding school report. Did the educationalists who looked after me want to say that they would be happier if I spent more time with people who did not understand my situation? Or were they saying that they had failed to help me with the difficulty of my situation and had to watch Heidi do their job? Why had I never been taken to a psychologist to perhaps get professional support in dealing with my emotions during this for me very difficult time? Was I really expected to cope with all the changes of the last 12 months on my own, without professional help? Apparently. In my eyes they had failed because I felt miserable inside.

As both reports about us were rather bad, we didn't make a long-winded case about it. We gave the reports to our father as evidence of our inability. To my surprise, Sue showed solidarity with us and said that the whole thing was not fair to us. Our father read and read and didn't react much. The only thing he said was: "How lucky for me that Bosch paid for your boarding school until Christmas and not me." He had thus saved DM 10,000 in boarding school costs. In addition, the

222

extra class was about 20 DM per hour, over four months that added up to another 4.000 DM. He went on to say that he would have to pay it after the holidays, so he hoped the reports would be better then. The actual core problem was no longer discussed. Basically, the boarding school could not do anything about the fact that we felt massively betrayed and robbed. We did try to speak openly with our father about what and how things had gone. But I cannot remember my father showing any remorse or apologizing for how things had gone. Perhaps we had already said everything indirectly by constantly criticizing what we were experiencing. None of us could turn back the clock and perhaps do or decide some things differently. Our lives had developed into what they were now. We could only move on from here. And now we should simply be enjoying our vacation together, as a family.

Stuttgart - Botnang 1979

When we returned to Germany from our skiing holiday, we finally had a home to return to after half a year. Our father had bought a condominium in a borough of the City of Stuttgart, called Botnang. There, on Furtwänglerstrasse, on the top floor of a high-rise building, we were to find our new home. After a very long drive, it was already dark when we arrived in Botnang. All around us, I saw nothing but apartment buildings. We seemed to have somehow landed in the middle of a concrete city. A little unsure, I asked my father: "Dad, what are we doing here?" He replied: "We still have to buy groceries. We don't have anything to eat at home." I was relieved to hear that we were just shopping here, because I thought we were supposed to live here. But then he pointed in a direction in the darkness and said: "Our place is over there." That had to be a joke, right? We didn't know where exactly he was pointing, but neither Carin nor I had a good feeling about this. Did he really mean that we should move into a concrete settlement?

He was serious. Fully loaded with our groceries, we finally arrived at our new home, full of anticipation. With the words: "Welcome to your new home", the heavy door was opened, and we were allowed to go in. We looked around this 4 ½ room place, with, as we were told, around 125 m². Before making this purchase, our father had already looked at a few places and he hadn't really liked any of them. The name of the seller of this apartment was Bauder, like us, but was not related to us. Our father told us: "When I saw the name on the doorbell, I thought how convenient, I just have to move in here", whereupon he bought the place. It was also convenient for him that all the rooms in this penthouse apartment were fitted with exclusive wood paneling, shelves and built-in cupboards, built to measure. Our father had bought the apartment with all the fittings, including the fitted kitchen and appliances, and in addition to that, took over most of the freestanding furniture such as tables and sofas as well. The apartment was almost completely furnished when we got there. It was unbelievable and a bit spooky. At the same time, there was also something friendly about it, because it was better than arriving in an empty apartment. On the other hand, this also had something uncomfortable about it, because the furniture was unfamiliar to us. It belonged to other people and was standing there in such a way that you couldn't tell whether the previous owners had moved away, or perhaps died, and had taken practically nothing with them. The living room was paneled all around with rosewood, there were shelves and drawers built in here as well and it looked very classy. Our mother would have liked that very much. She loved rosewood and our dining room and living room tables and chairs in Canada, were made if it. As we continued to walk around, we realized that our father had bought the beds and mattresses as well! Almost everything was there, except bed linen, towels and dishes. The only basic thing that we were missing when we arrived, was heat. This apartment was incredibly cold. How practical that was, because we already had our next joke ready: "Well done Dad, too bad it doesn't come with heating!". We girls were once again doubled over with laughter at this reference to what we sometimes felt was a somewhat backward level of development in Germany, especially when it came to the comfort in apartments and houses. There was of course heating, but it had been turned off when the family moved out a week earlier. At first, we didn't take off our winter boots, winter jackets, gloves or hats. But we discovered, to our great delight, that our bathtub had a built-in heater, which was the only one that hadn't been turned off when we moved out, so we had a warm bathroom! Mean as we were, we asked our father whether the Germans heated their bath water in this way? Again, we had something to laugh about, but by now it had become more of a roar. When we discovered, to our great delight, that there was running water in the apartment, we asked our father whether we had to fill the tub with cold water so that we could have a lukewarm bath the next day. We couldn't stop laughing! Our father had to put up with a lot from us!

On our first night in the apartment, we had the choice of either freezing or wearing some of our ski clothes, such as long ski underwear. When we saw each other in pajamas, sweaters and ski socks or even funnier combinations, we couldn't stop laughing and even our father had to laugh with us. All this laughter had the advantage that we got warmer and warmer, and it was also incredibly relaxing. Our father had to accept a summary comment from his daughters: "That was really a brilliant idea of yours, giving up our wonderful life in Canada and moving here instead."

The next morning, to our surprise, our apartment was relatively warm because we had turned all the heating up full in the evening and it had warmed up overnight. So, we were able to stay in our apartment on the first day dressed normally - what a luxury! After our ski vacation, we had a lot of laundry to do and wanted to start with that first. Then we girls realized that our apartment didn't have a laundry room like we were used to in our last home. After a careful but unsuccessful search, we asked our father where, please, we should do our laundry. He said there was a washing machine in the kitchen. Our kitchen was accessible from both the hallway and the dining area adjacent to the living room. The kitchen therefore had two doors, both of which were open. Since we had looked for our washing machine but hadn't found it, our father said somewhat jokingly, as if it were a matter of finding hidden Easter presents, that we would have to look behind the doors, which we then did. Lo and behold, we finally found what we were looking for! We would never have thought of closing the door to the dining area first to get to the washing machine, which was right behind it. We were extremely happy about our discovery, because it meant that we could finally actually do our laundry. At the same time, we were somewhat disgusted at the thought of having to do laundry in the kitchen, where food was stored and prepared. When we asked him if he was serious, our father replied that this was completely normal in Germany. Oh man, that was something that we would really have to get used to, dealing with food and smelly socks in the same room.

Our kitchen was also high-quality, with Siemens built-in units and Bosch appliances - another thing that impressed our father. However, much to our dismay, the kitchen was red, even a deep red, including the work surfaces. That also took some getting used to. To counteract our horror with a bit of humor, which was urgently needed at that time, we called the corner behind the door our "laundry room". Sue would always say when she ran the washing machine: "I'm in the laundry room". It was probably Sue, who was used to having to translate all sorts of things for us, who came up with this glorious "translation". We mocked our poor apartment at every opportunity, even though it was very high-quality und undoubtable had been expensive, but it was small. For what we were used to, it felt cramped that you opened the apartment door and found yourself standing directly in the hallway, even though it was spacious by German standards, we called the hallway area the "entrance hall". The bathtub was declared a "pool" and the terrace a garden. Our father assured us that this building, like most in Botnang, was a high-quality condominium. But that didn't help us much and, in our mockery, nothing was too sacred for us to make jokes about.

Botnang 1979, visit from Grandma and Grandpa, with Hans.

The fact that we were now the owners of a 4 ½ room apartment - and Carin, Sue and I owned half of it - was the next laugh. We asked our father what half a room was? He pointed to an open room that led off the hallway but was not closed off by an additional wall, which was to serve as his study. We couldn't help but ask whether a half room was defined by the fact that the upper half was missing or the lower half! Did a half room have no floor or no ceiling? How did you buy a half room? You go to an estate agent and say: I would like a half room, what do you have on offer? And the estate agent answers: "We have rooms without floors, but also rooms without ceilings". How we laughed! But perhaps this made us realize that we lived in a country that was small by our standards, where there was so little

226

living space that there were even half rooms! Now that was a frightening thought. Now I understood what my uncle Alex had said six months earlier when we were discussing my "year in Germany." "Everything is so cramped in Europe." It was true. On the same day, we received boxes of dishes, laundry, etc. All we had to do later was put our father's desk and a shelf in the apartment. The piano came with us too. We put the valuable leather couch with rosewood on the half-covered terrace so that we could sit comfortably there as well. Then a Persian carpet was put in each room and the place was ready. "Instant home," we called the result. Apart from the fact that our name was already on the door sign, the apartment had something else convincing about it. This was a fantastic view over the "Feuerbach Valley." As beautiful as our house in Canada had been, we didn't have a view there. It was only in this apartment that we were able to experience how wonderful it is to have a fabulous view for what felt like kilometers, offering forests, fields and pure nature. The view also included the Killesberg, the top side of Stuttgart north, and the outline of the Bismarck Tower in the distance. It was fantastic and will certainly have contributed to the high price of the condominium.

After a few days in our new apartment, we said goodbye to Sue, because she had to go back to Canada to study, and Carin and I had to go back to our boarding school. Our father had to start his new job that same month as sales manager at Bosch in Karlsruhe, as "Head of Sales for Africa, Asia and Latin America in the KH division". KH was the abbreviation for Automotive Equipment Trade (meaning car parts), Bosch's largest division. He was given power of attorney and commercial power of attorney by the company for his area of responsibility. He reported directly to KH/GL, the managing director, or, as we children said, the "boss" of KH. It seemed as if our father had been given a larger area of responsibility and had been promoted. Perhaps the company could not have found a more suitable candidate for this, after all, our father had years of sales experience in South America. Although he now had an apartment in Stuttgart, our father worked in Karlsruhe, almost an hour's drive west of Stuttgart. Yes, we had looked at a place in Karlsruhe-Durlach as well, but he did not know at the time in which city he would be working. A new sales and distribution center for the automotive equipment trading business had been opened there at the time. This was a large, light green building that was impossible to miss from the A5 motorway from Karlsruhe to Heidelberg, near Durlach, and was marked with the large red company name "BOSCH". We once again made fun of our father. So, we said to him: "Well done, Dad, an office

227

with a view of the motorway!" He had to put up with a lot from us and in this case, it was of little use that he explained to us that this warehouse was one of the most modern in Europe and delivered products to almost the whole world. We simply could not share his enthusiasm; we felt too deeply that we had lost our home for this promotion. He seemed to understand this a little better now and perhaps that was why he tried to explain to us the importance of the task, but all attempts were in vain. Perhaps he did indeed deserve praise, but we certainly did not have that ready for him. Instead, we jokingly asked him whether he had been "promoted" to forklift driver because he was going to work in a "warehouse". Sometimes he almost seemed in despair due to our comments and indifference towards his success. The situation was difficult for all of us. He received no recognition from his children. Instead, we criticized him at pretty much every opportunity. That had not happened when our mother was alive. She had taught us to respect our father's achievements. But the emotional wounds on Carin and me were still fresh and deep, and so we rather enjoyed causing our father pain.

Back at the boarding school, the cycle of school, tutoring, studying, school, tutoring, studying started again. I was back in my prison and forced to study again. Heidi, Carin and I consoled ourselves by counting the days until the next holidays. Thanks to Heidi, we had also rather crudely distorted what was actually a very beautiful Christmas carol. On our evening walks in the park, we sang the song with our own lyrics: "Hark the Harold's angels shout: XX more days till we are out, XX more days till we are free, from this penitentiary."

Much to my surprise, however, a change in the dreaded weekly routine presented itself to us. Fortunately, dance school was starting, meaning lessons in ballroom dancing. We were told that in Germany it was normal for girls and boys going to a Gymnasium, which was the higher level of schooling, to attend dancing lessons, at around the age of 15, to learn standard dances, or couple dancing. I understood the words "dancing and boys" and was excited. The dance school was to take place once a week and we girls from the Thadden boarding school were allowed to go, provided our parents agreed. We were also informed that this was a serious matter, and that standard dancing was part of the general education of "higher-class girls". Great, finally something more interesting, I thought. I got permission from my father, and we were off. We all took the bus into town together for our lessons. I liked the opportunity to get out of the boarding school once a week and to meet boys officially. I enjoyed dancing right away and so I went to the dance school on Saturdays as well, to practice. After two months, the course in which we had learned to dance the waltz, foxtrot, cha cha cha and rumba at the Nuzinger dance school was over.

Our farewell ball took place at the end of March. A tall, slim and attractive boy named Bernd invited me to accompany him to the graduation ball. I was thrilled that such a nice, charming boy had asked me. Carin was less lucky and had to go with one of the remaining boys. Our graduation ball took place in the King's Hall of Heidelberg Castle. Formal evening wear was required, but unfortunately, we had to sew our long evening skirts ourselves for this festive occasion. Our father said that we had learned to sew (from our mother and in school in Canada), so we should do it. Neither of us liked this idea at all, and we would certainly have felt better and more attractive if we had been able to buy something fashionable to wear, in town. But that was our father, stubborn and strict. The atmosphere in the King's Hall of Heidelberg Castle was stunning. It was hard to concentrate on dancing because the historic hall was overwhelmingly large and beautiful. What we experienced there was perhaps something that many Heidelberg tourists from North America or Asia could only dream of: attending a ball in Heidelberg Castle. So, our stay in Heidelberg did have a unique highlight, in a historical sight, with style and class. I liked the dance lessons and so I signed up for the advanced course. My sister, on the other hand, hated the whole thing and only did the beginner's course: she would have preferred to do gymnastics and besides, she did not find the German boys interesting.

It was nice for us that we now had a home again. We could now also enjoy our "home weekend" every other weekend. We took the train from Heidelberg to Stuttgart on Friday afternoons. Our father usually drove us back to boarding school on Sundays. Unfortunately, we didn't have many opportunities to do anything on these weekends because we didn't have any friends in Stuttgart that we could meet. After all, we went to school in Heidelberg, so how were we supposed to meet people in Stuttgart? We did once have a change of events, when Amelie came to visit. By now it had become clear that our father would not be able to have a relationship with the woman from Hamburg, whom we had met on vacation, because of the distance. I thought it was a shame because I liked her and her children too. Now Amelie was back, and we appreciated her more than before, because after all, she did make our father laugh.

At Easter, we went skiing in Leukerbad again. We liked the resort so much that we wanted to go there again. However, Sue didn't come with us this time. Firstly, she didn't have time because she was studying, and secondly, our father thought it was getting expensive to fly us three girls back and forth. We could understand the 'expensive' part, but it hadn't been our wish to be separated. It had come about because he had let our family fall apart. In this respect, he could talk about costs as much as he wanted, we were not at all receptive to this argument. In my opinion, family came before money. Apart from that, his cost problems were nothing compared to our homesickness and yearning to be there.

As our father was planning to rent another large flat in Leukerbad, he thought there would be enough space to take another person with us. We both said that we would like to invite Heidi. She was our best friend and had also become a kind of substitute sister. We could also well imagine that Heidi would like to come along, since we knew that she loved skiing. In addition to that, we thought that a bit of family life, even if it was a substitute family, would do her good. Heidi was delighted with our suggestion and agreed straight away. We also had no problems getting permission from the boarding school or her parents, which in hindsight surprises me a bit considering some of the wild nights we spent on holiday!

When we arrived in Leukerbad, we realised on the very first day of skiing that Heidi was not only a real Canadian, but also an incredibly good skier. Unlike us, she had been skiing all her life. She could even keep up with the local Swiss and Carin and I could only watch her in amazement. She didn't just take off, she also took the trouble to teach us a bit, but we still had to practise on our own. During the day, we went our separate ways after our lessons. Her route took us down the very difficult black pistes, while ours took us down the blue beginners' pistes. Instead, we spent our time together eating and going out in the evenings. Unlike the evenings with Sue, we didn't spend our time in the pubs. We had discovered a small disco in the village, which became our favourite place from then on. We went there night after night and danced to disco favourites, especially Boney-M. Heidi always had to laugh at the music and kept saying that music like that wasn't played in discos in Montreal. The amazing thing was that we were on skis all day long and still had the energy to dance in the disco at night. Perhaps we owed our stamina to the afternoon nap at boarding school?

After a few days, Heidi had found an admirer who came from Canada of all places, which led to a brief word of warning from our father. He told Heidi that he expected her to behave as her parents would expect her to behave. She said that She would, and that was the end of the matter. Apart from that, we all just had fun.

After two weeks of serious sports and lots of dancing, we had to give up our paradisial life and return to our boarding school in Heidelberg. None of us were looking forward to going back to the "institution", but we couldn't avoid it. We started singing our song "Hark, the Harold Angels shout..." on the evening of our return to the boarding school and counted down the days until our next "release".

I continued to have little success at school, except for one very important event for me. My German tutor, Dr. Rech, and I had amazingly managed to get my German up to grade nine level by the spring! I was now supposed to take part in regular German lessons with the other pupils. We had to read the book "Unterm Rad" (Beneath the Wheel) by Herman Hesse. I found it quite difficult to read and to comprehend, but I was willing to take part on the exam on it. The result was that much to everyone's amazement, I passed the assignment and with an average grade! I could hardly believe it. The best thing was that my classmates were happy for me about my success and even applauded! There seemed to be hope for me after all.

Candidate number three

There was also hope for our father. One weekend in spring, he brought a new woman with him to Heidelberg. Her name was Waltraut, and she was from Stuttgart. She had no children of her own but was a teacher. My father thought she might get on well with us as she worked with young people. She was only 10 years younger than our father, so I thought the age difference was acceptable. But a teacher? Was that good news or bad news? What was much better about this woman than her predecessors were her language skills. Waltraut spoke, understood and taught French and English and could therefore also understand us when we spoke English, which was always the case at home. She was tall, slim and a distinctive, attractive woman, not conformist but with an individual taste in fashion, somewhat artistic. I kind of liked her. She didn't live as far away as the woman from Hamburg and wasn't as small or as young as Amelie. She seemed to meet our father's requirements and ours much better. What was very impressive about her was that she was an academic and very cultured. She had travelled a lot, worked in the USA and even had a sister living in California who she visited regularly. She was therefore also familiar with life in or the lifestyle of North America, which made everything easier for us. But she had one thing that neither Carin nor I could cope with, and that was her name. It was so German that we had trouble pronouncing the sound of it hurt our ears a bit. In addition, "Wal-traut" had the connotation of "wall trout", which was neither feminine nor flattering. Waltraut was stress-tested through her job as a teacher when it came to teenagers and was therefore able to react calmly when we discussed our concerns about her name with her. She understood our language difficulties and we agreed to call her "Wally". She also had a good laugh, although she was more reserved than her predecessors. Her elegant reserve probably had something to do with the fact that her father once held a high position in an industrial company, her mother had a grand piano, and she came from a strict family. She was used to dealing with professionally successful men at home, which almost predestined her to get along with our father, as she would not be intimidated by him. She even understood my father's jokes, some of which were quite challenging! Candidate number three had a serious chance.

I was still "very good" at sports and had even received a certificate of honour for "outstanding achievements" at the Federal Youth Games. It had the signature of Federal President Walter Scheel printed on it. Not bad either, I thought to myself. A few weeks later, I received a winner's certificate for my successful participation in the Federal Youth Games, this time signed by the Minister of Culture and Sport of the state of Baden-Württemberg, Roman Herzog. In the same month, after successfully completing my advanced course at the dance school, I received my certificate for the German Dance Badge in bronze, awarded by the Allgemeiner Deutscher Tanzlehrer-Verband E.V., abbreviated to ADTV, a member of the International Council of Ballroom Dancing, from Nuzinger dance school. I could really be proud of my athletic achievements. I really enjoyed my sporting activities and needed them to balance out the pressure of my studies.

Six months after my father's return from abroad and his service for Bosch in Germany, his title and somewhat his job changed. From July 1979, he worked at Schillerhoehe in Stuttgart, the company's headquarters. In specific terms, this meant that he was now sales manager of the KH division, responsible for overseas sales, excluding North America, Australia and Oceania. My father had probably complained to the company that he had bought a flat in Stuttgart but then got a job in Karlsruhe. He didn't like having to drive back and forth every day, nor did he like having to report to a superior, which he was no longer used to. After lengthy negotiations, Bosch had probably realised that things had not gone well and that he had been kept in the dark for too long, which had led to the purchase of the flat in one place and the job in another. The change of job from Karlsruhe to Schillerhoehe in Stuttgart was therefore a concession by the company.

As far as we children were concerned, we were planning to live with our father in Stuttgart, after our year at boarding school. If he would have continued to commute to Karlsruhe every day, he would leave very early in the morning and return very late in the evening. Without this transfer, he would not have agreed to letting us leave the boarding school to move to Stuttgart and live with there.

When the school year came to an end, Carin had successfully completed year 11. I hadn't succeeded and was to repeat grade nine, which was a serious blow for me. I had never been one of the "failures" before, but now I felt like one. What I had previously taken for granted, namely finishing the school year reasonably well, was suddenly no longer possible. In addition - how could it be otherwise - I had to compare myself to my sister, who had managed the school year despite similar language problems. However, she had a clear advantage over me because she had attended first and second grade in Germany and had learnt to read and write here. But nobody was willing to take this advantage into consideration when comparing our progress at learning German. My father just couldn't stop comparing me to my sister year in, year out. That didn't exactly boost my self-confidence or my feelings for my sister. But even she, the talented linguist, the former perennial straight-A student, had struggled to achieve her goals that school year. My sister, the "mastermind", had only achieved an average of grade level four out of six (one being the best grade, compared to an A, and four being a D) despite her linguistic advantage and innate talents. But my father that didn't give it much thought that she had only reached a grade point four, or a D. I had a poor average of four, so as always, I was one grade lower than her, but my German was still so bad overall that I simply couldn't be transferred into grade 10.

In my school report, I only had the grades "good" in English and sports, but I wasn't satisfied with either grade. How could someone who speaks and writes English fluently be denied the grade "very good", an A? The reason given for the B was that I could not translate well enough into German. Really? Hadn't this comment itself already confirmed that I could speak English? But the real problem was that I didn't know enough German. Hadn't I already been sufficiently punished for

233

not being good enough at German with my five out or six or "poor", equivalent to an E in German, French and chemistry? Hadn't I already had four years of French lessons in Canada and therefore two years more lessons than my German classmates? Wasn't it obvious that I had a knowledge advantage? Did I have to endure a double punishment in one of my favourite subjects, French, of all things? It seemed to me and according to my impression, that some things were being evaluated unfairly. I had worked so hard. These poor grades and evaluations only discouraged me from wanting to continue putting in so much effort and diminished my hopes of ever being able to perform well enough. It was a very low blow to my morale. How could I only be "good" at sports and not "very good"? What was unathletic about everything I did? Could I only be "good" at PE at school? No, of course, it was again down to my verbal performance in the theoretical part of PE, as I was told. I could not explain things well enough in German!

It seemed to me that they didn't like me and that this rigid school took pleasure in giving a bad grades to someone who had achieved a lot. I accepted my five in chemistry, honestly. Chemistry as a subject completely passed me by in terms of content. These lessons would probably have passed me by in English as well. In physics and maths, I was graded as sufficient, at four, or a D. In these two subjects, I really struggled to understand the content linguistically. Physics also passed me by a bit, like chemistry. But I had always been a very good student in maths. Why should I suddenly no longer be able to master the logic of maths? Was I so bad that I could only get a "satisfactory", a C, in religious education, geography, music and art? Didn't I have quite a bit of knowledge in these subjects due to our lifestyle? Didn't I go to Bible classes and Christian leisure activities? Didn't I come from a cosmopolitan family where we children were expected to be able to recite the names of many countries in the world and their capitals and even find them on the globe? Didn't I have a real soft spot for art, which I had inherited from my mother? Hadn't we already visited some famous museums and art galleries, and couldn't I already identify various classical and modern artists? What was going on here? Had we encountered a school system that felt stronger by systematically denigrating the knowledge and performance of "foreign" students? Were only small units of specific knowledge tested, which were either memorised or not, and if you didn't give the correct answer, you failed? Perhaps yes, because learning success was measured here. But if you have language difficulties, you can't demonstrate as much success in learning as you can in your native language. Obvious and logical. Our father should have realised this too, as he had grown up in this

234

country. So, from the outset, our success at school had been sacrificed for his professional success. My English was undoubtedly better than that of my English teacher and my schoolmates. How could she only rate me as "good"? Was I a small, stupid, uneducated foreigner in their eyes because I hadn't learnt German fast enough? That's how I felt categorised, and my dislike of this country grew stronger and stronger. How can you discourage young people like that? I don't think the problem was with the school itself, but with the German school system. It only asked certain elements, the correct answers to which led to success. In other words, they wouldn't even recognise a genius because they wouldn't be able to perceive their knowledge of skills if they had another language as their mother tongue. If the genius could only count to 20 in German, they would completely miss the fact that they can count to 1000, with this system. Poor Germany!

Now I had to accept that I hadn't managed to fulfil the performance requirements like my sister. But what had these performance requirements been? Not just those of the school! Didn't anyone see the bigger picture? Our father was very disappointed with me and my results, and he emphasised that he had been paying for every single tutoring session himself since January. Not only that, but he had to pay for the second six months at boarding school himself, which was around DM 10,000, and he had expected a better result from us. But what did I care about the cost to my father and his employer to turn us into little Germans? We didn't want that, and we didn't want to be or stay here permanently! If our family had stayed in Canada, we wouldn't have had to fly to Germany in the summer and Bosch could have saved those flights as well. My father could have saved our two flights in the autumn holidays and Sue's flight at Christmas. Three overseas flights in half a year, which he paid for us, but not because we wanted it, but because **he** wanted it. So, it was his problem! For the money, he could probably have hired a domestic help for this time and left everything as it was, with or without Bosch. And with the money he had just inherited from his father, he would have had a nice financial cushion to reorient himself professionally in Canada, perhaps even become self-employed. Now all the Bosch gentlemen were burdened with spending money on us, apparently without having considered whether my sister and I would even be able to cope emotionally with giving up our home and being separated from our sister so soon after our mother's death. I certainly couldn't cope and at the same time I was supposed to perform at my best. That's ridiculous! Were there no psychologists far and wide at the time where these gentlemen could have sought counselling beforehand? Maybe there were, but they obviously did not look for them.

It is fair to question whether parents must always fulfil the wishes of their children, without taking their own wishes into consideration. If the children's mental health will suffer, then yes. After all, parents have a duty of care for their children. Yes, as a parent you regularly must put your wishes on the back burner. That's what I call acting responsibly. But that doesn't mean you have to do it forever, but you do have to do it sometimes.

It was now clear to Carin and me that we wanted to leave this boarding school. However, Carin's goal from day one had been "get out!". But now, since I had become quite bad at school, the boarding school recommended to our father, that I should stay at the boarding school. They thought I needed particularly strong control or a structured framework to cope with everyday life. They also said that at just 15, I was still too young to move to Stuttgart, as we had planned. At 17, Carin was confirmed to be mature enough to leave the boarding school and take care of herself as far as possible. The boarding school knew that our father was a single parent and still very career orientated. He was not the kind of man who would put his career on hold to spend more time with his children. So, the boarding school rightly assumed that we would have to organise our everyday lives ourselves. I was a little worried that this would be the case, but I was sure that Carin and I would manage it all. But I would never have admitted my honest reservations regarding the new and upcoming challenges. I had no intention of staying at boarding school alone without my sister. I realised that I didn't want to be separated from her. I also desperately needed a normal family life again to collect myself and focus, even though our family now only consisted of three people. I wanted my emotional wounds to heal in peace, and at home. I had already spent too many nights lying awake at boarding school without any attention or comfort. I felt that my desire to sleep within my own four walls again was absolutely justified.

Let's get out of here

The last school year had already started in August and lasted until the end of July. That means we had a school year of 11 months, instead of just 10 months like in Canada, followed by two months of summer holidays. We had all had enough of that school year. Heidi, Carin and I were overjoyed when the last day of school finally arrived. With our suitcases and boxes packed, we were ready to move to Stuttgart. But the end of the school year also meant that we had to say goodbye to our dear friend Heidi, which occurred with lots of tears but also in the usual way, with lots of laughter. Heidi was returning to Canada after grade 12, where she would be going to university. We would miss her terribly but were very proud that this sister had now also made it to university.

After a year at boarding school, Carin was determined never to set foot in a boarding school again. She had no intention of letting any house mother tell her what to do after the summer, at the age of 17. She chose a normal public school in Stuttgart and was determined to lead a normal life. I was determined to follow my sister wherever she went. Our father was now also living and working in Stuttgart, so I imagined that I would experience something resembling family life again. Against the advice of the head of the boarding school, I also intended to deregister from the boarding school. However, she wrote to my father that although Carin seemed to be doing well, I was not at all, I was too childish and still too dependent. Then there were my language and academic difficulties. We took note of this, but didn't listen to the justified doubts regarding my having success in Stuttgart. All my life I had followed the family on every move and now I had no intention of staying behind in Heidelberg on my own. For me, too, it was a case of "let's get out of here" from the boarding school. So, our father deregistered us both from the boarding school despite everyone's concerns about me.

As in the previous year, we had to find a new school quickly. Unfortunately, there was no high school in Botnang; the secondary schools were in the city centre. Unfortunately, our father hadn't thought about the school when he bought the flat. However, it was the case that all the secondary school children from Botnang commuted to Stuttgart every day, taking the tram. As our father worked, he wouldn't have time to take us to school in the mornings and wouldn't be able to pick us up in the afternoon either. Therefore, our only option was to find a school that we could reach relatively quickly and practically by public transport. We had a choice of two public schools, which were located opposite each other, in the west end of Stuttgart. One had previously been a girls' school, the other a boys' school, but both were now co-ed. Wally, who was now our father's girlfriend, was convinced that we weren't making the right choices. She said that I should without a doubt be going to a Waldorf school, being the Rudolf Steiner educational system, in which the pupils' intellectual, artistic, and practical skills, with a focus on imagination and creativity are educated and supported in a more holistic way. She was convinced that this type of school and teaching would suit me better and that there wouldn't be a strong emphasis on grades. I found the idea very interesting and was keen to pursue it. My father, however, categorically rejected the Waldorf school and said: "None of my daughters go to a school for dumbos." I asked him what he meant by that. He replied that they educate "beautiful minds", which he didn't mean in a positive sense. In his opinion, it was a school for children who were too stupid for regular schools, and we were not one of them. Well, I couldn't judge that objectively, but Wally was a teacher and could do just that. She knew the German educational system and the different possibilities. But our father didn't listen to her, he literally stifled her in giving her professional evaluation and judgement of the situation. Logical thinking told me that she had more of an idea about schools. I also felt that he had hurt her feelings by devaluing her qualified suggestion, which I didn't think was right. So, I decided to investigate the matter myself. As it turned out, the Waldorf School at Kräherwald was perhaps a kilometre away from us in a linear distance. But it was on the Killesberg, which we could only reach on foot through the forest. I didn't fancy walking alone through a dark forest. The public transport connection took us through Botnang, then up the Botnang hill, back down into the city, where we then took a bus somewhere else up the hill again. The connection was so unfavourable that I could have expected to be on the road for an hour each way during the day. As schools started before 8.00am, I would have had to leave before 7.00am and perhaps get up an hour earlier to get ready. But as I was certainly not an early riser, the whole thing seemed quite unrealistic to me. Even after one year living in Germany, my biological rhythm hadn't adapted to the German obsession with getting up early. Inwardly, my day still didn't start until shortly before 8am. Even getting up early at 6.30 a.m. at the Thadden had been too early for me, but I would never have made it any earlier! I was already secretly thinking to myself that perhaps I should have stayed at my boarding school after all. Much to my own regret, I had to decide against the Waldorf school. In hindsight, this decision was probably the biggest mistake we made at the time.

But maybe I was just a "dumbo" and we should accept that I should be trained in a dumbo-friendly way. Or maybe I wasn't a dumbo, but rather a bit overwhelmed due to the circumstances of the last two years and therefore blocked. Either way, wasn't I entitled to be treated according to the facts, regardless of the cause? In my father's world, however, there were no daughters who were daft or overburdened, only brilliant ones. In his eyes, he didn't have too high expectations of us either. We had all moved to and from different countries, changed languages, schools and school systems. Why on earth should anything be different this time?

Why shouldn't the third of his children master the move brilliantly? After all, we had experienced this many times before and had experienced our successes. Perhaps my father was right in his very high demands and expectations of us, which at least worked, towards the outside. He created the general conditions, and we had to respond. That was the way it had always worked so far. But hadn't my father overlooked one little thing? Had he not realised that he had always made the demands, but that it was our mother who had turned his demands into successes? Wasn't she the one who spent hours sitting with her first daughter in South America and doing homework with her? Wasn't it she who had always and everywhere chosen where to live, houses and schools, and not my father or us children ourselves? Wasn't it our mother who always made sure that we had an environment in which we could feel comfortable in? Wasn't she the one we could come to with all our questions, school-related and otherwise, and always get an answer? Wasn't it her who had been the haven of tranquility, our centre of peace, in our family? Had my father completely underestimated the role of our mother? Yes, he certainly had and now we had to carry on without her support. Carin seemed to think that we would manage without mother in Stuttgart, without any problems. I had ignored the boarding school's recommendations. Waltraut had given us expert advice about the school, but my father ignored her advice. Where would it all lead?

After we had decided on the schools with the shortest distance to school, Carin and I flew to Canada for the summer holidays. My friend Gabi from the Thadden came with us, for three weeks. She had been a good friend and support throughout the year. We were both very bad at maths at times and decided to study together for an exam. Surprisingly, thanks to studying together, we also achieved the best grades in the class test. Our maths teacher had initially suspected that we had cheated, but as we weren't sitting next to each other, that was out of the question. This joint victory and further visits of mine to her family home had resulted in a close friendship, although we were quite different in character. She had a strong political interest, while mine was still in slumberland. She was older than me and on her 18th birthday, a few weeks before our departure, she had energetically discussed the possible stationing of medium-range nuclear weapons in Germany with her more left-leaning friends. Everyone was obviously against this development. As I had no idea about any of this, she first had to explain the context to me. To summarise, I said that it was a good thing that the Americans were supporting us, protecting us from the Russians or defending us with their medium-range weapons if necessary. I thought it was great that they were prepared to do that! Defending ourselves against the Russians seemed basically logical to me. Growing up in North America, my thinking was decidedly anti-communist. I can't even say where this attitude came from, because we didn't learn it explicitly at school. But anything that wasn't democratic was hostile in my eyes. And that's roughly what I argued. My comments caused general dismay, if not even horror, to this group of peace-loving lefties. Gabi and I were so very different in many ways, and she had to defend me towards her friends. After this incident, we agreed to keep the subject of politics out of our friendship. As I liked Gabi, I really wanted to show her my home country. She had taught me a lot about Germany. And now, she wanted to see everything I had been raving on about to her, all school year. It would be her first trip to North America, to the 'capitalist aggressor', from the point of view of some of her friends.

At that time, a song by Supertramp called "Breakfast in America" was of-ten played on the radio. Gabi changed the lyrics and turned it into a Canadian ver-sion: "Take a jumbo, across the water, like to see Canada!" Then her modified version continued with: "See the boys in Mississauga..." Gabi was really looking forward to the trip. When we finally arrived, Sue took us to all the obligatory sights, just like our mother had done with her on her first visit to Canada, with Henny. It made me feel a bit like a tourist, but Gabi was thrilled with everything. She was most impressed by the huge dimensions and was astonished. What she liked best were the huge trucks, the type of trucks that didn't exist in this size in Germany. She liked the slogan "Keep on trucking", which was often a sticker on the back of the trucks, so much that we gave her the nickname "Keep-on-trucking-Gabi" or "Trucking-Gabi" for short.

We all travelled together "up north" with Ed and his family for a few days to Lake Muskoka, to their weekend cottage. This was where Gabi experienced the real Canadian lake life, including fishing and water skiing. The summer was very nice, and it did was good for us to be in Canada.

Unfortunately, I didn't get to meet many of my friends, again because we were once again staying in Mississauga and not in Oakville. That also made me sad. It was too inconvenient to get to Oakville at short notice and frustrated me a lot. But once we were in Oakville and visited two brothers who were originally from Bavaria. In the basement of their house hung Bavarian flags and a flag of the CSU, the Bavarian version of the CDU, the Christian Democratic Union, which is Christian, conservative and economic liberal politically central to right-wing. The left-leaning Gabi was horrified to see this CSU flag and said to me whether I real-

240

ised what kind of people they were? I certainly replied with a "Nope", as my political interest was still zero. I could only remind her that we wanted to leave politics out of our friendship and apart from that, we were so far away from Germany that German politics really shouldn't be the topic. She reluctantly agreed and we were able to relax again. However, she also had to accept that, although I hadn't realised it before, I was quite conservative and most of the people I knew were too and therefore more to the right than the left politically. She had in fact ended up with the capitalists in Canada, but still had a lot of fun, perhaps especially with them. After all, it was the capitalists who lived in nice houses and had weekend cottages by the lake, and not the politically left-wing ones.

My opinion of the many left-wing extremists in Germany in the 1970s was that it was modern to be against the establishment. But I didn't grow up like that and therefore had little sympathy or empathy for these people. In my opinion, it was easy and rather naïve to express left-wing views, if you lived in a rich western country. And the young people in particular, whose parents were doctors or otherwise belonged to a higher social class and earned a good living, made a rather ridiculous impression on me when expressing their leftish political opinions, rather than my being able to take them seriously. When Gabi expressed her opinion to me that everyone in Canada was quite conformist, by which she meant both fashionable and political, I asked her what was so bad about that? I explained to her that life in Canada was so nice that you didn't really have to fight against the system. There was no need to rebel against it, as most people in this fantastic country were doing well! That was an interesting realisation for both of us. All in all, it was an enriching and enlightening experience for both of us to see my country through her eyes. It was with a heavy heart that we parted from Sue, Ed and Canada at the end of the summer.

After the summer, Carin went to grade 12 at Dillmann-Gymnasium and I went to year nine at Friedrich-Eugens-Gymnasium. We had to take the tram from Botnang down into the city, which took about half an hour from door to door. From then on, we were really on our own during the day. We had to take the tram on the very first day and I was glad that I even knew the name of the stop where we were supposed to get off. Then we went our separate ways. I aimed in my direction, started walking and suddenly a car did an emergency stop right next to me and there was a terrible honking of the horn. I had walked onto the road, at a red-light pedestrian crossing. I hadn't even realised that I was crossing a road! That was not a good start for me. A very nice girl realised how lost I was, introduced herself and took me safely to school. I was very grateful to her for that. Then I looked for my classroom. Now, there I was in front of my new class, and everyone was staring at me, and I felt terribly uncomfortable. The atmosphere at this school was completely different to what I had experienced before, somehow more aggressive. Perhaps this was due to the terribly ugly inner-city school building, most of whose courtyard was tarred. The sight of it made me already long for the beautiful grounds of the Thadden School with its' huge trees, on my first day there.

There was only one empty seat in my class next to a boy called Udo, so I sat down there. He seemed quite shy to me, which was fine with me, because I hoped he wouldn't ask me so many questions about my background, that I didn't want to have to answer. The very next day, I met the nice girl at the tram stop in the morning who had taken me to our school the day before, as a sort of a personal escort. She introduced herself as Sonka and the nice boy next to her as Sven. They both went to my school and obviously had more experience than I did with travelling by tram and crossing roads in the city. I now realised how sheltered we had been in Wieblingen, far away from the city centre in a small suburb. In Oakville, neither trams nor cars had threatened me. This city life didn't seem suit me at all. But as the two people at my stop were very nice, they reminded me more of my friends from Canada. This gave me hope that I might be able to build up a circle of friends in this inner-city school, even though the inner courtyard was too tarred.

Our father worked all day and got his warm lunch in the company canteen. But we didn't get a warm lunch anywhere. He also travelled a lot for work and was often not at home in the evenings. Hence, he also missed dinner, which we had had changed to a traditional German snack time of bread, cheese, cold cuts and some pickles. For us, this meant that at the age of 15 and 17 we had to look after ourselves for the most part, even in the afternoons and evenings, including when it came to food. In the beginning, our father still went to the supermarket once a month to do the bulk shopping, but that stopped. He was now a member of a golf club again and went golfing at least once a week, either on Saturdays or Sundays, but sometimes on both days. He would set off early and return at lunchtime. In those days in Germany, you could only go shopping on Saturdays until 12.00 noon, which was left to us. We didn't have a real family life. I was lucky enough to be friends with Sonka and to be allowed to go home to her again and again. She was one of those people who lived in Botnang in a house and not in one of the "luxurious" flat blocks like many others. Her parents were both doctors and both worked.

It was probably also useful here if both parents worked and had income, so that they could lead a more comfortable lifestyle. This made me think of the parents of a friend from Oakville, who also both worked and could therefore afford a beautiful house. But it never occurred to me before that women could also earn money and thus contribute to the family income. My mother didn't work and that was completely normal to me. My role models seemed very conservative and possibly old-fashioned, maybe outdated. I had to realise that there were other ways of life than what I had experienced at home. As far as the house was concerned, I thought Sonka was very fortunate, and I would have loved to move in there! When I got to know Sven better, I had the impression that I was looking at the Stuttgart version of Matt. Sven was attractive, tall, slim, blond, obviously very intelligent, very athletic and very nice. And he also seemed to be a born leader, a classic alpha male.

There was a boy in my class, Martin, with whom I made friends with rather quickly. He was the only one of my classmates who approached me right at the beginning and started talking to me. I was very happy about his attention, and he was also very charming. He was friendlier than most of the others in my class, usually in a good mood and didn't seem to be bothered by much. When I confessed to him that I was repeating year nine, which I was quite ashamed of, he said: "It doesn't matter. I've done a lap of honour before." I was so relieved that someone other than me had failed! But unlike me, he didn't seem to mind. This was a completely new concept for me! It was probably possible after all, and this did reassure me, because for the first time I thought to myself, maybe it really isn't a bad thing if a school year doesn't work out. From home, I only knew the pressure of having to get everything right first time, but now I thought differently, thanks to his attitude. Who says we're all obliged to succeed straight away? I no longer felt obliged to do that and I felt less like a failure. Martin also invited me home and I thought he had incredibly nice parents. It always made me feel good to meet nice people, but at the same time I was a little envious of his good fortune to have such great parents. Repeatedly experiencing an intact family made me feel even more abandoned by my parents and empty inside. His mother seemed to me to be a strong woman who had her sons under control. Their household was also perfect, which I knew from home, and which always impressed me when I experienced it elsewhere. It was very cozy in their home, and she always looked very well dressed and groomed herself, even though she was also working! I wondered how she managed it all, because I had a mother who was often ill and didn't work and I thought that was normal. But this woman was a new role model for me. I also learnt about the German passion with this family: Soccer! The men would sit in front of the television on Saturdays to watch the sports. I also enjoyed being with this family because they were very nice and radiated a stability that was very attractive to me and which I deeply envied.

In October 1979, our father went for a spa treatment. He explained to me that Bosch was very concerned about the well-being of the upper management. He said that it was his duty and right to take a three-week spa every three years, so he had to do it now. I asked why he had never done this before, as he had been with the company since 1968. He said that this privilege only applies above a certain management level and that it only applies to the most senior managers working in Germany. The company had recognised that the management tasks were very strenuous and that you had to pay particular attention to your health. He was also obliged to take part in health checks. He also said that the "Bosch doctor" had told him that he urgently needed to take a spa to recover from his private stresses and strains. Interesting! With this explanation that he urgently needed to take a spa because the "Bosch doctor" had said so, he left us alone in Stuttgart and went to Baden-Baden, for three weeks. Our father was in the same country as us, but this country wasn't really ours and the city we were living in was still new to us. We had only been at our new schools for a few weeks. We couldn't drive yet either but had to walk or take the tram everywhere. Apart from Wally, we didn't know any other adults in Stuttgart, and she had to work herself. Wally didn't have the time to look after us. Or did she? Couldn't she perhaps have stayed with us in the flat during this time? Or would we have rejected such an opportunity?

During my father's absence, I felt totally abandoned and longed to return to my sheltered boarding school. My idea of a family life for three was probably a fantasy and I had to accept that it didn't and wouldn't exist here. Carin had, how could it be otherwise, a range of interests that she pursued and a large circle of friends. As a result, she was busy and often somewhere, but I wasn't. Sometimes I was at home with Sonka and her family and sometimes with Martin and his family. Both families were very nice to me and a little surprised that my sister and I were at home for three weeks without our father. I was grateful for every invitation, and I think my friends' parents certainly felt my gratitude.

Nevertheless, I now had to cope with the homework on my own, which caused a lot of problems for me. The real problem, however, was that I had learnt

'High' or proper German in Heidelberg, which was also spoken in school lessons there. But now I was in Stuttgart, and everyone was speaking Swabian German, a southern dialect, the students as well as the teachers! This led to my only understood half of what I what I thought to be a broad dialect. In class, I kept asking Udo what the teachers had said. He answered me regularly and with great patience. At home, I then repeated the lesson material, armed with a dictionary to translate what I had "translated" from Swabian into German into English. It was all very tedious. This was not how I had imagined repeating grade nine would be! I thought it would be easy for me as I had heard and seen the material before, even if not understood all of it. But everything seemed completely new and quite foreign to me. The additional burden of household chores, which weighed heavily on me right from the beginning, also got to me. My sister simply didn't join in the chores, as she wasn't interested. I wasn't particularly interested either, but someone had to take care of everything. Looking back, I don't know why our father didn't at least organise a cleaning lady to come around once a week and do the bulk of the cleaning. Instead, everything was left to us.

One day, between homework and housework, I was slumped over in despair when the phone rang. It was Erika from Heubach, who wanted to enquire how we and our father were doing. For some reason, she knew that he was away at his spa and now she thought she should be worried about us. I couldn't explain why she was interested in us; she was just an acquaintance of the family from the late 1960s when we had lived in Heubach. She had also sometimes picked us up from Schwäbisch Gmünd when we travelled from Heidelberg to our grandparents' house with our heavy suitcase. That had been a relief for us. I somehow was of the impression that this woman simply didn't have enough to do, despite being married and having two children, a few years younger than we were, but that she was happy to have an opportunity to drive her husband's car. Be that as it may. That day, her words of interest sounded so sincere and compassionate that I could only cry and didn't even manage to answer her question. It was the first time since we had been in Stuttgart that someone had asked me so directly how I was coping and how I was doing. She tried to calm me down on the phone, but it wasn't possible because I was letting pretty much everything that had built up inside me out of my wounded soul. She said briefly and simply, "Sweetheart, I'm coming to Stuttgart and then we'll go for a nice meal or a stroll or whatever you like." What a great reaction! What a wonderful gesture that touched me deeply in my heart, that someone took the time, to do something with me and my sister. It seemed like a godsend to me. And the fact that it was the very woman whom I disliked as a child, who now wanted to give me attention and time seemed almost unbelievably fortunate. Before we hung up, I asked her why she was prepared to do this, after all, she had to drive a whole hour to Stuttgart, and apart from that, she had two children of her own who needed her. But she replied that she was so sorry to see or hear me suffering like that, and as my mother Magda and she had been very good friends, she would of course do it for her good friend. Oh well, I was even more touched. She was sacrificing her time for her dear departed friend, although, I could not recall my mother ever having referred to this woman as her friend. In fact, there had never been any mention of her, and I was a little perplexed as to whether it was possible that I hadn't realised that there had been a strong friendship between these two women. Albeit I found that unlikely, as my mother and I did spend a lot of time together and we did talk a lot, also of her travels and experiences. She had once been upset about 'another woman'. Could this be her? But as it was right now, I was grateful for her caring commitment, even if I couldn't quite believe or imagine the story or her reasoning. I really enjoyed the afternoon with her.

Welcome to Strasbourg, France

It was precisely this kind of caring, of mothering, that I was missing. My father's girlfriend either didn't have the experience or the inclination for these basically simple, perhaps even banal things like eating together, going for a stroll, shopping or a motherly chat, which were decisive and crucial for my soul. They were the things that made the difference between a woman who had enormous knowledge and capabilities, as Wally did, and one who was simply warm-hearted, with whom I felt understood, as a teenager. But perhaps it was us, who had not allowed Wally's attempts to be motherly towards us. On the other hand, she was very committed to culture and education, which was a good thing. In this regard, she wanted to organise a student exchange for me during the fall holidays, and at the same time, do something to improve my French language skills. She was convinced that I would enjoy French again if I travelled to France and met people my own age. So, I agreed to her suggestion to take part in a student exchange, because I really liked the idea of spending a week in Strasbourg. Until then, I had only learnt French in school and was looking forward to experiencing it in France. I was hoping that they would find me a nice family there - for my emotional well-being -

with a girl my age who had similar interests to me. Maybe she would even do horseback riding, I thought. And this way, I would finally meet someone who shared my interests. I thought that would be great and hoped we could start a friendship for life!

On the day of departure, I was told that there had been a mix-up and that I had by mistake been assigned to a family with two sons. As a result, I wanted to cancel the trip, but my father said I should go anyway, as it was all about improving my French. Apart from that, he didn't have time for me, whilst I was on school holiday, and I would only be bored at home. We hadn't prepared an alternative plan for the holidays. So, I was once again left with no choice and I decided to experience Strasbourg, and off we went, even though I wasn't entirely comfortable with the idea. When we arrived, we received a friendly welcome. But when I saw the boy who was my exchange student, I immediately thought, this can't go well. He was a bit fat, very quiet and withdrawn and spoke almost no German. Unfortunately, I couldn't find anything in common and so I stood there, quite out of place, thinking about leaving with my father. But he had already given a "thank you" gift to give to the parents, then he said goodbye very quickly and left.

The family lived in an apartment in a historic building, possibly from early 1900's, which was beautiful to look at. What at first seemed like a romantic journey back in time in terms of living space, soon turned out to be a very technically backward reality. The light switches were, shall we say antique. And I remember the cold bathroom and the specific instruction to only take a short shower, otherwise the boiler would run out of warm water. The French seemed to shower even less than the Germans and so it was quite astonishing for this family that I went into the shower every morning. They were baffled by this concept. At least the older brother was more open-minded than the rest of the family and spoke pretty good English, so we talked in English. That was nice for the older brother, but didn't help me with my French.

At school, I was introduced as the exchange student from Germany, which didn't bring me any cheers. There was virtually no reaction from the pupils, and I felt a real aversion towards the Germans. I was also ignored during the breaks and was pretty much on my own, as the students had no interest in the "German". However, one girl did talk to me and said that she had been to Germany before and had met nice people there. Well, at least someone who didn't avoid me like the plague. But then came an English lesson that changed all that. I was supposed to read something aloud and I could already feel the little French people's excitement as to whether "the German" could do it at all. So, I read. Everyone was amazed when they realised that I was fluent in English. I would have liked to pretend towards the English teacher that we could all speak English so well in Germany, if only to put a damper on the French arrogance. However, I was not yet a real German who prioritised her own well-being over that of her country. So, I explained that I was from Canada and had only been living in Germany for a year. Lo and behold, I suddenly became interesting and during the next break, some of the little French guys who hadn't wanted to talk to me an hour before, came up to me and spoke to me in English. Although this was interesting for the French, it didn't help my French skills. Suddenly the "German" and the fat boy who had been made fun of before were interesting after all! That's how quickly sympathies can change! From this experience, I learnt to always tell French people first that I was from Canada. For the rest of the week, everyone spoke English to me, and I learnt a little French. I was glad to be able to leave again.

Back in Stuttgart, the classes continued. I had no sense of achievement, and I seriously doubted my decision to come to Stuttgart. Our father was still busy and so was my sister. Day after day, I sat in front of my books and had to teach myself everything. I thought about going back to my boarding school. I wouldn't have to worry about housework or food there. As far as school was concerned, I now understood what Steffi and Veri had told me: I was lucky not to be at a public school because they were worse than the Thadden. I realised that by now, because it really seemed to be almost all about just teaching facts, and that in the Swabian dialect! Inwardly, I had to accept that I was in a real mess, and I was coping much worse here than at boarding school. On top of that, there was something that I had never experienced before. In some cases, the pupils had a negative attitude towards the teachers. There seemed to be a fundamental disrespect, even if only subliminally, for the people who had the task of teaching them something. I had never experienced this before, neither in Canada nor at the Thadden School, and the reason for this behaviour was a mystery from me. Perhaps it was the age we were at, around 15, which predestined them to be rebellious towards authority. Or maybe it was because I was attending a school in the city centre for the first time and the interactions were simply more superficial and rougher. Whatever the reason, I didn't like it, and it didn't suit me. My whole situation was unsatisfactory, and I also knew that I wouldn't achieve good grades under all these circumstances.

It wasn't long before the Christmas holidays, which I was really looking forward to. By then we had all become keen skiers, and it was clear that we would be travelling to Switzerland again. This time, there would only be three of us, I thought. Then our father told us that Wally would of course be coming along too. I didn't have anything against it in principle, but I would have been happy if it had only been the three of us travelling together and we had our father to ourselves for once, so that we could have his undivided attention. At least I hoped that way we would be able to get closer to each other and talk. But after all, he was newly in love and why shouldn't he take his new partner with him? So, the four of us would be travelling together after all. Basically, I was glad that my father had a steady girlfriend, because a relationship seemed to do him good.

After our wonderful holiday, we came back, and the stress of school started again for me. In the meantime, however, I had developed a real fear of failure. On the one hand, I didn't want to imagine my father's reaction if I came home with another bad report card. Secondly, thanks to his very clear words, I now realised that I wasn't allowed to repeat grade nine again and if I didn't manage it, it would be the end of my school career. What a nightmare! I couldn't believe how quickly my wonderful and carefree life had turned into a package of worries with fears of failure and the future. Then I got my school report card and lo and behold, mine was bad. My father couldn't believe it and asked me how I could be so stupid as to still not be able to understand the school material, which I was now hearing for the second time. I was very hurt by his reaction and his comment because I realised that he couldn't imagine that I was overwhelmed by the whole situation. I was lucky that Wally was with us because she seemed to be able to understand me and defended me. She was also able to tell him that she had probably been right in recommending that I go to Waldorf school and that the result would certainly have been better there. Wally really realised that German was still a foreign language for me that I still had to master. I was glad that she was with us and could put my father in his place with her reasoning. I admired her courage in confronting him with her views. I had never seen that before. I wouldn't have been able to defend myself against the accusations and the constant comparison with my sister, who, unlike me, was better able to cope with the language and the new situation.

At first, 1 was almost like paralysed and didn't know what to do. In my desperation, I called Mrs. von Egen in Heidelberg and told her about my situation. She listened to me carefully and, in her generosity, spared me a lecture along the lines of: "I told you so." She said that I could come back to the boarding school and that we would certainly be able to do manage a successful completion of grade nine, but I would have to be prepared to do a lot for it. I was prepared to do that because I didn't want to accept that I wouldn't go back to school after the summer holidays. However, I was quite afraid to talk to my father about it. But he was on a business trip anyway and I had to wait until he came back.

Parenting via postcard

In February 1980, our father wrote us a rather exuberant postcard from Abidjan, Cote d' Ivoire, Ivory Coast, from a business trip to Africa: "...it's about time to come home. What a difference here compared to Lagos, it's a relief". I took it as if he was in a pretty good mood and therefore possibly open to a conversation on his return home. He came back, had a huge amount of work at the office and visited Wally in between. Suddenly he had to go away again, and I hadn't managed to talk to him.

In March, my father wrote us a postcard from Tehran, Iran. Only a year earlier, there had been a revolution there that had overthrown the monarchy and now the so-called "liberators" were oppressing the people. There was no room for open communication. He wrote: "I've been here for three days, I like it quite well, it's spring here". In terms of the text, it was a short and meaningless postcard. It contained no message, and I couldn't really do anything with it other than realise that it was spring in Iran. At that time there was political tension between Iran and Iraq. As I was at home with the flu, I had the radio on all day and listened to the news every hour. Every hour on the hour, there were reports of the possibility of an imminent war between Iran and Iraq, which made me completely nervous. I was 15 years old and already a half-orphan. The thought that my father could be involved in a war in a foreign country with even the slightest probability was unbearable for me. I didn't want to become an orphan. I could no longer stand this kind of up-bringing from afar and with greetings on a postcard. I felt completely abandoned by my father and it wasn't enough for me to just have my sister here, who was always out and about anyway. I wanted to have an adult here with me, a sensible and responsible adult. Whereas before I had "only" been afraid that my parents would be struck down by illness and taken from their lives too soon, now I was afraid that my father would be affected by an arbitrary act of war.

Back at home, my father told me in detail about his trip. He told me that he had someone at his side in Iran who was his contact person and accompanied him to his appointments. He explained to me that the postcard from Iran was so brief because he assumed that mail sent abroad would be censored. He wanted to write as neutrally as possible so that there was no reason for Iranian inspectors to destroy the card instead of sending it. I had understood his explanation and was now even more worried. I increasingly realised that he had been in a country where you were not allowed to express your opinion openly, which I disliked very much. He told me that it was so strict there under the current government that you also had to give a salute to the leader Khomeini at a given time or occasion. My father had witnessed such an occasion and told me that he had almost been arrested. In fact, he was arrested but was immediately released. He was in a group that was supposed to officially greet the picture of Khomeini, but he didn't join in. He was asked to do the salute as well, but he refused to do so. He said he was a foreigner and therefore not affected by such regulations. He was then arrested. His contact saved him by saying that this foreigner was a complete ignoramus and that he apologised for his behaviour. This story disturbed me beyond words. I thought my father was quite a nutcase who recklessly jeopardised his freedom, just to get his way. I thought he was crazy and incredibly irresponsible towards me. I was sick with grief, and he had also risked being arrested.

But I was wrong about his motivation, because I couldn't recognise the deeper meaning of his protest. He told me that after the Nazi era he had sworn never again to salute a dictator or a power that was not based on free will. I was amazed at his determination and straightforwardness. On the one hand, I was proud of his principles, but on the other, I could only hope that his determination would not put him in danger again.

Now was the right time to express my wish to return to boarding school to my father. He looked at me with a look I didn't understand, but didn't say anything about the subject. Perhaps he hadn't realised how serious I was and how bad my school performance was. He didn't pay any further attention to me and my concerns but did what he always did: he worked a lot in the office and visited Wally in between, went golfing and then on a business trip. I was desperate by now.

In March, my father wrote us a postcard from Lagos, Nigeria. It depicted locals in traditional dress, standing next to each other in a row. He couldn't resist a little joke and wrote: "Here are some of my spark-plug customers, they are still waiting for their cars!". His little joke became the basis of one of our other family

251

jokes. Whenever we saw people standing together and didn't know what they were doing there, the comment would be "These are Dad's spark-plug customers, but they're still waiting for their cars!". We always thought it was hilarious and laughed about it for a long time.

It was only when he returned from this trip that we found the time to talk seriously about my problems. He finally got on the phone to Mrs. von Egen. He didn't know that I had already checked the situation beforehand. So, they had a brief conversation. He then agreed to my request that I be allowed to return to Heidelberg immediately after the holidays.

Heidelberg 1980

Since I had failed in the real world, I was very happy to be "locked up" and looked after in my boarding school. I was allowed back into the "little house", with my former house mother and was very relieved to be able to live in orderly conditions again, without having to worry about housework, food, shopping or anything like that. There was only one free place in the little house, so I inevitably ended up in a room with Katrin, who was about two years older than me. She seemed very mature and enlightened to me and was a mixture of what I had never encountered before, a hippie, rebel, vamp and lawyer's daughter. That was a bit too much for me and at first quite intimidating. She made it very clear to me that she was not at all happy about having a younger girl in her room, and on top of that, such a well-behaved, well-adjusted, conservative one. So, I tried to conduct myself as quietly and inconspicuously as possible. After all, I had experienced such unfavorable and sometimes hostile feelings from my sisters at times, and I was good at staying out of their way. Since we were very different, I could only hope that it our sharing a room would work out, until the summer holidays. After all, I had no other place to go. It had to work. I had to make it work.

I was placed in a different class, which was new to me. There was only one free seat available there, in the front row, so I sat there. I knew that from now on I could not waste a single day when it came to studying, and I concentrated on the lessons accordingly. The first English lesson came, and I felt relieved that at least I would understand everything in this subject. But then I was in for a big surprise. Our English teacher had studied in Great Britain and had a very strong Scottish accent. She was a very small, slim woman, dressed very conservatively, and had an ugly face. I had never seen anything like this woman before and never heard an accent like that. When she started reading, I was amazed at the different ways of pronouncing "my" English. When our teacher read out the title of a story called "A crooked roof", I had to ask her what she had just said. I had heard something like "e gruggd ruff" and couldn't imagine what that was. When I posed my question, she and the rest of the class understood that I could indeed speak English. Yet still, I only partially understood her explanation for my question. Then a girl from behind gave an explanation in an English accent that I didn't recognize either, but which I at least understood! The girl was called Conny and, like me, was German, but had lived in Malaysia for a few years. I was so happy to have a like-minded person in my class, another German-foreigner! Conny was half a head taller than me, had a broad back and somewhat resembled a soccer player. I later learnt that she played tennis. One day, when one of the girls asked me to come with her to watch Conny play on TV, I grasped that she played professionally. That was impressive! In any way, Conny and I could laugh a lot together, and we did, especially in English class, which later led to our English teacher letting us stay in the hallway during class because we were disrupting the lesson with our constant giggling about her accent. So, we spent a few hours in the hallway and even played Mastermind, until we decided to go back to class because we had a sneaking suspicion that there might be a catch to our not being in class.

In the first week with the new class, I soon had French lessons. I was supposed to read aloud, which worked reasonably well. Then I was supposed to translate the text from French into German, which didn't work as well. I explained to our teacher that I could translate French into English very well, but not as well into German, and thought she would be able to understand and accept that. But she didn't. Instead, she insisted on the translation into German, which I found quite annoying. Why was she so intolerant? I offered to translate into the language of one of our subjects and not into Swahili! How could someone who knows languages be so petty? I couldn't comprehend it. It should be about me proving to her that I understood the text, but I could only do that with the direct translation from French into English. Instead, I stuttered around in German, and no one would have ever guessed that I had been learning French since the 6th grade. There was a girl sitting directly behind me who recognized my problem and whispered the translation to me. I was very grateful for her support, even if it meant we were cheating. Her name was Ariane, and she was also German. But, as I quickly discovered, she had very good language skills. Unlike the other girls, she could already speak English well and some French, which she had probably learned during her time of going to school Switzerland. I was also very impressed by her whispering skills. Ariane was a whole head taller than me, had long blonde hair and sparking blue eyes. She had amazing energy and a positive attitude, which I particularly noticed because most of the other girls didn't have either. With time, as we got to know each other better, I came to grasp that she seemed deeply hurt inside. Perhaps that was precisely why she had the ability to show compassion and help someone who was stranded, like me. I liked both girls straight away and so I had made two new friends on my first days at school. With time, my roommate Katrin got used to me and, to everyone's surprise, we were fine with living in the same room. We sometimes even went into town together on Saturdays. She went to the bars, drank beer and was hit on by the Americans. I sat next to her and hoped that we would get out of there safe and sound and that she would still be sober. During the week, however, I was swamped with a lot of studying material and, as I was used to, I also had a few hours of tutoring. This time, however, my attitude towards learning was different; I wanted to learn, and I absolutely wanted and had to get through the school year. I couldn't and didn't want to get used to the idea that I was a failure at school. Unfortunately, that was the impression everyone who got to know me during those years had. Very few people understood that I was struggling to integrate into this country and with this language. They certainly couldn't imagine that I had not had any problems at school before. I was German, so I should be able to speak German. That is what I was told and what was expected. But the fact that I was so-to-speak a reintegrated person, a returnee, was not really considered. I still felt like a foreigner.

Already then, it was fashionable to simply denigrate a lot of things that came from North America. It is possible that some Germans did this to compensate for their feelings of inferiority towards the still-present occupiers. They lumped "my" Canada and the USA together, and probably added other countries as well, and called it "America," which would be roughly the same as lumping all German-speaking countries together under the term "European German-speaking." I was simply told by the teachers at my school that the Canadian school system was probably no good, if I had never had any problems at school before. How arrogant and ignorant they all were. And how unfair they were to me. Can a young person - especially in puberty - really endure so much in one or two years and still perform at their best? No, not me, I was emotionally overwhelmed by everything and even having a higher intelligence is of little use, when the soul is suffering so much that the brain goes blank. That was the situation at the time, but unfortunately this possibility was not even considered. My failure in the German school system had nothing to do with the quality of the Canadian school system.

That same month, I received a postcard from my father from Johannesburg, South Africa, at the boarding school. He wrote: "How are you, have you settled in well at E.v.T.? It is nice there. It is bearable here too, wonderful autumn weather." I was under the impression that my father was doing well, since I - his problem child - was no longer in Stuttgart and he did not have to worry about me. He was now paying others to do that. He really enjoyed his work and all the traveling, and I realized that this way of life was exactly what he was after, and he enjoyed being involved with many different cultures. I gradually began to understand that he had perhaps been doing the same job in Canada for too long and had perhaps become bored because he could not work internationally there. It was sad for me to realize that "my" Canada, or at least the job he had had there, had not fulfilled him. In stark contrast to him, I did not need so much variety and a multicultural environment. Canada was enough for me to be very happy; I loved the peace and stability we experienced there and the incredibly friendly people. It was a shame, I thought, that he had not managed to find a working environment there that was just as international and varied. I simply had to accept that we had completely different needs. What made me happy bored him. What fulfilled him overwhelmed me. We were completely different, and I was at the mercy of this fact. These realizations gradually gave me the feeling of surrendering to everything I had to accept.

Nevertheless, this time everything was different at the boarding school. I met a lot of nice girls, including one who lived near Stuttgart, named Tina. I was very happy about that, because it meant we could take the train to Stuttgart together and meet there at the weekend. She was also relatively new to the area and didn't have any friends there yet. This led to another friendship, although Tina and I were very different, right from the start. She was incredibly active, almost restless and, to my taste, much too thin. I, on the other hand, was more inactive, quiet and still had my steamed dumpling proportions. My father later said that we looked a bit like "Laurel and Hardy". That was his view. Tina couldn't stand my father. This antipathy was mutual. She was the only person who later described him as mean and selfish, which really impressed me. At first, necessity had brought us together, but that was better than if neither of us would not have had anyone, right? My father should have been happy that I had a friend at all and one whose family background was similar. She had lived with her family in different countries, "like us" and so she knew what it was like to be a newcomer. Perhaps that was the only thing we had in common and perhaps it was the inner emptiness because of the friends we had left behind in the distance, that brought us together. Tina, Ariane and I travelled every other weekend by second-class train to Stuttgart, Ariane, then on to Munich. It wasn't easy from the start, as I liked both very much, but the two of them didn't seem to get on very well. But that's just how it was at boarding school, strangers were thrown together and not everyone could get along.

At school I had to catch up on a lot of lessons. It was downright catastrophic how much I had missed and how much I still had to learn. Mrs. Schmid and I realized that it was rather unlikely that I would pass the school year. But I was ambitious and so I voluntarily studied for hours every day. One day, in my frustration, I said to her that I wouldn't have to go through all this if my mother hadn't died, and she said, "You're not the only one whose mother died." Oh really, I thought to myself and asked her for a specific example. She said, "Why don't you talk to Doro? She lost her mother even earlier." So, I did, and that's how I met Dorothea, who was a baroness, but everyone just called her Doro. She seemed very nice, capable and content. She had been living at the boarding school for several years and seemed to be an integral part of the institute. She knew everyone, including all the teachers and educators. She held additional duties, such as the school road-crossing guard service, which she even headed. This girl seemed genuinely happy to have her place at the boarding school. However, she gave me the impression of a child who had received little love and attention. Sometimes she seemed a bit like a wet dog, a little neglected, but happy to have the warmth of the living room. She told me that her mother died when she was only five years old and that there were several housekeepers until her father remarried. I thought to myself that I had was more fortunate, in two respects. Firstly, I had my mother for eight years longer than she had hers. Secondly, I did not have to be brought up by a stranger. I was very happy and grateful about both things, and it eased my pain. On the other hand, I tried to explain to Mrs. Schmid that Doro had it better than me, because at least she had not lost her home and her homeland, and she did not have to cope with a new school system and an almost foreign language. My argument was correct, but I still received little understanding. Because, as I had often heard in Germany: "But you are German, and this is your home country." Back then, I could not react to this statement or correction from others as I do today. Today, I can clearly say: a passport does not make you a local. In my heart, I was Canadian, and one is a local from where one's heart belongs.

And so, a friendship with Doro began back then, and it was she who, when I asked whether other girls had "problems" too, drew my attention to other and sometimes quite brutal blows of fate suffered by the girls living in the boarding school. The house mothers were not allowed to tell us about the difficult or serious cases, for reasons of discretion, because the girls were supposed to have a "normal" life at the boarding school, without being burdened by the prejudices of others. Contrary to appearances, this boarding school was not exclusively for "higher class", privileged or spoiled daughters, who only knew the sunny side of life. There was a series of girls there who had little to laugh about at home, regardless of their parents' financial status. Some didn't even have parents. Some had a parent who was mentally ill and unable to look after their children. That's how I found out that there were also girls at the boarding school who were there with the help of a scholarship, which in turn was made possible by donations from former students. This way, girls whose parents were in financial distress were also accepted. I was very surprised by the social aspect of the Elisabeth von Thadden boarding school, having falsely thought that it was 'just' for rich kids. But then I was told about the founder of the boarding school, who was a deeply religious, convinced and practicing Christian. She was such a staunch Christian that even during the Hitler regime, she hid girls and women of Jewish and non-Aryan origin on her property, i.e. in the very buildings that we used. Whenever possible she also helped people to escape abroad. Her opinion of the Nazi regime was well known and led to her school being closed. She herself was arrested and sentenced to death in 1944. The most astonishing thing about this story for me was that it was said that Elisabeth von Thadden walked to her execution praying and singing. My opinion of the "Thadden" changed completely with this new knowledge and insight. I began to understand that this was a school whose basic ideas were good and that it represented much more than I had previously realized. From then on, I was proud to be at this very institution.

Fly Daddy, fly

In May 1980 my father wrote me a postcard from Kuwait, from the Sheraton Hotel. He wrote: "36°C, sunny, soon it will be even warmer, that's Kuwait. Lots of sand, lots of oil, lots of cars and lots of nice people who want nothing more than to be happy and earn lots of money!" Admittedly, I was always happy to receive a card from him. He was thinking of me and the other girls were quite envious of my many interesting postcards from other countries. At the beginning of June another postcard arrived from a business trip to the Far East: "After Singapore, Jakarta and Manila I've landed here. I'm still doing well; I hope you are too - again." This was in reference to the fact that I was very worried about my school performance and had been rather desperate at times. I received another card from the same trip with the text: "This is still Tokyo, but tomorrow it will be Peking. I just talked to Sue; she is fine - so am I". It was a very nice card of Mount Fuji with a flower landscape in the foreground. Along with his signature, he drew a "happy face", a smiley with slit eyes! He just couldn't resist making jokes and I was of the impression that he was getting increasingly better. He had immersed himself in his new job and was developing professionally. In contrast, I had great difficulty coping with my tasks and was not developing particularly well. His rise - my fall.

In June 1980, he wrote another card from Jeddah (KSA). The picture was "The Holy Mosque at Night". He wrote: "Today I am in Jeddah, tomorrow I am going back to Riyadh. It is still very hot and sandy - but business is going well. Best wishes, also to Mrs. Schmid". I wasn't sure what he wanted to express with the greetings. Had he taken a liking to my house mother, or did he just want to say hello in a friendly way? Or maybe he was grateful that someone was looking after his daughter, and he wanted to express that with the greeting? But maybe he was happy that he could continue to travel to his heart's content without having to feel guilty about leaving his youngest daughter unsupervised at home.

The end of the school year had come. I had barely made it through the 9th grade. It had been another nightmare school year, and I was glad it was over. My father said that I didn't deserve a summer vacation because my school performance was so poor. I thought that was very unfair considering that it was the change of country and language that had turned me into a student with learning difficulties. Despite his opinion, he did agree to the trip to Canada, but the real reason was that I should stay somewhere for the summer. He had to keep working and traveling and didn't want my sister and me at home for the six weeks of school vacation. So, he passed us on to Sue, who had in the meantime started working, and understandably did not really like the whole thing. We seemed to be completely redundant, and I didn't feel welcomed anywhere.

After we had spent the summer in Canada again and again in the wrong place, namely in Mississauga instead of with our friends in Oakville, I went back to the boarding school in Heidelberg and was happy to have a place where I could live and be looked after in terms of food and other things. I was allowed to live in the little house again - with my still very valued and cherished Mrs. Schmid - and was able to move back into "my" old room, where I had spent the first year. My new roommates were Susanne and Heide. Susanne came from Karlsruhe and had come to the boarding school because she had missed a lot of school, due to health reasons and was now supposed to concentrate exclusively on her academic performance at the boarding school. She was a tall blonde girl, slim and lanky. She didn't look at all sporty and wore thick glasses that made her eyes disappear, so that at first you could hardly see that she had very beautiful green eyes. She dressed very conservatively and over the course of the school year taught me the meaning of some brand names, such as Burberry. On the outside, she seemed quite cool at first, just as I imagined a cool northern German to be.

Heide came from Saarland, a small state in the southwest of Germany bordering onto France and explained to me that she had missed a lot of school because of a death and had now come to boarding school to catch up. She didn't really say much more than that. She didn't seem particularly interested in anything other than studying. Fashion-wise, with her skin-tight jeans, she looked somewhat of a rock-band groupie. The only thing that sometimes made her somewhat distant eyes flash was when she talked about her younger brother, Bernd, racing go-karts. She was sure that he would become a great racing driver one day. She infected us with her conviction so much that we also stuck stickers on our notebooks with the names of go-kart races or racetracks. Contrary to both of my roommates, I was still Canadian-sporty conservative in my style of dress. Since I had only just barely made it to 9th grade, I too had to concentrate very hard on my schoolwork. So, there we were, three girls, all very different, all of whom had been through something terrible and now all of whom had to concentrate. Would that work? My new roommates were quiet and initially quite reserved, so I did what you do at boarding school, you don't ask any more questions. But I didn't have the feeling that I would warm up to these two girls either and thought to myself how good it had been with Veri and Steffi.

You never know when you get to know someone at boarding school, whether the reasons they give for being there are true. They could be partially true or completely made up. So, it was always interesting to hear what they said, but you had to assume that it might not be true. Then there were also girls who gave no reason at all, the quiet ones. I once found out that a girl was at boarding school because her mother had committed suicide, but didn't want to leave her daughter alone. So, the mother first tried to kill her daughter with sleeping pills and when she thought she had succeeded, she committed suicide. The daughter survived and was now - anonymously - amongst us. I knew for sure that my mother had died, and my father had no time for me or, to put it another way, that he was a successful businessman. So, I had one dead parent and one absent, which is why I had to be looked after. I was always suspicious when the girls had two parents who were both still alive and together under the same roof. I always asked myself: Why were they at boarding school? And I had the feeling that it might be worse for the girls this way around, if everything at home seemed intact from the outside, because then something might not be intact after all, otherwise the girls would live at home, right? But they either did not want to, couldn't or weren't allowed to talk about it openly.

I had called my father to tell him about my new roommates, Susanne and Heide. As always, he asked the girls' last names. When I told him what Susanne's last name was, he said, "Ask her if her father's name is Dietward. If so, tell her to give her father my regards." I was a little surprised that my father thought he might possibly know my roommate's father. How could he, when he had lived abroad for most of his adult life? But still, I told Susanne what my father had said, and she passed it on to her father during the next phone call. Then I heard from her, "My father said that if your father's first name was Hans, then I should send him my regards back." During the next phone call, my father explained to me that they had both worked at Pfaff for years and therefore knew each other. Since the greetings had been formal, but not warm, I assumed that the two had probably not been friends. Susanne and I could hardly believe this coincidence and, precisely because we both suspected that our fathers had not gotten on well, the fact that we were now sharing a room together was quite strange for us.

I was increasingly doing better at boarding school. Compared to my first year, I had nice friends this time, which made things much more pleasant. In that respect, the criticism in the boarding school report from the first year was correct, that I should have made more of an effort to socialize instead of isolating myself with Carin and Heidi. But at the time, I was still in such shock because of all the changes that I had to cling to what was familiar. The shock had now worn off and in its place, I felt an emptiness at not having anyone at home to look after me. In addition to the emptiness, there was also a bit of despair due to the enormous pressure of having to pass 10th grade at the first try, because there would not be a second chance to do so. The cycle of school, homework help, studying and more studying started again. I was very happy to have Ariane with me to help with my homework. She tried to make learning easier for me by explaining things I didn't understand. In addition to that, she always knew how to make a joke, sharp on the edge between tolerated and disruptive, into the otherwise dry homework sessions, with her unique sense of humor. At some point she told me that her brother was at a boarding school in Switzerland, where he didn't like it at all, which is why she wrote to him regularly to cheer him up. So, I joined in and wrote him a letter or two. It felt good to help another suffering person in this simple way, and as she assured me, he was also happy to receive the mail. It was only then that I found out that Ariane's father had recently died and that she was also a half-orphan. Perhaps that was what brought us together.

To my own surprise, I didn't really miss my sister. On the contrary, I was glad not to have her around me, because when we were at boarding school, she was so full of hatred towards the school that under her influence I had not even thought of seeing the positive sides of the school. I now felt a bond between the girls at the boarding school, because we were all in the situation of not being able or wanting to live at home. The reasons were various. Some simply wanted to go to a better school, that they did not have in their hometowns. Others were half-orphans, orphans, children of divorce or children of single working mothers or fathers. Sometimes I felt as if we were mostly a bunch of leftovers. That connected us in our humor, in our helplessness, in our hopelessness. Because here we were at home. Even the girls who did not particularly like each other at least had respect for the others, because you never knew what the other girl had been through. In this sense, boarding school was an enormous life lesson, a unique experience to develop or improve our social skills. For some girls, boarding school offered a surrogate family, with surrogate mothers and siblings, arguments and reconciliation, rules and discontent, but also security and protection. For some girls, it was more than they had at home, wealth or poverty. Speaking of poverty: I once found out that the head mistress "Benita", who some of us found to be too strict but who nevertheless had a good, if partly hidden, heart, even bought a winter coat from of her own money, for a girl who got almost nothing from home.

On my travel weekends, I noticed that my father and Carin seemed to have everything under control in Stuttgart. Carin had a lot to study for her A-levels but still had time for friends and activities. She had also signed up for a student exchange with a girl from Australia, and when I came home one day, she was there. She was blonde and with an Australian sunshine radiance, quite extroverted, and gave the impression that she could become a real party animal one day. She was wearing a coat made of kangaroo fur, which I had never seen before, and we couldn't help but ask whether it was easier to jump in a coat like that. She found our fall weather incredibly cold. Carin and this girl made fun of the German weather and all sorts of other things. She was most pleased that she had ended up with us instead of a typical German family. It wasn't good for her German skills, but she had a lot of fun with us.

Wedding

The fall holidays came and with them, Sue and Ed's wedding. My father and I would fly together from Stuttgart to Toronto via London. First, I had a rather unpleasant incident at the airport in Stuttgart. My father and I went to passport control together, he was waved through, and I was not at first. The police officers asked me where I was born and I answered: "In Caracas, Venezuela." They looked at me very suspiciously but then let me go. My father and I were then separated for a physical search. I went to the women's booth, he to the men's. In the booth, a second policewoman joined the one already waiting there and asked me the same questions as before and more. I then thoroughly was tapped down and searched, all over my body, which I found quite unpleasant, and I also had to take off some items of clothing. The whole thing became too much for me, and I was under the impression that there had been a misunderstanding. So, I asked if they could get my father to come along, but this only irritated these women more than it helped me. They said no to my request and instead asked me more questions: where I was flying to and for how long and why via London and what I was planning to do there. I answered: "To Toronto for a week, for my sister's wedding and we are flying via London because that's how my father bought the tickets." Meanwhile, somewhere I heard my father arguing quite loudly with someone. That seemed to have helped because a male colleague investigated my cabin and said that they should let me go, which the policewomen were reluctant to do. I was relieved and was about to leave when one of the policewomen grabbed my hair and pulled down hard. I was horrified! What was this crazy woman doing to me? I shouted at her accordingly and said that it had hurt and why on earth did she dare to pull my hair?! She simply said that she just wanted to make sure that I was not wearing a wig. After having felt unjustly attacked, I was very happy to see my father, who was obviously upset and very happy to see me again. I told him everything that had happened and he called for the chief officer in duty in such a tone, that had the policemen follow his orders. My father apparently mentioned some important names from the worlds of business, politics or the judiciary and threw around legal terms and threats, which worked. The chief officer in charge listened to our story, then spoke to the policewomen and then apologized to us for the whole thing. His explanation was that one of the policewomen thought that she saw a resemblance in me, to a wanted terrorist. Great, I thought, that too! I could not believe it. She seemed to have missed the fact that I was only 16, and the woman they were look-ing for was perhaps 20 or older. This policewoman thought my passport was a fake, my appearance a cover, that my father was my father was a lie, and that I was a threat. But luckily everything was cleared up. For me, though, it was a very frightening experience. There they were again, Germany and its' terrorists. It was what I had thought three years earlier in Canada: I don't want to move to a country that has such problems. And now this problem had become mine too, even if only for a short time. Accordingly, I was happy, happier than ever, to leave Germany.

When we arrived in Canada, there were a lot of things waiting for us to do and some waiting to be paid, by my father. Carin had flown separately because of a chemistry exam, but soon we were all together. It was a nice feeling and the first time in a long time that the four of us were together. My father had already paid for the flight tickets for himself, Carin and me, but also for Sue's best friend Henny, because she was invited and was to be the maid of honour. The four of us girls stayed with Sue in her apartment. My father preferred a hotel room for himself. The final preparations had to be made quickly. I drove with my father to his tailor in Toronto, where he had picked up the suits that he had ordered there on his last visit. My father only wore tailor-made suits and that tailor in Toronto remained his tailor. The beautician who would do our make-up for the ceremony came to see us for a make-up testing session, and the dresses had to be tried on. Sue's wedding dress still had to be finished and paid for. Then there was the going-away suit for Sue's honeymoon, the flowers, the food, the church, the priests, the band, the banquet hall and the limousine. There was a lot that Sue had prepared, and it was very impressive. We had a lot of appointments and invitations, but the whole thing was also a lot of fun. The night before the wedding we celebrated with the bridesmaids and after the others had gone home, we stayed up for a long time. Sue and Henny continued celebrating, which was probably their farewell to Sue's bachelorette life. Before going to bed, Carin and I hid all the alarm clocks we could find, so that the next morning Sue, hungover and cursing, had to go looking for them at 6:00 a.m. She had an abnormally early appointment at the hairdresser and was probably not feeling well after the little sleep she had gotten.

The wedding was to be an ecumenical ceremony in a Catholic church in Mississauga, with a Catholic priest and a Protestant pastor. Ours was our faithful pastor Knaack, the Catholic priest was called Bonk. So, Carin and I had something to laugh about again: the Knaack and Bonk wedding! We thought that sounded incredibly funny! Unfortunately, we were simply not old enough to have respect for an ecumenical wedding, which was a real novelty at the time. Pastor Knaack had to grin when he saw us again, the sisters who had once been his difficult confirmation candidates, the "pliers" as he had called us. I don't know what he really thought when he saw us, but he was surprisingly friendly towards us. On the day of the wedding, it was pouring with rain and Sue said that was a bad omen for their marriage. My father calmed her down and said that she had to look at it this way: with the weather being like this, things can only get better! Sue looked fantastic, despite the rain. The wedding was beautiful, the large church was full to the last seat.

Then we went to the banquet hall, which was perfectly prepared for 320 people. After the photo session, the first guests arrived, and we stood at the entrance and greeted them all with a handshake or a kiss. It seemed like a very long time before the hall was full and our hands were sore from all the handshakes. This small inconvenience did not spoil the fantastic atmosphere in the hall. Speeches were given and the multi-course menu left nothing to be desired. The dancing that followed gave us exercise and joy. The whole evening was magical. At the end, the young bride and groom said goodbye, and everyone was visibly moved by their happiness, for which they had been preparing for years. It had been a wonderful celebration.

Shortly after this wonderful event, everyone returned to real life. Back at the boarding school, the girls asked if it was true that I had flown across the Atlantic, just for a week? I had to answer that it was true. However, I always added that I had flown for my sister's wedding. Despite the explanation, some classmates were speechless about this long journey for such a short stay. Many of them had never boarded a plane before and very few had even been overseas. I tried to put the matter into perspective because I noticed that the whole thing had not gone down well with them. They seemed jealous and some were downright angry that I could do something like that, but they could not. For some, traveling like that was an ostentatious display of financial superiority. I couldn't believe how hostile some people were being towards me, due to this matter. What I was experiencing was pure envy. I then told only a very few carefully selected girls, including my roommates, that 320 people attended the wedding. The others would have been overwhelmed by the dimension of the event.

I also discussed this hostility from some girls with Ariane when she came to see me on one of our boring Sunday afternoons, when there was nothing else to do but drink tea. Apart from being in the same class and homework supervision together, we were in the meantime also sometimes going to the orthopedist together and occasionally went shopping in Heidelberg on Saturdays. I was the one of us who always had extra pocket money. My father gave me 50 DM a month, which meant I had more than twice the extra pocket money, than the amount of monthly allowance, which we were officially given by the boarding school. In contrast to most of the other "interns", I was well off in terms of pocket money. Ariane was not the only one who always had less than I did. But that Sunday I told her that I didn't understand this hostility from the other girls. After all, it wasn't showing off to go to your sister's wedding! It wasn't my fault that I had to travel far to take part in the occasion. The girls didn't see that this international lifestyle was not to be envied, but on the one hand it was the result of the hard work of my father, and on the other hand it brought me little joy. They seemed to confuse my family situation with that of a luxurious jet set who flew to Monaco or somewhere else to party. In my family, we spent a lot of money to see each other, and I was annoyed at the false envy I was shown. And I said to Ariane that one girl even went so far as to accuse me of only being interested in surrounding myself with rich people. Ha!

How wrong I thought that was! I didn't choose my friends based on their wealth, but on whether I found them nice or not. She looked at me and said, "You have no idea, do you?" and I asked her what I was supposed to have no idea about. She said: "About my grandfather." I didn't know what her grandfather had to do with the subject of hostility, but I suspected that she was trying to tell me something. She continued by say that her grandfather was a successful businessman. OK, I told her, you don't have to be ashamed of that. None of us are responsible for the jobs or careers our parents or grandparents have. My grandfather was also successful, having been the director of a mid-sized company, and my father was successful as well. So, she came out with it and explained to me that her grandfather was one of the biggest entrepreneurs in Germany. It turned out that he was a publisher and founder of what was one of the largest publishing firms in the country and in Europe. OK, that was a different dimension to what I was familiar with from my family. But I did not like her more or less because of it. I did, however, find it strange that she always had less pocket money than I did.

It was lovely for me and the others when the time of Advent began, which was traditionally celebrated very devoutly at the Thadden. With the simplest and perhaps most beautiful things, such as fir branches and candles, our dining hall was decorated in a warm and inviting way for Advent. We all sat together like one big family and sang Christmas carols. This probably warmed all our hearts, and for some, maybe even more so, than being with their own family.

For Christmas, we, the almost-family, Dad, Wally and I, went to Arosa in Switzerland. Of course, as always, we were looking forward to the upcoming skiing adventure and, especially this year, to a new ski resort. But the sentiment was different than usual, and this seemed due to Wally's. She was sad and after a few days my father had to speak frankly to me. He had already received the suggestion of a transfer in the fall, which he had told us in passing, but we did not take it seriously, because he had only just been transferred. But now it was already the case that he had agreed to this transfer. I could not believe what I was hearing. He had only been in Germany for two years and now he was not only going to be transferred, but also to a different country?! But how did he imagine that this was going to happen? We had only learned the German language to a certain degree, enough to cope with school. I was still having difficulties at school and my sister was in grade 13, and therefore about to take her A-levels. He couldn't seriously think that we could cope with another change of country and language! No, definitely not! Or could he? Perhaps if we moved to an English-speaking country, our problems could be solved. Possibly, but he was being transferred to Spain, as I soon found out. I was speechless again. How should we learn Spanish as well? He couldn't possibly be serious! But he said that he was being serious, and the move would be to Madrid. There are also German schools there that we could transfer to, he added. After the initial shock, the basic topic of "transfer" was followed by my first thought about the country that he was talking about. Spain, that sounded warm and lively, and to me, perhaps interesting. Moving there might be an option after all. But what about Waltraut? She had already been with our father for a year and a half. Would she just let him go? Did she have any say in this situation? Would he move without her? Or would she move with him, perhaps as his wife? There were so many questions and few answers. But, as always, there was an ultimatum. Immediately after the skiing holiday, my father was already heading to Madrid. I found it all unbelievable and, what's more, that we were once again faced with a fait accompli, a final decision. When Carin joined us a week later and we discussed the topic with her, she simply said that she would not go along with another move and wanted to finish her damned high school diploma in peace. Topic closed.

At least we had a lot of fun skiing thanks to a group of young, attractive, funny and a little crazy Swedes. In fact, they were very cute! Despite my rolls of pudge, I tried to impress them with my now amazingly good skiing. These Swedes were full of mischief and so, it was perfect timing as a sort of laughing and silliness therapy, against the stress that we were experiencing, due to our father's newest development. Every day they had lunch at the ski hut, and so I also wanted to join them sometimes. Normally, our family ate as we had been doing so, in our apartment for lunch, instead of at the expensive ski hut. When I told my father about my wanting to join them for lunch up at the ski hut on the mountain, my father said, much to my surprise, that it was no problem. The Swedes were very polite and courteous people, he explained, and if they asked me the next day if I wanted to have lunch with them, I should just answer: "Jag har inga pengar", which translated means "I'm hungry". So, I remembered my little sentence and looked forward to being able to use it when the time came. And it did. They politely asked me, like every day, if I wanted to join them for lunch and I answered proudly and visibly pleased with myself: "Jag har inga pengar". Lars then said that it was no problem, I should come with them, and he would invite me. Not bad either, I thought. Of course, they asked me where my Swedish knowledge had come from so suddenly, to which I explained that my father had taught me this sentence and other important things like "Snö" and "Snöboll", meaning snow and snowball. The boys were rolling around laughing hard and I had a vague suspicion that something was wrong. They explained to me that when they asked me if I wanted to come to lunch with them, I had answered "I have no money", not "I'm hungry". I was so embarrassed that I wanted to crawl under the table! Apart from that story, I had a lot of fun with "my" Swedes. And as for our daily daring races, during which my thigh muscles trembled and burned with pain as I raced downhill, the boys sent me a postcard to my boarding school: Lars crashed in a race and broke both of his arms, the day after I left.

Madrid, Spain 1981

In January our father started his job in Madrid. Of course, we had not had the opportunity of being involved in the decision-making process. During the skiing vacation we simply exchanged ideas, but after a decision had already been made on his part. But he insisted that this was not his doing. He had been entrusted with this task by Hans L. Merkle, the highest official at Bosch, the top of the top. The situation in Spain was critical, because Spain wanted to become part of the European Union. In the decision-making process, the politicians also wanted to obtain the opinion of a committee of leading economic experts. Such discussions were scheduled, and it was therefore necessary to know exactly whether it was worthwhile for German companies to invest in Spain in the long term, given that the dictatorship there had only ended a few years prior. In the new, developing democracy, too much was still uncertain, and employers had to assume that socialist legislation was too strong, making economic activity unprofitable. In short, my father explained to us that he could speak Spanish and hence Mr. Merkle had asked him to go there to find out what the situation. I was floored. I hadn't expected such a heavy-weight explanation. It all was much more and weighed heavier than just securing income or advancement in the company. The expansion of Europe, what a fantastic cause! I couldn't even be angry with my father for having to leave at such short notice. I was very impressed that he was able to contribute something to it directly or indirectly. And, as he also added, he didn't particularly like being in Karlsruhe or Stuttgart. He simply couldn't get along with his colleagues and superiors, who basically deeply envied him for his foreign assignments and experiences but would never have admitted it. Instead, they put obstacles in his way, blocked his suggestions for improvements, such as the visual and functional standardization of the "Bosch Services", initially in Germany and later across Europe. They rejected it with comments like "Not everything you experienced abroad can be transferred to us" and were simply petty. My father had to admit that the matter he was now pursuing had a deeper meaning for him personally. He was not happy at Bosch in Germany, so he was happy to leave again. His suggestions regarding the "Bosch Services" were implemented during his stay in Spain. However, one of the "petty people" received praise for the wonderful idea, not my father.

In Madrid, my father ran a Bosch subsidiary called FEMSA, together with a colleague. In January, he sent me a postcard, writing: "Finally found a postcard and the time to write. To go to school every day is a very hard job - I prefer working! So far, I like Madrid. After snow the first day it's nice and warm now". The card with the "Plaza Colón" was signed with a happy face with huge eyes. I got the impression that my father was doing well and was quite cheerful. That was to be expected, because he had also told me that he was incredibly excited, specifically about moving to Spain, of all places. He further explained that he and my mother had been indescribably happy during their years in South America. They loved everything Latin American. Now my father hoped to experience some of that in Spain. I hoped so for him too, after I realized that his repatriation to Germany had not been a great success either. And the way he spoke so lovingly of my mother and himself, having been so happy in South America earned him some extra points of credit with me. And Wally had not gone with him; she stayed in Stuttgart.

Shortly after I had received this card, I returned to the "little house" from school one day. Mrs. Schmid was already there to greet me, and I sensed that she had bad news, because she had an extremely worried look on her face that said: I must tell you something. The news was about the political events in Madrid, which she was trying to explain to me. There had been an attempted coup by rebels against the Spanish government in Madrid and I was trying to understand her and at the same time evaluate whether this posed a danger to my father. Mrs. Schmid looked worried when she told me this, because she didn't have any more details either. Suddenly, I felt lost. Where was my father? How was he? She said that we hadn't received any bad news from or about my father and that this was basically good news. She was sure that he would call as soon as possible, but apparently there was a problem with communication with Madrid. All we could do was wait.

That same day he reached Mrs. von Egen by phone, who then gave me the good news that everything was OK with him. I could have cried with joy and relief, but at first, I was still shocked and numb. I had to process all this first. That same week I was able to speak to my father on the phone. He calmed me down and assured me that he had not been in danger or was he now. The whole situation had been so critical that King Juan Carlos of Spain spoke to the people, because democracy as well as his own position were at stake, if the rebels would win. My father played down the situation with the words "There are only traffic diversions in place, and I have a longer way to work." But I didn't quite believe him.

Shortly afterwards we had a week of carnival holidays. Since the whole move to Madrid had not yet been decided or finalised in detail, it was still unclear who from our family would move there and who would not, I was supposed to visit my father there. He wanted to show me the city and we were to discuss the possibilities for my future there. I was very nervous about taking this trip, because flying alone was still not my thing. I would also be flying to a country whose language I did not speak, and which had been facing a possible violent takeover just a few weeks before. Part of me didn't want to go, but the flight was booked, the ticket had cost over 1,000 DM at the time and for that reason alone, I would not have dared to back out. And I also wanted to see my father. To make my flight on time, the school gave me exceptional permission to leave early on the last day of school before the holidays. Everyone, the head of the boarding school, the head of the school, as well as the director, were excited for me. Mrs. Schmid was ready to go in her little red car, at the onset of the long 15-minute break, between the 3rd and 4th lessons, and drove me directly to Frankfurt Airport. I almost felt sick with disconcertment. I had asked my father beforehand what I should say at the border control or at customs to explain that I was visiting and had nothing to declare. He kept it short and said: Just say: "No hablo español", which simply means I don't speak Spanish. I didn't really trust him after the Swedish "I'm hungry" stunt. But he assured me that I could trust him this time.

I flew directly to Madrid with the Spanish airline Iberia. The seats were so small that I felt cramped. There wasn't enough room under the seats for my bag. The stewardesses spoke only Spanish, and I remember the food as being lousy. Next to me sat a very cultivated and well-dressed Asian woman who was clearly feeling the same discomfort as I was. When we were given the written customs declarations in Spanish, we looked at each other and had to laugh. Then we put our heads together and, speaking English, we muddled through the forms that needed to be filled out. What a bad advertisement this flight was for Spain!

Finally arriving in Madrid, I had walk out of the plane with the woman who had been sitting next to me, towards the exit, when it got loud around us. A man seemed to be ranting and raving and when I looked at him, I realised that it was addressed at me. He waved me over and as he was wearing a uniform; I followed him. He continued to rant and had probably complained that I had not come over to him when he first asked me to. I smiled politely and said the only Spanish sentence that I knew: "No hablo español". My bag was on a table in front of him and he was demanding something. It took me a while to realise that he wanted my passport. He looked at it with interest, then his eyes got big, he looked at me quite angrily and snapped at me with words, of which I only understood: Caracas, Venezuela and español. Dressed from head to toe in mouse grey, as befits a travelling private schoolgirl, I continued to stand there, smiling politely and repeating my sentence: "No hablo español". Obviously, the little hot-headed Spaniard did not believe that I did not speak Spanish, since I was born in Venezuela. Now I understood his problem. That was a bad turn for me, but it was not my fault. As a kind of punishment for still not believing that I did not speak Spanish, he examined every inch of my bag in detail. He even took out the huge bar of Toblerone chocolate that I had bought for my father, opened the packaging and emptied that as well. He pointed to it and seemed to ask what it was. I smiled at him politely, as usual and said in English that it was chocolate. He was visibly disappointed that there were no drugs or anything else in it, because I am sure he also thought my passport was a fake and me too. After a long pause for thought on his part, I said firmly to him: "No hablo español", packed up my things again and continued going my way. I wasn't sure whether he would run after me and my heart was pounding accordingly. When I finally saw my father, I hugged him tightly and he hugged me too. I don't think we had ever been so happy to see each other, in our entire lives.

We drove to the Eurobuilding Hotel, where he was staying and had booked a small suite for the duration of my visit. On the way there, I got my first quick impressions of Madrid, a beautiful city that was clearly a world metropolis with a glorious past. The fantastic buildings radiated something that let the visitor know that they are a proud people. Everything I saw struck me with reverence and was very impressive. We went out to dinner that same evening, but at a time when I had to be in my room at the boarding school. We took a taxi to the "Plaza

Mayor", an absolute architectural and historical highlight of the city. There we entered a narrow restaurant that was loud, warm and smoky. My father assured me that it was one of the best local restaurants as we went down to the basement, where we met up with work colleagues and friends of his. I was greeted warmly and was told that my father had been really looking forward to my visit and that they were happy for him. These Spaniards had a warmth that in Germany would only have been expressed in a formal handshake. I liked their mannerism very much and, although I felt quite queasy after this long and eventful day, I tried to talk to them. For dinner I was given something that I couldn't identify either visually or by smell. It was a specialty of green and brown color, solid and liquid mixed and with a floating oil mass on top. Accordingly, I was delighted to have to eat this without letting on that the broth disgusted me. After this "delicacy" I had to go to the toilet because I had the feeling that this food wanted to leave me as quickly as possible. Since I had been away for a while, my father asked me upon my return, if everything was OK. My big eyes and a barely suppressed, tormented expression on my face made him suspect that I was not well. Since he was still in the middle of his business dinner, we quickly agreed that I should take a taxi back to the hotel, by myself. We would tell the Spaniards that I was simply tired because I had already got up at 6:30 a.m. and had a flight behind me. So, my father put me in a taxi, gave me a banknote with lots of zeros on it and told the driver where to take me. My salvation seemed to be in sight. Then we drove a route that seemed completely different and longer than the one we had come. I tried to tell the driver my observation in English and said that I was sick and that he should hurry up. After a long drive we finally arrived, and I gave him my banknote. After a quick calculation I had calculated that I still had to get a few hundred back, but I was already feeling dizzy. So, I signaled to him to hurry up. Then he gave me a whole handful of change. The money was completely foreign to me, and I was not able to deal with it. As my food was making itself known again, I showed the porter my handful of change and said that I had probably been ripped off. I couldn't stay to argue and ran to my room as quickly as possible. When we got there, the broth and I separated and I went to bed, completely exhausted. When my father came back shortly afterwards, he checked on me. I must have looked miserable because he got me a hot water bottle and medicine for or against diarrhea, dizziness and vomiting. The next morning, I felt surprisingly well again. I suspect it was all a bit too much excitement for me. Nevertheless, I stayed in bed that morning. It was not until the afternoon that I went for a walk, through Madrid, and ended up in the luxury department store "El Corte Inglés". I was endlessly impressed and excited by everything I saw there. It was a shame that I wasn't one of those super rich kids with a credit card and a high limit on it. I only had a little cash, so I just looked around and had enough for a magazine.

That same evening, we were invited to the home of a Spanish business-man and his family in their villa. Our taxi took us to a residential area that prom-ised considerable financial success on a scale that I had never seen before. And I was excited to see what awaited us there. I only asked my father not to force me to eat spicy or fatty Spanish food. When we got there, we were invited in by the but-ler, who led us to wait in the study, or smoking room. This one made my grandfa-ther Paul Bauder's study look like a spacious storage room with books. The ceiling height was higher than I had ever seen in a private home. In the study, the walls were covered in leather and my father, who had been there before, explained to me that it was high-quality leather. The huge and pompous furniture with its decora-tions and gold seemed more like something out of a film to me. On the walls hung lavish portraits of the family members. I was in awe when the host arrived, for whose appearance I was already quite excited, but not at all prepared. This man came up to my father loudly and beaming with joy and greeted him warmly, as if they had known each other forever. I did not fail to notice that the small white-haired man was no taller than me. Then he came straight up to me and greeted me just as warmly, as if I were a close relative. He spoke to me exuberantly and I as-sumed he was welcoming me. My father had to translate. Our host was obviously very wealthy, but did not speak English. After the men briefly discussed something more serious, we headed off to the next room. On the way there, I told my father that I had observed that the man did have a lisp. My father had to suppress his laughter and explained to me that this was the Spanish pronunciation, to which I simply said that he could not possibly be serious. Who lisps voluntarily?! When we arrived in the next room, which was the size of a small hall, the lady of the house was sitting there, a real grande dame in elaborate clothing, with lavish jewelry and a hairstyle that only a hairdresser could do so skillfully. I felt that I was dressed too modestly here, but there was nothing I could do about it. Our hosts were full-blooded Spaniards, and I came from a Swabian-cosmopolitan Protestant family. Other people were sitting and standing around the Señora, her children, friends and employees. Everyone greeted me individually and warmly. It was incredible! Much to my relief, the children all spoke English, even though I had never heard this way of pronouncing and intonation before, it was funny.

The very next day I visited the German school, which I was very excited about. Unfortunately, the young people mostly spoke Spanish to each other and so, even though I was introduced, I felt quite out of place. During the break we went to a city café, which would have been unthinkable at the Thadden. But here everyone was relaxed and enlightened, in a southern style. They were not just city people, but obviously part of a metropolis where the clocks ticked differently than in a small German suburb. I couldn't stop being amazed. The girls were fashionably dressed, they all smoked and drank real coffee. They wore make-up and wore valuable-looking jewelry. But what impressed me most was that they all spoke fluent Spanish, as if no other language had ever existed for them. But I knew that they could also speak German, English and some of them even spoke French. When I asked - which probably seemed stupid to them - why they all spoke Spanish to each other, the leader or head of the girls, the one with the blonde hair, short skirt and the most conspicuous gold jewelry, explained to me that Spanish was such a fantastic and passionately lively language that you just had to speak it! Oh, I thought to myself, and I really felt like a country bumpkin. Oh dear, I thought to myself, how am I ever going to fit in? Besides, how was I ever going to learn Spanish fluently when I couldn't even speak good German? I had my doubts about whether I could handle the move. But I didn't know with whom I should share my concerns with. Or how.

The following day we visited the golf club that my father wanted to join, in the north of Madrid, "La Moraleja". There was a fantastic clubhouse that made his Solitude golf club near Stuttgart, where he was a member, seem very modest. This was a completely different dimension, and my father said that the price for membership was correspondingly higher. But he said that he would negotiate with Bosch about how much of it they would cover, because after all he had been transferred by the company and expected that they would accommodate him in this regard as part of the transfer. That sounded logical to me. We then drove through a residential area that was under construction, like the "Paradise Homes" in Oakville. Villas, houses and spacious semi-detached houses were being built directly next to the golf club. I was immediately enthusiastic about this area! Finally, a residential area with houses and greenery instead of concrete high-rise luxury. All my negative impressions of the flight, passport control, food and lisp were swept away in one swipe. My concerns about school had also disappeared and all I could see in front of me was our new family life, like what we had had in Canada. But my father translated the many zeros on the big posters for me and said that he couldn't afford this. But I didn't give in and searched the building sites until I found the smallest of the houses with only seven rooms, plus the one for the "housekeeper", the live-in staff, as was also common in South America. My father became more lenient, but he still did the math. He said that this "small" house would cost a lot more than the condo we had in Stuttgart. Since I wasn't in the least attached to the apartment and now saw my future in Madrid anyway, for me it was just a question of the technical processing, and I would possibly move into our new happiness during the summer holidays. But my father asked me how I imagined him spending so much money on a house? At that moment I was furious with him and didn't hide my indignation. Why, I asked him, would he work so hard, accept international transfers and let our family fall apart if it didn't pay well? He said he earned well, but not brilliantly. That's when I finally lost my temper and said that he couldn't pretend to me that he didn't earn enough as co-director of a company with over 1,000 employees to be able to take out a mortgage for a semi-detached house! He looked at me a little taken aback and after a long pause he said: "You're just like your mother." I took that as a compliment and then asked him whether his family meant nothing to him and whether he didn't think we deserved a home? I saw the solution to my longing for a house and a family life in front of me and was happy about my future in Spain. After that it was quiet between us, and we drove away. My first visit to Madrid ended shortly afterwards and I was sure that I would really enjoy this country with its warm-hearted people.

Back at my boarding school, my father wrote a postcard from Egypt in March. It depicted the Giza pyramid group. He couldn't write more than "Also from Cairo, your daddy sends you warm greetings." Perhaps he didn't have enough time, perhaps it was his mood. What wasn't written was that he had been there 21 years previously, with our mother, prior to the trip, was melancholy about the memories of that time. He had expressed a longing for the good old days and for the first time, how much he missed her, his wife. Perhaps all his memories really came flooding back to him there. After his return from there, when he came to Stuttgart at one of his long weekend visits, he didn't say a word about it, neither about the trip to Cairo, nor about his feelings for his deceased wife. He seemed withdrawn and lonely.

At school, my stress about studying continued and I tried to imagine how I would cope with learning another language, as of the next school year. Sometimes

I felt downright dizzy at this seemingly unsolvable situation. But I knew that I needed a family life and that if my father was now living in Spain, I would move there too. It was not yet clear what Carin would decide to do. She was in her last year of school and was studying tirelessly for her A-levels. The only thing that was certain was that she would study, but where or what was still completely open. She could move almost anywhere to study, if she spoke the language of the university. In practical terms, that meant that she could stay in Germany and study. But if we sold the apartment in Stuttgart, she would be all alone, without family of course, but also without the apartment she had already lived in for two years. If we bought the beautiful house in Madrid, she could perhaps study in Madrid, and we would have a family life as of three again. But she was considering moving to Toronto to study because she wanted to pursue her goal of returning to Canada. There she would be close to Sue again, which wouldn't be bad either. However, for the first time in my life, I would no longer have her close to me. I didn't like the idea at all. The three of us didn't really get a chance to talk because our father was either at work in Madrid or away on international business trips.

There was only one way to finally come to a decision regarding moving there or not, and that was that we should visit our father in Madrid together over the Easter holidays. My sister and I were both excited. I had told her beforehand about our possible new home and she was excited and curious about everything that Madrid and its surroundings had to offer. At first, we had thought that Carin and I would fly to Madrid alone because our father finally wanted to spend time with us and look after us. At the same time, it was only too understandable that his partner, Wally, would feel excluded by such an action. Apart from the fact that she was still in love with my father and wanted to spend time with him, she was also excited about Madrid. Now my father had to make a decision that would do justice to both his partner and the children but would also suit him. So, he decided that all three of us should come to Madrid together. We girls had mixed feelings about this decision. On the one hand, we felt that we had an exclusive right to our father, and we really wanted to be alone with him for once. On the other hand, he always seemed to be happier when he had a partner with him, so for his sake we pretended that it didn't bother us, that she would also be coming along. We were all competing for his attention. Apart from that, we did have important decisions to make, which affected all four of us significantly. So, the three of us flew together from

276

Stuttgart, probably all with mixed feelings. Surely, she would have also preferred to be alone with him.

When we got there, we had a full program planned and were also supposed to take Spanish lessons at the Berlitz school during the day, on weekdays. In our intensive course, after six hours of lessons, we still had a lot of vocabulary to learn. Of course, Carin was more brilliant at learning the language than I was. But I was happy that after a few days I could order my orange juice with: "Uno zumo de naranja por favor". In the meantime, our father was living in an apartment hotel in the Eurobuilding, which meant that he had a living room in addition to the bedrooms. Living like this was completely normal for our family; new country, temporary accommodation, learning the language, getting to know a new culture.

The art that Madrid offered us would have kept us busy enough. We spent half a day twice in the Prado Museum, where we focused almost exclusively on classical Spanish art and included names like Greco, Goya and Velázquez in our general knowledge. I had seen a picture of the Prado Museum in a travel guide about Madrid while leafing through it, and I said to my father: "Look at this beautiful house!" He and my sister replied somewhat dryly: "It's not a house. It's a museum." They both called me megalomaniac, although I did say that I had only seen the picture briefly and had not looked at it more closely. In any case, I found everything that we concentrated on to be largely difficult and dark art. I was moved by how gloomy, dreary or hopeless many of the paintings were. It occurred to me that Spain must have had very difficult and cruel times. Spain was indeed passionate, for better or for worse and I was deeply moved, impressed and a little worried.

In the following days we visited many historical sites in and around Madrid. We drove to the "Real Sitio San Lorenz de El Escorial" (Royal Castle of Saint Lawrence of El Escorial), a castle and monastery complex from the 16th century, in which the remains of the royal family had been kept for centuries. This gigantic building takes your breath away, even from afar, as you approach it. As an allusion to my comment about the Prado, my father said on the way there that we were going to the "King's summer house".

On the way there I had to ask my father what kind of car he was driving. Since my last visit he had gotten a company car, a Seat in a bright green shade. He said it was the top model from Seat, whereupon we all rolled up in laughter! When he showed us the top speed of the top model on the motorway, we almost had to laugh with pity! We asked worriedly what the other cars looked like, if this one was the top on the line. Our judgement was harsh and mean, but we only knew our father as a Mercedes driver and this square car did not have the slightest chance of matching the safe driving experience of a Mercedes. The joke was that the car was equipped with a top-notch Blaupunkt stereo system, which was clearly visible from the speakers in the doors and elsewhere. To demonstrate, he turned the volume up step by step until the speakers vibrated and the power of the stereo system sent us into pure roar. Shortly afterwards the whole car vibrated, and we said he had to turn it down before the car started to fall apart. Finally, we said that he was now equipped, that he could leave his car, turn the stereo up and have an open-air disco around it.

Toledo, Claudia and Carin.

Overall, we had a lot of fun together on this trip. We also visited the city of Toledo, and everyone bought the local costume jewelry with floral motifs as inlays. In this short time, I developed the feeling that the four of us had a chance as a family, even though we were all so different. But my gut feeling also told me that not everything had been discussed between Wally and my father. When I asked her if she could imagine moving to Spain with us, she said that she had a job in Stuttgart. That seemed strange to me, because there was certainly work for an educated and multi-lingual woman like her in a city as big as Madrid. Perhaps she could have worked at the German school? But her statement was also a bit strange to me, because I couldn't really imagine a working woman at my father's side. My mother didn't work, and it would have been difficult because of all the moving and us children. I knew my father as a conservative man whose wife didn't work. And since I had the impression that he wanted to have a wife again, she had to fit in with his ideas, including looking after the house and children and, of course, cooking. Was the love between the two of them so strong, that Wally would exchange her independent life for a traditional wife, "housewife" and substitute-mother role? Or maybe my father had expanded his horizon in the past years, having dated women who were working, and was now ready to appreciate an independent woman at his side. Raising the children was only of limited importance, since I was the last one who was still a minor. But the fact that Wally couldn't cook seemed to be a problem. Was it really something so trivial that our shared happiness shouldn't work out? I was too young to understand any of it, and not able to analyze it. The situation and its solution seemed so simple to me, but in my point of view, the adults made it very complicated.

We came back from Madrid, and I was full of hope and joy that we would move to Spain in the summer, with or without Wally. Perhaps Carin could go to university there. The house would also be big enough for longer visits from Sue and Ed. How exciting it all was! After we got to Stuttgart, we received a postcard from our father, this time from Hong Kong. He wrote: "Have a glimpse at Hong Kong, it's beautiful. Have a nice April". In a phone call that followed shortly afterwards, I told my father how excited and enthusiastic I was about moving to Madrid, to which he replied, quite unexpectedly for me: "You're not moving to Madrid." I was again speechless. I should not move to Madrid. Why not? Where should I move to then? What about our family? He was my father and couldn't possibly just leave Germany and not take me with him. How was I supposed to cope here without my parents? I didn't even want to live here! This wasn't my home! First, my father took our home away from us, forced us to live here and then he moved out of the country. I couldn't believe it! He said that it was too far for me to take the bus from La Moralecha to school into the city every day, and that even if the German school was a full-day school and I was looked after during the day, I would still have to take the bus home afterwards. He said I would be gone for maybe 10 hours a day. But that was exactly the good thing about it, I thought! We could have breakfast together and later in the evening we could have dinner together. I couldn't see any problem in any of that. I would need the time in between for my homework anyway, so I would effectively be busy all day. Apart from all the technical details, I would be 17 in the summer and almost an adult. He had to give me a chance, like Carin had gotten her chance with Stuttgart – at 17. I practically begged him for it. The conversation was tough and ended with his saying that Mrs. von Egen shared his opinion. What was I hearing? Mrs. von Egen was involved in our decision-making, and I didn't know the first thing about this?! I felt so betrayed again and countered that she had only said that so that I would have to continue to go to her boarding school. No, my father said: "I cannot and do not want to take responsibility for you here in Madrid." Apart from that, he said, he had decided not to buy a house in Madrid because the political situation was not yet stable enough to invest in property in the long term. With these two arguments I was defeated and devastated. And that was the end of the conversation.

It wasn't long before I asked Mrs. von Egen for a conversation. On my part, it was certainly one of the most unfriendly and rude conversations I've ever had with her. But she took it well, with supremacy and forbearance. In summary, she told me in no uncertain terms what she had also said to my father, that she thought I could not look after myself in a foreign country, especially one of which I didn't even speak the language. In addition, I would not be able to cope with a big city. She went on to say that I had grown up in a sheltered environment and that a metropolis like Madrid entailed far greater dangers than I could imagine. I was overwhelmed by her argumentation. Although I knew she was right, I couldn't have admitted it at the time. My hopes of leaving Germany had been enormous and now they were gone in with one single blow. My longing to live with my only living parent was huge and would remain unfulfilled. The prospect of a future in Spain was tempting and promising, but it was no longer mine. I couldn't say all of this to her but being a very good judge of character and human nature, she had most likely known all of this, even before our conversation. The only thing I could think of at that moment, regarding the whole thing - as a kind of punishment for feeling betrayed by her - was to assure her that I would not be returning to boarding school after the summer holidays, and thus her efforts to keep me here were in vain.

I felt like my father had pushed me away for good. Under these circumstances, with my future now completely uncertain, I was supposed to make it through the school year. It was stress, stress and more stress. Then I got the bad news that almost broke me at this stage of my life. Shortly after this news, I called my sister Carin. Throughout our lives, it had always been her who had comforted me in difficult times. For example, when we were "parked" in the Black Forest for weeks as small children and didn't really know when or if our parents would come back. In any case, she had already heard about our father's decisions. Now she told me that she had decided to move to Toronto to study. What, my sister was leaving me! Was I supposed to stay in Germany by myself? Please don't go! Don't leave me as well, I begged her.

For the first time in my life, I didn't really want to carry on living because I felt so dispensable or redundant. None of them needed me, but I needed them. With this, and my declining performance and correspondent bleak prospects of studying, I couldn't see any prospects for the future. I felt lost in a country that was not foreign, but still not mine, and I was very alone. My family had left me, and I couldn't and didn't want to be without them. It doesn't always have to be due to a war, like it was when my parents were young, to take away a young person's hope for a future. I had lost my mother, then my home and my friends, then I was separated from one of my sisters by an ocean. Then boarding school – which did have some positive aspects. Then my father moved away and now my second sister was also separated from me by an ocean. The only option left for me was to continue living in a country that I didn't want to be in. This was certainly all too much for me. During this time, the motivation to carry on living diminished day by day. If only I were dead now, I would have nothing to worry about. And I would be in heaven with my mother and could tell her everything that had happened since she left us. These thoughts were the only ones that pleased me, and I thought about how I could facilitate my own death. The last four years had been too stressful for me. Unfortunately, no one around me noticed enough. I had lost too much of what made my life beautiful and worth living. I looked the same outside. But inside, there was a whole different story. How many losses can a young person cope with in such a short time? And how can one cope with the fact that the losses are accompanied by personal failures? The last three years of school had been unsuccessful for me, sometimes near torture – but without a positive result. Now I was supposed to get by without any family support here and now, to continue preparing for a future that had no prospects for me? Today I am amazed that I did not give up back then and end my life. But that was most likely due to a turn in events.

I must have given my sisters the desperate impression that I would not survive if I stayed behind in Germany alone. We talked about how we could solve this problem. One of them had the brilliant idea that I should move to Toronto, to be with them. They did not want to leave me alone either and said that since Toronto also had boarding schools, they would sort it out. By this they meant convincing our father that this was the only solution. Again, I was stunned, but this time in a positive way. It looked as if I might not have to get by without support after all. And the hopelessness that I had, now took a hopeful turn.

How my sisters managed it, I do not know. But they had both always successfully fought for what they thought was right. Before I could even process what had happened in the weeks of spring 1981, a few weeks later we flew to Canada to stay with Sue and Ed for the Pentecost holidays, to discuss all the options with them. Carin went to visit the university she wanted to go to. Sue and I went to look at potential boarding schools. It was extremely stressful for Sue to have us there - once again – and to make sure that we found a suitable place somewhere to stay. However, this time it was much easier than three years before. She spoke the language, had her own car and she also knew where we had to go. But she did not have much time because she was working full-time. Sue works in a bank and was working more hours a week than her husband. Ed worked in his father's office. This meant he was more flexible and could do things with us from time to time. He was there for us, as we had always known him to be. And we, the well-rehearsed trio, enjoyed being together. For us, he was not just our sister's husband. He was like a brother to us, and a loving one at that. Sue and Ed were looking for a house at the time and so we drove with Ed to various building sites. The whole thing was very exciting, and we could only be happy for the two of them when they decided to build their own house. Ed assured us that once the house was finished, we would be welcome to come and stay with them anytime. What a great prospect!

Geneva, Switzerland

With renewed energy I returned to boarding and to school, having the spiritedness for a positive future. I could count the few days left until my release, towards a new life. It was tempting for me to count the hours I still had left to spend in a German school, as I did hate the school system that much. But I didn't have the time for that. I still had to fight for my grades to even pass the school year. This was the prerequisite for me to be able to go to school in Canada after the summer holidays. The head of the school, Mrs. von Rad, took me aside to have a serious talk with me. Apparently, my performance had slipped a little further in the last few months and my passing grade 10 was seriously in jeopardy. That was not surprising given the circumstances. Thanks to my father and his employer, I just couldn't get any rest! They had ruined my school career. Nevertheless, I assured her that, although I still didn't understand anything about chemistry and was bobbing around between grades five and six, I would manage the school year. After all, I would be allowed to return home afterwards, and I wasn't going to miss that.

Fortunately, we had diverse week-long school trips ahead of us and I was able to escape the clutches of the school for the time being. I had signed up for a trip to Geneva because I knew that there were many international organizations there that had a magical attraction for me. We would travel by train from Heidelberg to Geneva with about 15 girls and a teacher. We were all very excited and curious. Only Ariane, who had also signed up for this trip, was missing when we left. She was at her grandfather's birthday party and was supposed to fly directly from there to Geneva to join us. The teacher, who I didn't know before, but who was leading and supervising our group, said to the assembled crew: "The young lady won't be joining us until Geneva. Apparently, she's too good to take the train with us." I was speechless! What nonsense was this woman saying?! Ariane had traveled with us every other weekend in second class by train all year. Sometimes the trains were so full that we only had one or two seats, and we had to alternate between standing and sitting every half hour. She was by no means too good to take the train. I told this teacher that and made it clear that she had just announced utter nonsense. But I only got angry looks from her and, to my surprise, from some of the external girls who didn't even know Ariane. Even during the train ride, the "anti-Ariane" group seemed to have formed, and they were not just gossiping about her. They were literally talking shit about her only being able to fly. I tried to counter this grumbling and complaining with facts. I explained that she had not flown once all year. That didn't interest the "higher-class daughters". The climax of this slander campaign, which had been fueled by this stocky teacher who was a head shorter than me but had such a wide bottom that one had to wonder how she didn't fall over, was still to come when we arrived at the train station in Geneva. The fat cow said that we should hurry to our hotel because who knows, "Maybe the young lady will land on the roof in a helicopter!" and "We don't want to miss that." The girls, who I had only hours before considered to be classmates or girls from parallel classes, followed her, giggling and cackling. Now they seemed to me like a pack of half-savages who were on the trail of sensationalism to delight themselves at the expense of an innocent young woman. I couldn't believe it.

In the hotel lobby, the teacher said smugly that she was going to give "the young lady", who was trying to arrive at the same time as us, a good scolding. I was shocked. What kind of nasty person was she? Where did this deep hatred come from that made her so unfairly denigrate one of the pupils entrusted to her protection? Things happened here that I couldn't explain and that really scared me. I went to my room and put my things away, so that I could go to Ariane as quickly as possible to warn her of the impending attack. But I missed her. She was already in her room and when I got there, she was sitting on her bed, completely distraught and crying. Another girl and I tried to comfort her. But Ariane was hit hard and deeply hurt. She wanted to leave straight away, but we decided that we were not going to let that cow win the battle. Ariane said to me: "If only I were called Bauder like you. You fly around the world all year round and nobody cares." It was almost right, because after I had experienced similar but milder attacks after the fall holidays, I had decided not to tell the others anything about my trips, except that I was visiting my father or my sister, for example. I didn't say where they lived. Or, I even lied and said that I was meeting them in Stuttgart. But it was for my own protection and so I didn't attract their envy and anger. What really lay behind my family situation and how much I was suffering from it was of no interest to anyone. Just as the girls were neither willing nor able to deal with the facts with Ariane. The whole thing was disgusting and for us it put a huge damper on the mood of our entire trip to Geneva.

We still managed to see all the sights. We went to the Red Cross, where we looked at a huge room with endless index cards with the names of missing people. At the United Nations, we looked at a huge conference room and then had lunch in the canteen on the top floor of the UN building with a view over Lake Geneva. Geneva and Lake Geneva were beautiful. These international organizations were simply fantastic and inspired me to want to do something meaningful later in my life professionally. I finally had goals, even if they were very vague. Now I was sure that one day I wanted to work for the United Nations here or in New York. This trip was a wonderful end to my three years in Europe. It was marred, however, by the fact that I had to experience how unbelievably ugly these German girls and women could be, and so I only wanted one thing: to get away from them forever. In this country, it seemed to me, you were not allowed to come from a family that was successful, including financially. In the eyes of the less

284

successful, you were one of the bad guys. What a twisted world, I thought to myself. After all, it was those who ran companies who provided work and income for others. This was met with envy and resentment.

But I had also made good friends at the boarding school, Doro, Conny, Ariane and my roommate Susanne. I would miss them and thought it was a shame that we were now going our separate ways. But that was just the way boarding school was. We lived together for a while, then we would go separate ways.

After having studied very hard, Carin passed her Abitur, high school, or A-levels in Stuttgart, with only an average grade. That was an enormous achievement for her, but the final grade was still regrettable. If she hadn't had to deal with a language change, she would undoubtedly have remained an A student and would have been able to graduate with honors. She would certainly have received a scholarship to a university, which is so important in North America where universities must be paid for, if she would not have had to leave Canada and could have completed high school there. Unfortunately, she was cheated out of this opportunity. Nevertheless, she celebrated her personal success extensively with her friends in Stuttgart, and at a barbecue in the Kräherwald, the local forest, several of them burned some of their books. Carin burned them all. Dad and I were very proud of her for passing her Abitur. The work she had put into it, the effort, had been enormous. As a reward, she was allowed to return to her home country, study there and start her future life.

In contrast, I had only just passed the school year, but I was promoted to grade 11. I was given a certificate and told that I now had the intermediate school leaving certificate. Whatever it was, I wasn't interested. I was practically packing and with my thoughts, had one foot in my home country. For me, the three-year horror trip, which was, however, positively interrupted by some lovely holidays, and meeting some very nice girls, was over. I was indescribably happy and just wanted to go home. My uncle Alex had been right in everything he had said. I shouldn't have gone to Europe and the family only had a chance if we had stayed together. My father had achieved professional success, but the price we had all paid for it was far too high.

Whilst I wanted to be dead just a few weeks earlier, I now had the opportunity to build a future for myself. But my father's transfer to Spain had separated him from us for good. I don't know how he felt about having his own three daughters living on another continent forever. He had let the family break up, sacrificed it, so to speak, and now had to live with the consequences. Somehow, we had lost our father. At least we three sisters, all of whom were Canadians at heart, would find each other again and be reunited. My hope of returning to my homeland at some point had fallen by the wayside, somewhere in the last three years. But thanks to the fact that my sister Carin had never lost sight of her goal - returning to our homeland - I was now able to follow in her footsteps. Europe has shown us many beautiful and interesting sides. We had been able to experience Switzerland several times, had our ballroom dancing graduation ball was held in a real castle, we somewhat got to know the stunning charisma of Madrid and much more, including amazing art and architecture. But as impressive as the historical buildings were, as nearby as the various languages, as varied as the cultures may be, my heart was still a beating Canadian one, and so I wanted to end my "Europe adventure" and simply fly home, to where I felt most comfortable.

We stood at Frankfurt Airport laden with huge suitcases and knew that we were only a few hours' flight away from having our Canadian homeland under our feet forever.

Acknowledgements

I would like to thank the following people and companies for their helpful information, interesting conversations and support:

Carin Bauder, for going through the journey with me, of reliving and remembering the many details, experiences and changes of our childhood.
Margret Kelbass, for the many conversations we had, to help me become more familiar with my mother.
Charlotte Grimm (née Bauder), my father's sister, for information about my grandfather Paul Bauder.
Klaus Maier, Mayor of the town of Heubach.
Dietward Horn.
Heidi Ribkoff (née Stiefenhofer).
Robert Bosch GmbH in Stuttgart for allowing me to look at my father's old personnel files and for various informative conversations.
Waltraut Mayer, my father's former partner.
Ann Mulvale, Mayor of Oakville.
Janet Hayes (née Monteith) and Shelli Harrison (née Pundsack). We had a lot of fun in 2004, remembering some of the details of our youth, which we partially spent together.
Martin Holl, my mother's brother.
Susanne Bauder Fujarczuk.
Hildegard Schmid, for the many interesting conversations, the critical questions and the proofreading. Without her support I would probably have given up on this project.
Brigitte Bauder.
Much gratitude goes to Tonya Harmon, for helping me with the English version!
To everyone else who supported me directly and indirectly in this project.

Copyright © 2009, 2025 Claudia Bauder
Publish: BoD · Books on Demand GmbH, Überseering 33,
22297 Hamburg, bod@bod.de
Print: Libri Plureos GmbH, Friedensallee 273, 22763 Hamburg

ISBN: **978-3-8192-2775-2**